PROJECT AND PROGRAMME MANAGEMENT

Fabio A. Guilherme da Silva

TAP

Toronto Academic Press

Project and Programme Management

Fabio A. Guilherme da Silva

Toronto Academic Press
224 Shoreacres Road
Burlington, ON L7L 2H2
Canada
www.tap-books.com
Email: orders@arclereducation.com

ISBN: 978-1-77469-788-7

Toronto Academic Press publishes wide variety of books and eBooks. For more information about Toronto Academic Press and its products, visit our website at www.tap-books.com.

ABOUT THE AUTHOR

Fabio Guilherme da Silva is an academic, analyst, and software developer with over 25 years of experience in the field. He obtained a Bachelor's in Mathematics (with a specialisation in Informatics) from the State University of Rio de Janeiro (UERJ) in 1994, and began working as a software developer and business analyst right away. He worked on projects for numerous companies in Brazil, including giants such as TV Globo, Halliburton, UBS, and the government of the State of Rio de Janeiro. In 2010, he obtained his Master's in Information Systems from the Federal University of the State of Rio de Janeiro (UNIRIO), and in 2015, a Doctorate in Computer Science from the Pontifical Catholic University of Rio de Janeiro (PUC-Rio). His research was dedicated to the use of artificial intelligence in games and interactive storytelling, and for both of these latest two degrees, he was awarded a full scholarship from the Brazilian government. During his doctoral degree, he worked as a researcher at ICAD/IGames/VisionLab at PUC-Rio, producing reports that helped win some game copyright infringement cases in court, including one for Zynga. In 2012, he was awarded an Honourable Mention (Interactivity) by the International Telecommunication Union (ITU) for his work. He then worked as a lecturer at PUC-Rio and FUCAPE Business School before leaving Brazil in 2018 to work for companies in Argentina, Germany, the USA, and the UAE. He currently lives in Portugal where he works as a researcher and assistant professor at the European University of Lisbon, focusing his research and teaching on Artificial Intelligence, Games, and Programming Languages. In addition to his pursuits in Computer Science and IT, Fabio also holds a diploma in International Relations and is fluent in eight languages. In his free time, he enjoys travelling, sports and playing music, having already toured and played in multiple countries in Europe and the Americas.

Contents

List of Figures

List of Tables

List of Abbreviations

BI	Business Intelligence
DSDM	Dynamic Systems Development Method
ICT	Information and Communications Technology
IPMA	International Project Management Association
IT	Information Technology
PMBOK	Project Management Body of Knowledge
PMI	Project Management Institute
PMO	Project Management Office
ROI	Return-on-Investment
TQM	Total Quality Management
WBS	Work Breakdown Structure
WIP	Work-in-Progress
XP	Extreme Programming

PREFACE

The application of specialized knowledge, skills, tools, and processes to create something of value for others is project management. Examples of projects include software development for a better business operation, the construction of the facility, the rescue effort following a natural disaster, and the development of sales into an expansion into a new market. For many people, program management can mean a variety of things. Everyone would agree that managing a multitude of projects is what program management is all about. In reality, this includes the majority of businesses that are managing multiple projects at once. Most organizations are involved in this. Everyone would concur that managing a program entails having the ability to step back from specific issues and gain an overall picture of the procedure.

In recent years, numerous organizations from both the private and governmental sectors have begun to recognize the importance of project and program management in bringing about positive change. It still holds true in prosperous times as well as difficult ones when merely surviving is essential. Both conditions present possibilities and challenges; thus, a business-led management strategy is advantageous. Projects as the main tools for managing change, and it is believed that anyone who does not understand their importance would have a very difficult time succeeding.

The discussion of the books starts with the fundamentals of project and program management, followed by the central principles of project and program management. Also, the key role players and their responsibilities in project and program management are described in detail in this book. The project and program management processes and approaches are also explained in detail. The significance of project and program offices, essential for the success of projects, is described in the book. Managing risks and opportunities while working on projects is discussed in detail. Lastly, the challenges and future trends of project and program management in businesses and organizations are explained in detail at the end of this book.

This book comprises of eight-chapters; the first chapter discusses the fundamentals of project and program management with emphasis on the project life cycle, types of project management, and key differences between project and program management. The second chapter deals with project management principles, including regulations from cultural environment principles to implicit principles of project and program management.

The third chapter is about the key players and their responsibilities in project and program management, along with the project and program environment. The fourth chapter deals with the approach of managing a project and program that includes the initiation phase, planning phase, execution phase, and controlling and monitoring phase.

The fifth chapter describes the significance and role of program and project offices for successful project and program management. The sixth chapter deals with addressing and managing risks and opportunities in order to complete the projects successfully. The seventh chapter is about the future of project and program management in several businesses of the 21st century, and the eight chapters is about various challenges that a project or program manager faces during project or program management.

This book has been written specifically for students and scholars to meet their needs in terms of knowledge and to provide them with a broad understanding of project and program management. We aim for this book to be a resource for academics in many subjects since we believe it will provide clarity and insight for its readers.

—***Author***

CHAPTER 1

INTRODUCTION TO PROJECT AND PROGRAM MANAGEMENT

UNIT INTRODUCTION

A project is essentially a job with a specific goal in mind (El Khatib et al., 2022). For instance, constructing a new home is a project, with the completion of the home serving as the project's end. Similar to launching an innovative product for a company, developing new software or apps is a project. Projects can be used to finish a wide variety of activities.

To plan, organize, and manage the complex and varied activities of new manufacturing, corporate, leadership, and technology projects, project management has been established (Springer, 2019). The ability to transform ideas and actions into new efforts is a characteristic that all undertakings have in common. The actions that will result in a consequence can indeed be predicted with 100% precision due to uncertainty and risk. There are several instances of projects that have been completed late, beyond budget, or perhaps not at all. Such disasters occur far too frequently in various economic, industrial, and (mostly, it appears) public sector enterprises.

For many people, program management can mean a variety of things. It is conceivable that this book will contribute in a little way to the manifestation of the numerous phrases and applications for those terms that are associated with this subject (El Khatib et al., 2022). Everyone would concur that managing a multitude of projects is what program management is all about. In reality, this includes the majority of businesses that are managing multiple projects at once. Most organizations are involved in this. Everyone would agree that managing a program entails having the ability to step back from specific issues and gain an overall picture of the procedure. They need to view the entire mosaic (Pellegrinelli, 2008) (Figure 1.1).

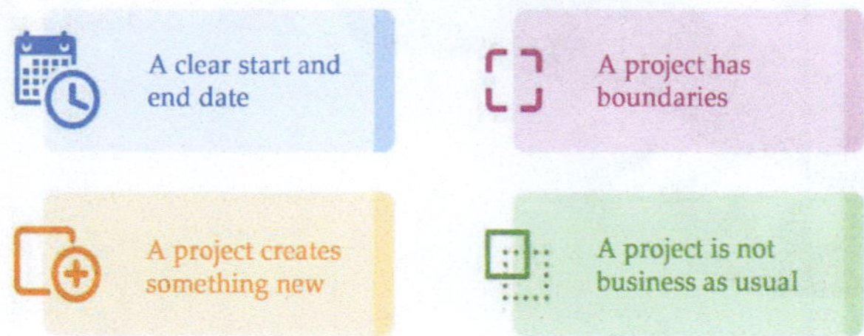

Figure 1.1. Illustration of various project features.

Source: Kissflow, creative commons license.

Learning Objectives

At the end of this chapter, readers will be able to learn the following:

- Fundamental concepts of project and program management.
- Various roles and responsibilities in project and program management
- Dimensions of a project.
- The concepts of the project life cycle
- Difference between project and program management
- Difference between MRP and program management

Key Terms

- Agile Method
- Critical Path Method
- Customer
- Dimensions
- Family tree
- Leader
- Life cycles
- MRP
- Phases
- Projects
- Sponsor
- Stakeholders

1.1. BASICS OF PROJECT MANAGEMENT

A systematic area for managing projects is project management (Cobb, 2011). During the past century or so, project management has evolved as it has been clear that without a disciplined strategy, people struggle to complete projects successfully. Project management's main goal is to guarantee that projects are finished and that the intended outcome—a new home, computer system, or product—is realized. Beyond this, project management involves getting there that destination predictably, which typically entails doing so at a specific cost and within a predetermined window of time.

Readers will discover as they read this book that structure, control, enough attention to detail, and relentless action are the keys to successful project management. For project management, there are various methodologies or approaches (Clough et al., 2000). One brings them up because if they speak with a qualified project manager, they might hear them. Popular project management approaches include the Critical Path Method, Prince2, and Agile (Figure 1.2).

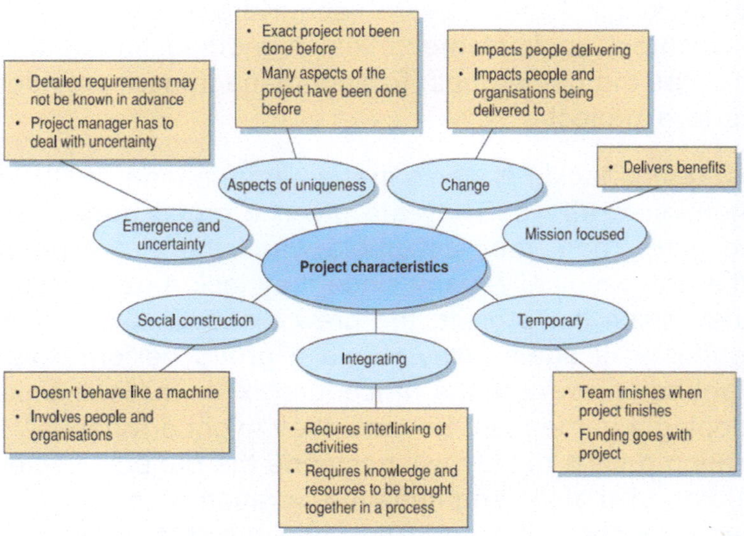

Figure 1.2. Illustration of the project characteristics.

Source: Harvey Maylor, creative commons license.

As the project manager, it is his/her responsibility to comprehend project management well enough to put its rigor and structure into practice and guarantee that their project is completed within the time and budget they want. This will not be as difficult if readers follow the instructions in this book. The duties of a project manager include the following:

i. Ensure a clear understanding of why a project is being done and what it will produce (Rosenau & Githens, 2011).
ii. Plan the project – to understand how long it will take and how much it will cost.
iii. Manage the project – must make sure that while the project moves forward, it accomplishes the goals they have set while staying within the budget and schedule constraints.
iv. Complete the project properly – to ensure that everything the project produces is of the anticipated quality and functions as needed (Bibarsov et al., 2017).

Project management is a combination of tools, strategies, and expertise that, when used correctly, can help create superior project results. Attempting to run a program without project management is akin to trying to play football without the need for a game plan. The coach would gather the team and ask, "So, how would we play this game?" It is expected to obtain more scores than the other squad, which requires scoring goals. Now, everyone, go out there and do whatever is necessary to win (Wirth & Tryloff, 1995)."

What are the team's odds of victory? Not particularly high. What is lacking? A strategy for achieving success. The game plan's synchronized implementation. A method for modifying the game plan as the game goes. Project management provides these features in a project.

Did you Know?

In 1969, the Project Management Institute (PMI) was formed in the USA

Most teams tackle projects in the same manner as the football team mentioned above. They are given a group project and then begin to play. Then, they assemble when there is a problem, of which there are typically many since they lack a game plan. If and when they finish the project, the crew disbands with the hope of never enduring it again. Why would a group perform this? First, they might be unaware that a procedure exists that will assist them in developing a game plan. Second, they might erroneously believe that creating a style of play will postpone the project. Neglecting to make a plan ultimately lengthens the duration of the job. Following a technique conserves time in the long run (Marçal et al., 2007).

Project management gives a procedure one can obey, a series of steps that will assist in addressing some fundamental issues before plunging into completing the task. Questions like what are you trying to produce? What are the specific wants and requirements of the customer? Who is going to be accountable for doing the work? How much longer is it going to take? What is the price going to be? What could go wrong? How could you prevent potential issues? These questions are answered at the beginning of the process to ensure that the work will go smoothly and effectively.

A system of project management will not only assist in planning but will also assist in keeping a project on track and fixing issues as they appear along the way (Figure 1.3).

Figure 1.3. Schematic of the importance of project management.

Source: Kissflow, creative commons license.

1.2. KINDS OF PROJECT MANAGEMENT

1.2.1. Directive Project Management

A directive method is an antiquated form of management. The project manager is assumed to be the best candidate for project planning and control. Planning is done by the project manager, who subsequently assigns duties to the teammates. After that, they check in with each team member to ensure they finish their assignments on schedule. Most of the team member's communication goes to the project manager. It is the leader's responsibility to find a solution whenever an issue arises (Figure 1.4.).

The directive style has a variety of significant drawbacks, despite being effective in some situations since it takes less time during project planning (Dlakwa & Culpin, 1990):

i. The entire project takes more time since the implementation stage (the longest stage of any project) takes longer owing to uncertainty, miscommunication, and reworking (having to repeat work since it was not executed the first time correctly).

ii. Teammates have limited knowledge of the overall project or how their job fits it.

iii. There is relatively little project commitment or dedication on the team.

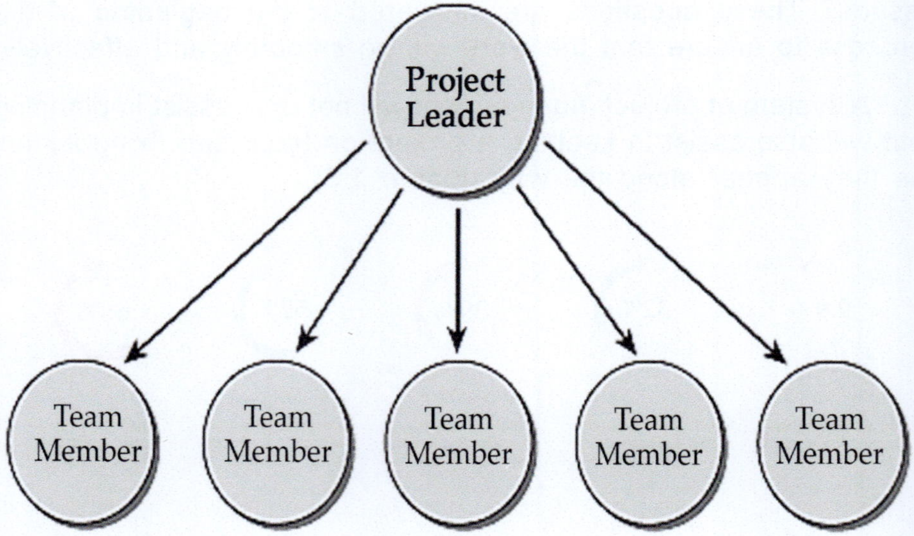

Figure 1.4. Illustration of fact that communicative approach is directive.

Source: Paula Martin, creative commons license.

1.2.2. Participatory Project Management

Participative project management is the newest project management technique. The project manager supports project management by guiding the team thru the planning processes.

Under the project manager's leadership, the team will monitor the project's progress as the tasks are carried out (Kim & Huynh, 2008). Decisions regarding the work are made collaboratively, and communication flows from teammates to the project manager and within the team (Figure 1.5).

The advantages of a participative strategy are:

i. Each team member recognizes how their contribution to the project integrates into the greater whole.
ii. More concepts are produced.
iii. Improved decisions are reached when all parties are involved.
iv. Participation fosters a sense of ownership, which enhances dedication and responsibility.
v. The morale of the team is generally higher.
vi. Less rework needs to be done.
viii. Individual and group performance is enhanced.

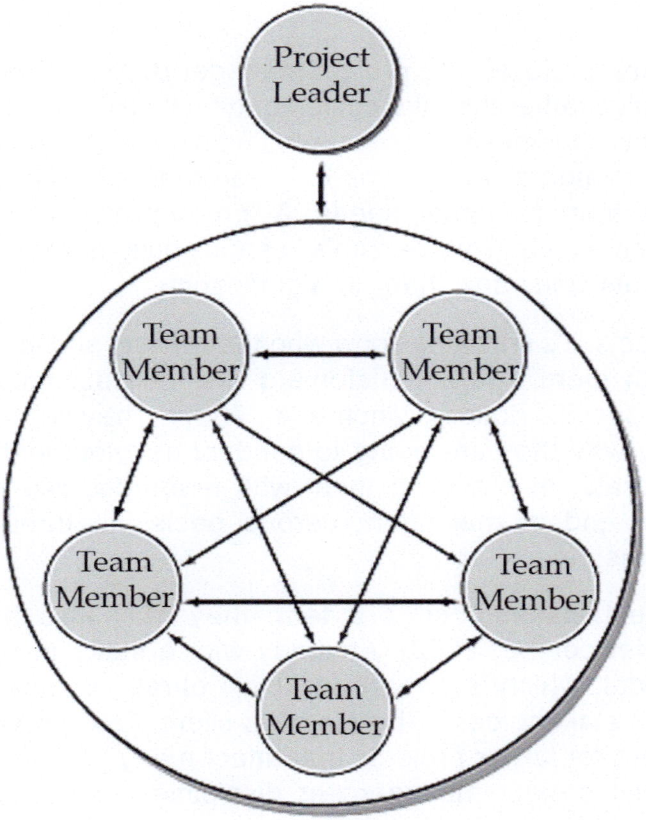

Figure 1.5. Schematic of a communicative approach that involves a participative style.

Source: Paula Martin and Karen Tate, creative commons license.

In most cases, more remarkable project outcomes can be achieved using a strategy emphasizing participation. The participatory approach, known as the CORE PM approach, currently has the widest applications (Blomquist et al., 2010). People are essential to both directive and participatory methods of operation. Without the collaboration of individuals, nothing can be accomplished.

1.3. THE PROJECT'S CUSTOMERS AND STAKEHOLDERS

Every undertaking is completed because somebody wants it to be. In project management jargon, the individual who wants it done is called the project customer. The customer could be anyone, employer of a firm, someone who uses firm goods and services, someone they collaborate with at work, or anyone else.

A single customer or a collection of clients are both acceptable (Aapaoja & Haapasalo, 2014).

On some projects, the project manager deals with a customer representative rather than the customer directly (Heravi et al., 2015). For instance, "business analysts" who work on numerous business initiatives evaluate and compile "requirements specifications" documents from customer needs. A "product owner" is a role in the Agile technique. This person's responsibility is to describe the client's wants and rank them in significance.

In projects, it's crucial to know who the client is and to collaborate closely with them. Project customers are held accountable for a number of specific duties (Winch et a., 2007). They will be involved in deciding why they are going to conduct development and what it will generate, in providing them with resources like individuals and funds, and in making numerous decisions throughout the project's lifespan.

A project stakeholder is a term they may also hear about projects (Newcombe, 2003). Anybody with a stake in a project is a stakeholder, which is a more inclusive phrase than a customer. One kind of stakeholder is the project's client. There may be many stakeholders for larger projects that affect many people, and there is a specific project management discipline called "stakeholder management" for dealing with them.

Remember

Not all projects are conducted commercially or for profit. Most not-for-profit organizations, including national and local government departments, professional associations, charities, and disaster relief agencies conduct projects that fall into this category of management projects.

1.4. THE PROJECT TEAM

There are many different duties that must be completed for the project which the users are about to handle. One can be the project manager who completes all the planned duties for a very uncertain project. Several persons will be involved at various points during the life of larger projects. The group of people is referred to as the project team, and it is this group that they will be in charge of managing (Edmondson & Nembhard, 2009).

Managing team members for a project differs from typical line management work (Oertig & Buergi, 2006). There is typically a line manager who oversees the project team members daily. On the project, they are exclusively working for them. They could need to do other jobs that have nothing to do with their project. It's possible that after the project is finished, they will not work with the team again. They must be able to manage, inspire, and lead the team despite this (Bond-Barnard et al., 2018). To do this, they must have a clear idea of what they must perform and how much time they must devote to the project they supervise. Moreover, they must ensure that they use this time to focus on their project rather than simply performing other duties for their regular management. Discussing this with each team member's regular manager and getting their consent that they will be available for the project and be under their management supervision while they are working on it are the first steps in making this happen (Figure 1.6).

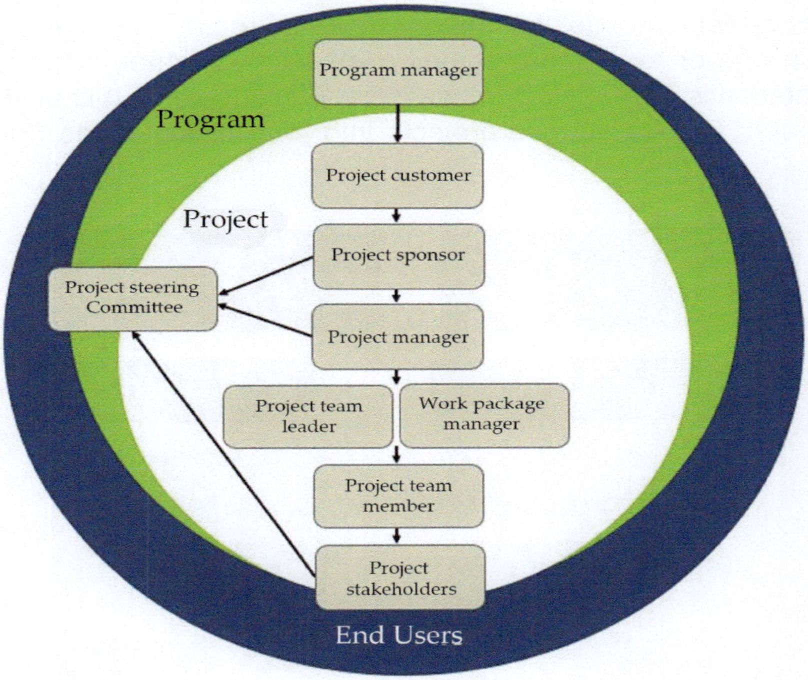

Figure 1.6. Diagram representing the steering committee of a project.

Source: Queensland Government, creative commons license.

1.5. DELIVERY AND DELIVERABLES

Project managers and those frequently involved with projects frequently use the word "delivery" in their conversations (Lynch & Roecker, 2007). Delivering a project refers to completing it and accomplishing the goals it set out to achieve. Delivering the project is consequently their responsibility as a project manager.

Delivery is a helpful term because it eliminates the need to repeatedly write "completing the task to the estimated duration and price with the desired outcome." Deliverables are the products or services that a project produces (Whyte et al., 2016). Using the examples given above, the deliverables from each project are a new home, new software, or new goods. The desired deliverables in a project are identified at its inception, and their performance as a project leader depends on their ability to deliver them on time and within budget.

1.6. DIFFERENT KINDS OF PROJECTS

The primary distinguishing feature of a project is its originality. It is a risky venture into the unknown. Even recurrent projects will differ in one or even more commercial, organizational, or physical characteristics from their predecessors. Nevertheless, it is possible and practical to categorize projects into four distinct kinds (Figure 1.7).

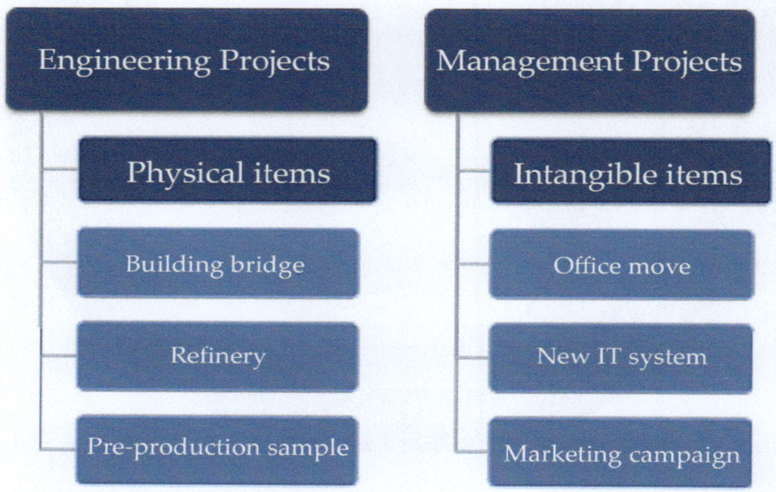

Figure 1.7. Schematic of different kinds of projects.

Source: Free Management e-Books, creative commons license.

1.6.1. Engineering, Construction, Petrochemical, and Mining Projects

The projects that fall into this category are the ones that come to mind first and foremost whenever the topic of industrial projects is broached. The real work, also known as the fulfillment phase, should be carried out at a location that is open to the elements and is typically located some distance away from the contractor's main office (Jiang et al., 2008). This is a characteristic that is shared by all of these situations. As a consequence of this, they are frequently visible to the general population.

These projects come with their own unique set of risks and organizational challenges. They may need a significant investment of resources and demand stringent control of growth, finances, and quality. However, this is usually not the case. Because operations are frequently dangerous; health and safety concerns require heightened attention, which is especially important in physically demanding tasks such as building, tunneling, and mining. The cash and resources required for some huge industrial projects might be too large for one firm to find (Jiang et al., 2008). Thus, the involvement of numerous different experts and contractors is expected to impede organization and communications. It is also possible that the key players would cooperate through a collaboration or strategic partnership business created mainly for the project.

1.6.2. Manufacturing Projects

Manufacturing projects culminate in the creation of electronic or mechanical devices, machinery, a ship, an aircraft, a ground vehicle, or any other product or specifically made hardware. Although the end product may be designed specifically for a particular customer, internally conducted research and development projects for items offered in all market segments also fall under this manufacturing classification (Kasvi et al., 2003).

Manufacturing projects are typically carried out in a laboratory, plant, or home-based setting where the organization can easily practice on-the-spot management and offer an ideal environment to accomplish and oversee the work. In fact, perfect conditions do not always exist. Some manufacturing projects need work outside the home base, such as installing and activating a machine or piece of equipment on a client's facilities, client training, and post-project maintenance and assistance.

Complex products developed and produced by a coalition of enterprises, often with members residing in various countries, present a greater challenge. A typical example is aircraft manufacturing, in which the engines may be designed and made in one nation, the wings in the other, and the assembly process in a third (Bangerter & Clark, 2003). Due to organizational intricacy, national rivalry, agreements, long-distance communications, various languages, and opposing technological standards, international production ventures are prone to greater risk and challenges in management and coordination.

1.6.3. Information Technology (IT) and Management Projects

This type of project demonstrates that every business, regardless of size, may anticipate requiring project management competence at some point in the future. These are the projects that come up when companies move their corporate headquarters, create, and launch a new computer system, start an advertising campaign, get ready for a trade fair, create a report on practicability or another study, reorganize the company, mount a stage production, or usually start engaging in any operation that requires the supervision and coordination of operations to generate an outcome that is not primarily recognized as a product of hardware or development (Nobelius & Trygg, 2002).

Even though management projects do not typically culminate in a visible and concrete development like a piece of hardware. A great deal frequently relies on their effective ending. It may be necessary to make a significant financial commitment. A few well-known incidents in which, for example, failure to properly install a brand-new computer system has generated significant operational breakdown, presenting the responsible management to public disgrace. These breakdowns have occurred as a result of the failure. The importance of efficient project management in these endeavors cannot be overstated compared to that of the largest building or industrial project (Herbsleb, 2007).

Remember

Not all projects are conducted commercially or for profit. Most not-for-profit organizations, including national and local government departments, professional associations, charities, and disaster relief agencies conduct projects that fall into this category of management projects.

1.6.4. Scientific Research Projects

Pure research projects are a true exception. Sometimes, they result in enormously beneficial discoveries. On the contrary, they can consume huge sums of money over an extended period without producing pragmatic or economic results. Since they aim to expand the bounds of human understanding, research undertakings involve the greatest risk. Typically, it is challenging or impossible to specify the stated goals, and the possible outcomes may be unknown (McGregor & Little, 1998). Thus, academic research projects are typically inapplicable to project management methods applicable to industrial, manufacturing, and managerial projects.

However, attempts at management over pure research projects must be made. Money, as well as other resources, cannot be wasted without oversight or limitation. Budgets must be established in accordance with existing resources.

Conducting regular management evaluations and reconsiderations of the project's economic worth is a suitable method for managing an actual scientific research project. During each of these evaluations, a decision may be made to terminate the project (often referred to colloquially as "drawing the plug") or to announce new financing to permit it to go on at least until the next review. Even though this is worrisome for the scientists engaged, the project sponsor is not anticipated to invest resources into a large hole indefinitely (Poon et al., 2004). This method, in which project funding is contingent on the results of periodic inspections, is called stage-gate control.

Even though the research operations may fall beyond typical project management methodologies, the provision of lodging, communications, machinery, and research materials may well represent Type I, II, or III capital investment projects that may and should be appropriately managed.

1.7. FIVE DIMENSIONS OF A PROJECT

One of the basic principles of project management will soon be explained. Even though it is simple, it is effective and powerful. Spend some time making sure they comprehend this.

Assume the endeavor is as easy as redecorating a few rooms in their home. Project managers thus take a seat and give this decorating some thought before deciding to adorn their living room and dining room and to paint each wall with three coats (Gransberg et al., 2013). They do the math and discover that with standard paint brushes, the job will take four days and cost them £200 in paint. Much more quickly, a buddy of mine has a machine that can spray the walls. Sadly, it does not always function and has a tendency to spray paint everywhere, including any exposed furniture close, so they decide against using it. The following information has clarified some key elements of their project:

i. The scope has been established. The project manager refers to what their project entails as its scope. Their job here is to repaint the dining room and living room (Reis & Renzulli, 2018).

ii. The quality has been specified by them. On all the walls, they have chosen to apply three coats of paint. How people judge quality depends on the output a project generates; there are many different ways to measure quality. The majority of outputs, nevertheless, can be produced in some form with varying degrees of quality. They can make the deliverables more or less labor-intensive by altering the quality level. Quality can be a vague but crucial idea; additional examples include a deliverable's robustness or dependability or the way it is presented. How well a deliverable meets the needs of the project customer is a useful way to define quality.

iii. Project managers are aware that it will require four days. They are aware of the price: £200.

iv. Project managers are selecting the low-risk choice because they are aware of the level of hazard they wish to incur. The use of a spray-painting machine is an additional, high-risk option. Although using this machine could speed up their work, there are hazards to their furnishings and a chance that it will not operate (Iveroth et al., 2013).

Although business undertakings are more complicated than this, the idea is still valid (Van Den Hamer & Lepoeter, 1996). Once they are aware of these five factors, users can swap them off to achieve the best outcome. For instance, criteria are frequently made for projects, such as that they must be finished before Christmas or cost no more than £50,000. If they do not think they can accomplish this, they might be capable of satisfying these requirements by altering the scope and the caliber of their deliverables or by choosing a higher-risk strategy.

Project management places a lot of emphasis on the concept of risk, especially as projects grow bigger and more complicated. There are typically more uncertainties, unknowns, and possibilities for unexpected outcomes as tasks become more complex (Mirbagheri & Khajavi, 2013). This is not just a case of bad prediction; risks and unknowns are just a part of everyday existence. The majority of a project manager's time is spent attempting to determine risks and figuring out what can be done to mitigate them. In this book, they shall deal with straightforward risk management. They must gain a deeper grasp of risk and risk management to advance to the position of professional project manager.

1.8. THE LIFECYCLE OF A PROJECT

Each project goes through different phases as it develops. Depending on the sort of project, these stages change (Martinsuo, 2020). A project to create a new car, for instance, has distinct stages than a project to create an ad campaign for a brand-new washing detergent (Figure 1.8). Nonetheless, projects must generally go through standard processes such as:

i. Planning the project and working out how it will be done.
ii. Specifying in detail what the project is for.
iii. Completing the project as planned and producing the deliverables.
iv. Verifying the deliverables are what they initially desired and meet the requirements
v. Closing the project down (Labuschagne & Brent, 2005).

These five steps defined are a simple project lifecycle.

The methodology being chosen affects the project's lifespan as well. During the past few years, this has been a topic of discussion and growth within the project management community (Kujala et al., 2015).

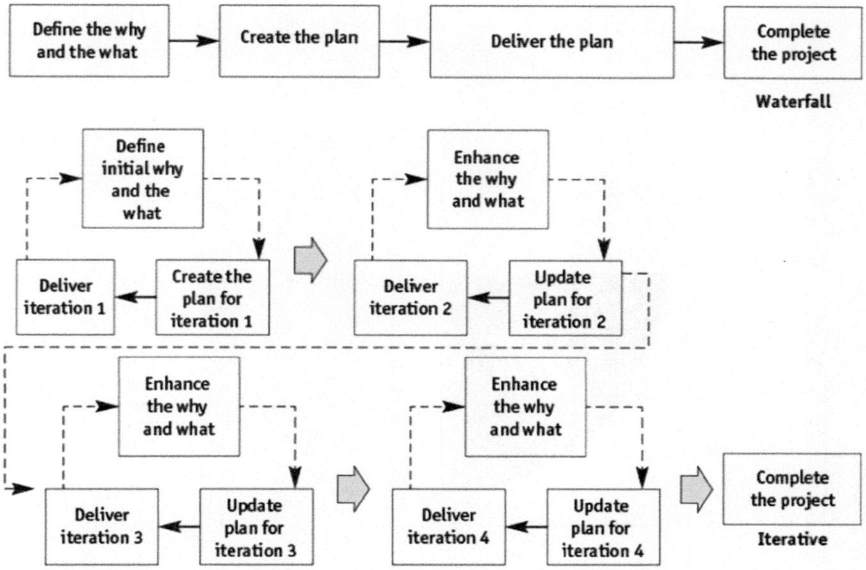

Figure 1.8. Illustration of the project life cycle.

Source: Richard newton, creative commons license.

For instance, compared to a traditional project, Agile uses a significantly different lifespan. Although this complexity is beyond the scope of this book, it is important to understand the distinction between an "iterative" and a "waterfall" lifetime (Martinsuo et al., 2019). With a waterfall project, they essentially complete each phase once after going through the lifetime.

Using the aforementioned lifecycle, they begin with specifying and end with project closure after completing each step once in the order provided (Somers & Nelson, 2004). Similar actions are performed in an iterative lifetime, but they are repeated numerous times.

There are various justifications for choosing a waterfall over an iterative lifecycle. It is outside the purview of this book to delve deeply into something that has been the subject of hundreds of books and articles. But in plain English, iterative lifecycles allow them to go forward rapidly with prototypes that meet customers' often straightforward needs and then gradually improve the deliverables as they gain knowledge from the development process.

Readers now have all the information needed to begin going and are now prepared to assume the responsibilities of a project manager and start carrying out their project. Readers truly can complete their project as they read the ensuing chapters of the book (Figure 1.9).

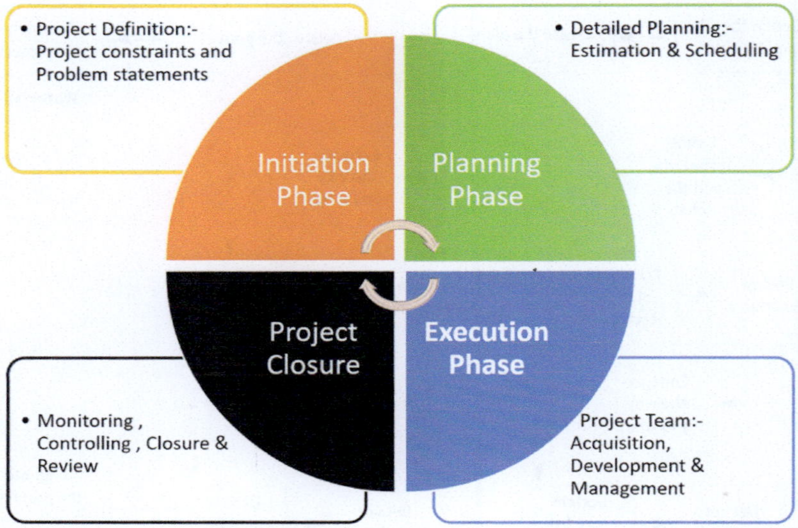

Figure 1.9. Schematic of stages of project management.

Source: Matthew martin, creative commons license.

1.9. PROGRESSION OF PHASES

Each stage expands and improves upon the stages that came before it. If an excellent job is not done during commencement, then the following three steps will be difficult. If enough effort is not put into planning, it will show in both the implementation and the way one wrap things up. If the project is not executed well, the whole thing will suffer (Wehrend & Meinecke, 2001).

> **Did you Know?**
>
> The first recorded instance of program management dates back to the 1950s, when the US air force used the approach to manage complex weapons development programs.

After each phase is an approval procedure that needs to be carried out before going on to the following stage, this prevents from moving on to the subsequent step before it is ready to be entered. Phase gates are the last approvals that must be obtained before moving on to the next phase.

One advantage of receiving approvals after every stage is that it helps to keep project costs to a minimum because they rise rapidly from project commencement through planning and execution. During closeout, the expenses then start to decline significantly. One may cut costs and avoid wasting time by ensuring one has all of the bases covered before moving on to the next stage. It's helpful to have go/no-go decision gates, like phase gates, that compel a decision to move forward with the project if one is spending a significant amount of resources, whether in the form of money or people's time (Cairncross et al., 2006). If the project is medium or lengthy (lasting more than six months), one should also include sure go/no-go decision gates during the execution phase to ensure that everyone is on board with what is going on and that the client and the company still require the outputs that are created. Stage gates are these executions go/no-go decision points, and the sponsor must set them.

1.10. PROGRAM MANAGEMENT

Program management is the process of managing multiple related projects in a coordinated way to achieve specific strategic business objectives, It involves overseeing the planning, implementation, and evaluation of several projects that share common goals and dependencies (Zighan & El-Qasem, 2021).

Everyone would agree that operating a program entails having the ability to step back from specific issues and gain an overall picture of the procedure (Levin & Green, 2016) (Figure 1.10).

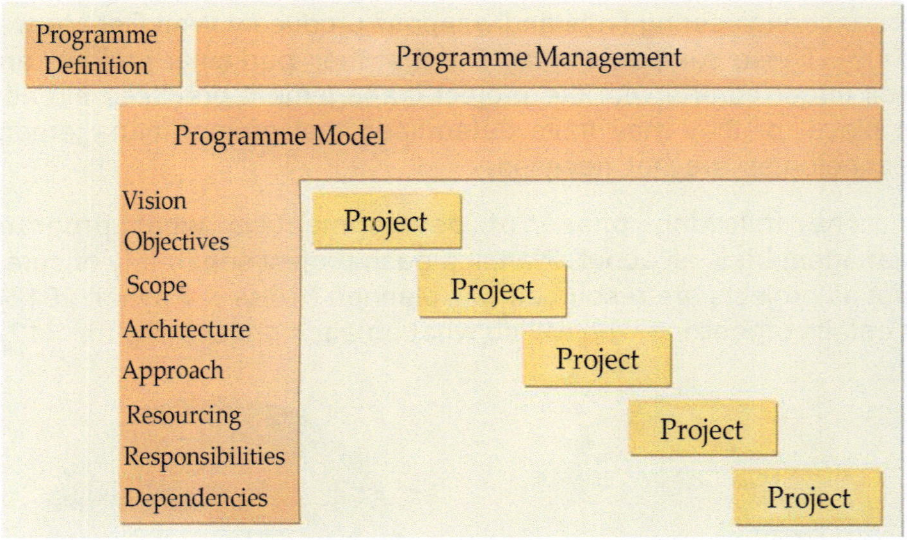

Figure 1.10. Image of the basic program management framework.

Source: EPM Book, creative commons license.

1.10.1. Managing the Program

Here, a broad range of organizations are being discussed, including government agencies like the extremely helpful Health, Environment, and Taxes departments. The fascinating Department of Employment is another option (Nicholas, 2004) (Figure 1.11).

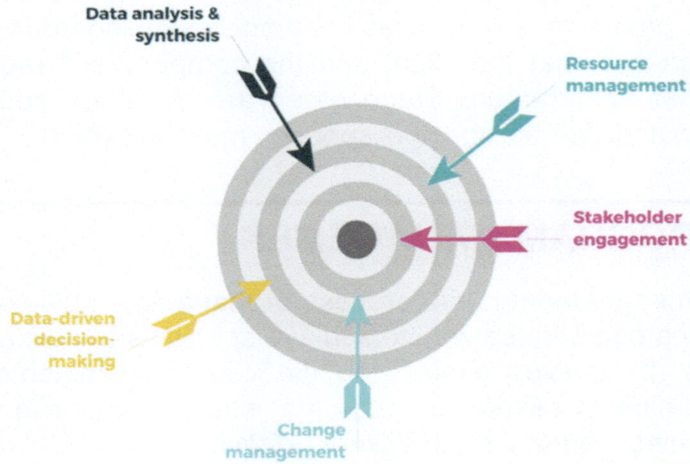

Figure 1.11. Diagram representing essential skills of a program manager.

Source: Elizabeth Harrin, creative commons license.

All types of organizations oversee programs. These include everything from office supply stores to software development firms to contract engineering firms and weapons producers (Van Der Merwe, 2002). These companies may find that their particular projects are well under control with the project management practices already in place, or they may have determined that project management technologies are not necessary.

The following phase of development is what program management is all about. Planning each project separately ensures that all projects are resourced and planned (Reiss & Rayner, 2012). It entails organizing who will do what on each project (Figure 1.12).

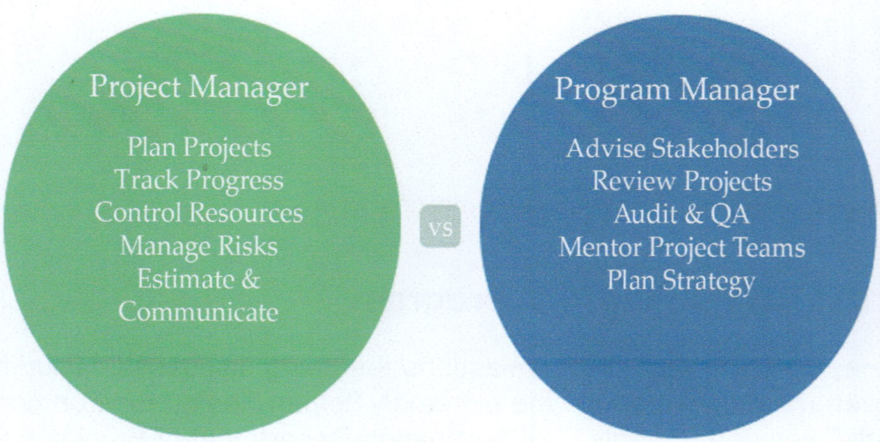

Figure 1.12. Representation of responsibilities of project and program manager.

Source: Esther Cohen, creative commons license.

1.10.2. Not Many People Work on One Project at a Time

These days, few project leaders are working on a single lonely project because the trend toward product management is so strong. Most tasks are manageable within organizations with numerous other endeavors and projects (Rosemann et al., 2012).

The heavy engineering and building sectors are two of the rare market segments that heavily rely on project management yet avoid program management because, typically, each project is managed independently, apart from other projects. Such projects are frequently physically separated, which is a lovely way to say they are trapped in a remote valley closed off by snow for three months of the year or in the middle of a desert.

The project manager must battle to assemble his team from the company's specialists when a team is formed to construct a bridge, a tunnel, or a zinc mine. The most talented individuals are in high demand and are presumably engaged in other global endeavors (Simons, 1991). Project manager consults with heads of departments, other project managers, and personnel staff. Someone hires from inside their organization, from other companies, and, very infrequently, through the Job Center. This is the core group of people who agree to work for the next few years on building the dam, bridge, or road. Most join the project team as full-time employees.

In an effort to promote teamwork, many project managers gather the team around them and take over the west wing of the fourth floor of the corporate headquarters, set up an office on-site, or rent a location apart from the main office (Rosemann & vom Brocke, 2014).

Table 1.1. Difference Between Project and Program Management

Program Management	**Project Management**
Many simultaneous projects	One project at a time
Personal relationship with skilled resources	Impersonal relationship with unskilled resources
Concentration on resources	Resources less important
Need to maximize utilization of resources	Need to minimize demand for resources
Project tend to be similar to each other	Project tend to be dissimilar to each other
The team must ensure that the project's aim helps the organization forward	The team do not care what happens to the project after they finish their part
Concentration on the corporate objectives	Concentration on the project alone
There are loads of available tools	There are few available tools

Source: Geoff Riss, Creative Commons License.

Project managers want the project to be everything to their crew (Ehret, 2004). They know there will be many diversions from men and women, smokers and non-smokers, and company automobiles. The last thing they want is for the team members to be lent out to handle a specific aspect of their previous job, to be presented to a client regarding a future job, or to serve on the advisory council for the bowling green (Table 1.1).

When the project team is established, controlling and directing contractors takes center stage in project management. The project manager and the team beg and plead with the contractors to prioritize the job in their in-trays while also planning and looking forward.

The project team typically works with businesses rather than people (Easterby-Smith et al., 2021). In essence, one assigns the management of the contractors the responsibility for worrying about resources.

So when people hire a builder to build them a house, bridge builders do not become engaged with specific painters and welders. Project managers might be familiar with the bricklayer their builder uses, but suppose the brickie wins the pools and leaves for Bali with his IQ in the double digits, leaving them without a bricklayer. Instead of going to the Employment Center, they go to the construction company because it is their responsibility to replace the pool winner with someone else who will occasionally lay bricks and continually demand tea (Null, 2017).

Contractors who are not helpful face a strong and motivating consequence from the person building the house or bridge: they risk being fired, replaced, or unpaid. A bridge builder will prioritize the success of his project well above the commercial success of his contractors (Vollmann et al., 2000).

Dams, bridges, and large tunnels—but not their garages—are examples of these uncommon and great feats of human creativity and capability. The companies they are collaborating with will be referred to as "them" and "they" by the team.

Project managers for tunnel construction often remark, "We need more carpenters from Cumberland & Sausage." They do not say, "Hey, let's acquire some more chips at the labor exchange." These individuals are in charge of a project, not a program (Artto & Dietrich, 2007).

Things are considerably different when operating a program in a software company (Morris, 2010). The projects are typically smaller, and the project manager must contend with numerous coworkers, each in charge of a separate project. Many are competing for the same design engineer or computer at precisely the wrong time. Instead of hiring contractors, the project manager for IT typically uses staff members paid by the same compensation division as him.

The software engineer frequently has absolutely no consequences for the coworkers (Rohloff, 2009). Although realizing that all of the organization's projects contribute to the business's success, which is something an engineer cares about somewhat, they still value projects as vital. To achieve the business objectives, one must collaborate with the other project managers.

The engineer and the project are borrowing the resources (Loushine et al., 2006). On Tuesdays, or worse, after 7 o'clock, one might have access to the mainframe computer. Everyone who contributes to the initiative does so voluntarily. Even though this favor may be formal and covered under the donor's job description, it is still a favorite. The majority of resources labor on numerous unrelated assignments and numerous other initiatives (Sherman & Chappell, 1998). As their resources work at their desks and terminals while performing whatever tasks they are assigned, the project manager might not notice when one loses someone from the project right away. They most likely contribute to the initiative on a freelance basis.

The unique resources and their functional superiors' priorities are their own. That's not accurate. Although their objectives appear to be their own, individuals are frequently pulled in different directions between many urgent and high-priority responsibilities.

Because no one could have predicted that a fire would damage the printing works over the weekend, sometimes "unplanned" is acceptable (Lee, 2009). Typically, the term "unplanned" refers to something that might have and should have been planned eons ago but has been sitting in a senior suit's inbox while struggles with more pressing matters like the paper clip supply or the secretary. Several senior managers suddenly understand that because they did nothing about "something," "something" has become essential and vital (Yang et al., 2011). They, therefore, play the system, exert pressure, and siphon funds from other carefully thought-out enterprises. Who said that life is supposed to be fair?

The crew is scattered in this setting. The likelihood of getting the crew to stay put and work for an extended time is vanishingly slim (Young et al., 2014). Gathering everyone for a project meeting now and then is the project manager's only chance to accomplish this admirable objective.

At these sessions, everyone seems highly enthused about the project, eager to participate, and ready to contribute. People often experience that as a result of projects. Its effect on people is often exhibited by effective project managers.

Regrettably, the team members will participate in other project meetings where they will grow enthused about the project, eager to get involved, and ready to contribute. They begin to forget about the initial idea and the current promises as a result (Sanchez et al., 2009).

Some considerate project managers would gather the entire group at a distant location (the neighborhood hotel), where the strategy is explained, and the team dynamic is strengthened, and communication channels are opened.

1.10.3. Timeline of Projects and Programs

People can confidently expect that a fascinating and dramatic endeavor will follow a recognizable life cycle. It will start, go on, and come to a conclusion.

For most projects, there will come a time when the project team members will gather and reflect, "There, they did it. Somebody built it." Meanwhile, a powerful person in a suit, who showed no interest in the undertaking and undoubtedly made no contributions, will be the one to announce to the media, "There, we did it. I constructed it" (Melton et al., 2011).

Projects are born to live and die, just like individuals. The programs do not. They continue endlessly. On paper, a project plan can be created with a timeline across the top. They often have an end date well down to the right, and a start date towards the top left corner.

By the way, plans created in the Middle East occasionally deviate from this guideline. Project plans are occasionally drawn from right to left since Arabic, Urdu (India and Pakistan), Ivrit (Israel), and Farsi (Iran) are all written that way.

Let's now think about a program plan. A schedule can still be created on a single piece of paper if by "program" one very massive undertaking is meant, such as the moon landing. Nevertheless, a single sheet of paper can no longer be utilized if a "program" is defined as several internal or external projects ongoing throughout the business (Walenta, 2016).

They require an indefinitely long scrolling piece of paper on which projects appear, move over to the left, then vanish to arrange this. Old, currently finished projects get erased and drop off into the past while new projects are constantly being added to the right (in the future). There is always work to be accomplished (Marnewick, 2016).

These days, it's hard to find scrolling pieces of paper that go on forever. Somebody scoured the Sasco catalog and drove the local stationery store- guy bonkers. People looked through catalogs of miniaturized desktop aluminum dustbins to hold paperclips and tiny brushes to clean their phone but to no effect. There are not enough pieces of paper that scroll indefinitely.

Some define "program management" as a group of projects, each advancing a single objective (Cooke-Davies, 2003). These individuals are perfectly content using a standard, flat piece of paper. The program does come to an end in this situation.

1.10.4. Difference between MRP and Program Management

How does MRP come into the picture if assignments are about one specific purpose while programs are about multiple concurrent objectives? This section gives an overview how these three concepts—project and program management, as well as MRP—fit together (Cwikla & Jalocha, 2015) (Figure 1.13).

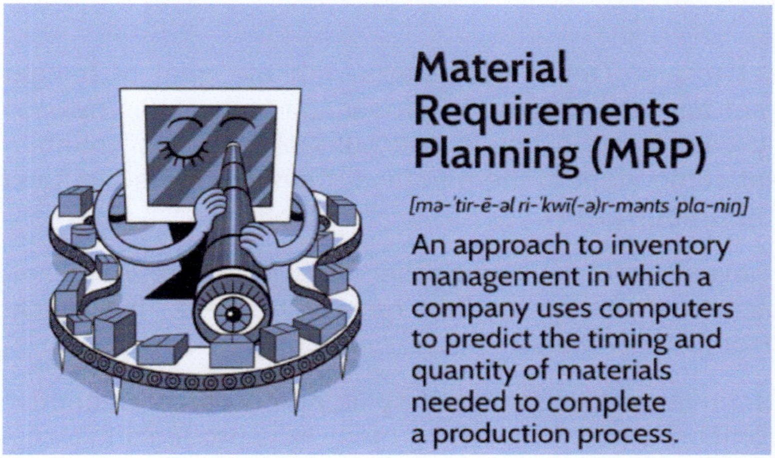

Figure 1.13. Definition of material requirement planning.

Source: Will Kenton, creative commons license.

Planning for material requirements is known as MRP, and it has to deal with the production process. Readers are now at the point in the "project" to "process" spectrum that is most remote from a single project (Ashurst et al., 2012). The one-time, large-scale project, such as the Eurotunnel, is at one end. Such endeavors frequently take on enormous, extraordinary, and curiously romantic forms. Several joint projects are smaller, more well-known, and fit into clear categories in the middle band of this specific spectrum. The continuous-flow procedure, which comes right at the end, involves letting oil, tomato juice, or another flavorless substance flow along a production line while being treated as it goes.

MRP is utilized to aid in planning the process's conclusion. Many in the production industry use the term "projects" to refer to the type of product development work, which tends to muddle the matter considerably (Blumberg et al., 2014).

When process experts discuss projects, they refer to the steps necessary to introduce a new tomato juice to the market. They come up with a brand-new type of tomato juice; perhaps it already contains Worcestershire sauce (Alam et al., 2010).

This concept has to be turned into a marketable product. They must arrange for the procurement of the ingredients and obtain approval from numerous authorities both inside and outside of their company. They must plan and create their marketing campaign in addition to designing and organizing packaging. They may create TV commercials or hire a freak to shout "Purchase Tomato Juice with Worcester Sauce Now" at local radio stations when records are playing (Bartl et al., 2013).

There is a lot to do, so they should have vehicles available to distribute the goods.

Hence, a project exists. The project starts with the goal of bringing this product on the market and ends when the production team takes over or when the product is being consumed in hotels and pubs all over the country. Since this is the investment component of the equation, manufacturers aim to shorten the time to market (Bartlett, 2017).

The lesser the investment, the earlier the return, and the less likely their competitors will release a similar product before they are; the quicker the product is released onto the market.

Project experts have a program if they imagine for a second that a manufacturing corporation is now introducing many new products to the market. They may easily think of the early marketing efforts for several new items, the pre-production modifications made to manufacturing equipment, and the research and development operations as part of a program. It possesses all the traditional indicators of various projects utilizing the expertise of numerous functional departments (Smith & Telang, 2018).

The production control tools and concepts like MRP and JIT can be used once the project is finished and the product is on the market. JIT, or just-in-time manufacturing, is another name for short-cycle manufacturing (Fatemi & Lankenau, 2004).

They are getting to know one mentality far too well if they thought short-cycle manufacturing built motorcycles for midgets. Like most notions, this one is straightforward: automakers are quite typical. Why do they inquire, "should they carry a sizable inventory of parts to support their production lines, such as brake drums and windscreens?" Stockpiling costs a lot of money since they have to tie up big sums of cash, break, and lose a lot of it, and employees have the bothersome habit of slipping expensive items down their trouser legs just before limping off to their homes for tea.

Each component must also be moved and unloaded before being stacked, moved about on a forklift truck, lost, found, and finally fed down to the production line where the automobiles are manufactured (Luehrman, 1998).

Why are they doing this? They want the production line to continue operating, is the reply. Stopping the line because they lack wiper motors would be extremely expensive. This was fairly accurate and lauded as being very wise until computerization allowed us to estimate what cars will be produced and when reasonably. All they need to do is list the components of each type of car and schedule each type of car. The computer can then generate a list of the required parts and a schedule for each. Wait a minute, how do they break down the list of parts? An automobile is at the top of a family tree-style hierarchy that is broken down into its key components, which are then broken down into smaller components at the next level, and so on (Reuvid, 2010) (Figure 1.14). Here is a brief illustration :

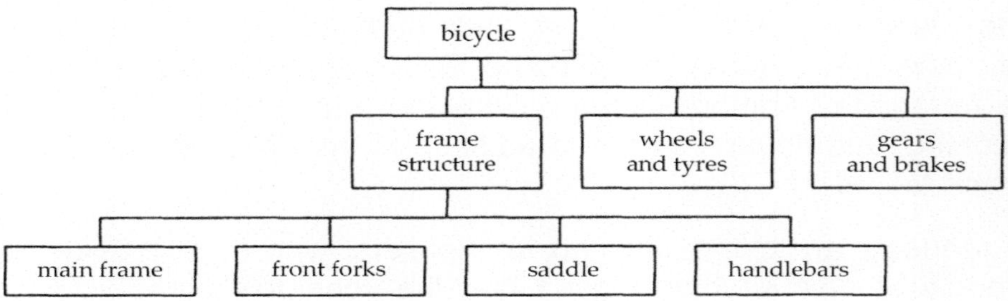

Figure 1.14. Diagram of the family tree for bicycle manufacturing project.

Source: Geoff Riss, creative commons license.

Indeed, it is not a car, but it is still far greener than a car. This is sometimes called a component breakdown structure (Reiss, 2002). They may create a bill of materials by taking this diagram and turning it into a list with the same structure but the boxes represented as headings (Figure 1.15).

- bicycle
  - frame and structure
    - main frame
    - front forks
    - handlebars
      - bars
      - grips
      - stem
      - locating nut
    - saddle
      - seat
      - seat post
      - fixing bolt
  - wheels and tyres
  - gears and brakes

Figure 1.15. Illustration of the bill of materials for bicycle manufacturing project.

Source: Andrew Farell, creative commons license.

Does this resemble a job breakdown structure in any way? Given how similar the concepts are, it should. There is a distinction: A deliverable's components are listed in a component breakdown structure. The item they deliver after the task is referred to as a deliverable. The same components are listed in list form on the bill of materials (Blichfeldt & Eskerod, 2008).

The work required to obtain, produce, and assemble these components is also covered by the work breakdown structure (WBS). Tasks like "Interview potential saddle suppliers," "Place order for saddles," and "Wait for delivery of first saddles" would be included in the WBS. 'Doing' words can be found in WBS diagrams and lists (Cobo-Benita et al., 2016).

They now have various automobiles with all kinds of absurd names and option packs thanks to the JIT idea and the general computerization of the automobile manufacturing process. Their intelligent and astute choices are all entered into the computerized ordering and manufacturing system when they order their new Fraud Acronym 2.0lt XLS Gti 16V Aero-deck 4WD RWS Econogreen in Terracotta ('Another one in brown, Joe') with the two-tone brown trim, air conditioning, and driver's airbag in addition to the optional ice-warning alert and ski rack (Yu et al., 2018).

Oncoming requests are communicated to suppliers, who must provide the goods on schedule. Just a second, wasn't that the scheme's name? Just in time, not "bring the goodies," please. The suppliers must load their articulated lorries with the correct automobile parts in the proper sequence as directed by the production line and then back them up to the factory's side doors. Their ski rack might be hidden in the rear of the appropriate truck if they stop it on the way to Halewood (Chang & Rieple, 2013).

The motor maker feels considerably better overall because of the much-reduced stockpile, decreased risk of theft and wastage, less financial commitment to stock, and decreased warehousing. The vendors are working quite hard to keep up. Sometimes people wonder if JIT means that the inventories are in supplier-owned warehouses rather than manufacturers-owned warehouses.

A second ingenious strategy is concurrent engineering, and many people will gasp in disbelief that no industry has always been using it. If they do not believe in concurrent engineering, they have a team of designers who work out the entire design for their new vehicle, bicycle, or anything before construction. The construction sector is probably one of the worst in this regard. The architect spends hours planning their hotel down to the last hinge and bracket using a hot drawing board or CAD system (Engström et al., 2023).

After the design is almost complete, the quantity surveyor assumes control and compiles a book called a bill of quantities that lists every component. This provides a detailed list of all the concrete, drainpipes, and doorknobs.

This book is distributed to construction companies that submit bids to build the hotel, and the job is often awarded to the company with the lowest bid. The work begins on the construction site among a sea of mud and continues through the concrete frame and foundations to the roof. The inside work starts after that, and the door hinges are installed much later.

They might notice a soft nudge that the building might have started long before each hinge was conceptualized. It will be possible to start some construction work concurrently with the design work if it follows a logical pattern (Gurca et al., 2021). As a result, the project will be completed more quickly, delivering the client to their hotel considerably earlier. Concurrent engineering is the term used to describe this.

The phrase "over the wall" may also describe this. One set of persons receives compensation for carrying out certain tasks and realizing certain goals. The design team aims to produce a comprehensive package for the new product because they are paid to design.

To create and test prototypes, another team is compensated (Clarke, 2010). Once they get the design, they scream hysterically about how those dreadful designers couldn't design their way out of a paper bag, how they seem to have no idea how to create things practically, and how they will be last in line for bread when the revolution occurs. Following an appropriate amount of groaning, one of two things occurs:

i. The idea is rejected as impracticable, igniting another round of whining within the design team;
ii. The engineers grudgingly get on with the job (Risius & Spohrer, 2017).

The objectives are flawed in these situations. The goal of the design team should be the same as everyone else's: to release a fantastic product that is profitable. They create barriers between the groups when they put the designers and engineers in separate rooms and ask them to design, engineer, and so on with other groups.

Because the team was housed in one area, the Chrysler Viper automobile was released to the public at a record-breaking rate. The barriers were torn down, but they all made it work. The pressure to get items to market fast clashes with the stringent quality and safety regulations that frequently apply, as well as the complexity of current development initiatives.

With all of this in mind, it is clear that program management will be essential in guiding these development projects through the concurrent engineering phases, setup phases, prototype, and test marketing phases, and JIT production. Hence, no conflict exists between MRP, program management, or project management. Program management is probably for them if their company specializes in producing expensive goods in small quantities. MRP is their man if they are in the mass production of inexpensive goods (Sirkin et al., 2005). In either scenario, program management may be very beneficial during the research and development stage as they attempt to market new items, but MRP will enable them to manufacture their new product efficiently.

1.10.5. No Plan is an Island

Project management software has been used by the industry for several years despite the nagging suspicion that the tools were not truly what was required in the first place (Lussier, 1995). In addition, people like to believe in Santa Claus, and Michelle Pfeiffer would like them if one had the chance.

Even while people claim that "these project-management tools help," "their competitors are heavily invested in project management," and "the MD says it's a good thing, so who are they to argue," there remains a nagging feeling of unhappiness (Håkansson & Snehota, 1989). In general, word processing, spreadsheets, and accounting systems appear to do what is expected of them. Project-management software appears to have been overlooked and is feeling down. Stuffing a duck because they are feeling down is not appropriate.

Perhaps the name has something to do with that unhappiness. A disc or three of project management software are grossly oversold. These products are expected to manage projects by consumers (Brass Island, 2011). What a ridiculous notion—next, they will think that diet pills work and that politicians and advertising executives are telling the truth. There are many excellent software tools available to assist with project planning, but none of them could operate their way out of a paper bag. When their thoughtful and naive manager receives a copy of a book on program management, they anticipate that it will assist in project management, but it does not. Instead of solving their difficulties as expected, it makes things worse. It assists in identifying issues; it might do so early on, while there is still time to take action, but it does cause issues for them. To solve the issues, they must take action (Fabeil et al., 2020).

Hence, just under its name, project-management software is a little disappointing. Even if they were more properly referred to as project-planning systems, they might still feel something is missing.

The computer is an island in project management where no bottles carry messages. It is a small, isolated area where the resident of the desert island listens to his eight records, burns the entire canon of Shakespeare to stay warm, and models his creations (Nair & Chelliah, 2012).

The word "eight" served as the paragraph's keyword. The important word is "models," I'm only joking about checking if they are still awake (Scott-Young & Samson, 2008).

Modeling the project is what project management software is all about. Modeling the installation of the roof, testing the software and delivery of the printing press may not have any impact on the project. The project is impacted by the decisions that are made as a result of the modeling's ability to assist people in seeing a little into the future. Not the tools but the people who have an impact on the project.

People would probably agree that weather forecasting is a modeling process and has no impact whatsoever on the weather. Michael Fish's forecast for tomorrow helps them choose what to wear to the races or the picnic. The model is the foundation for their decisions, just as in project management (Unlucan, 2010).

If they are older than eight, they probably have witnessed projects where one person diligently plots away in a corner. At the same time, another manages the same project, completely unaware of the plan. They have even worked on projects where when the planner comes to visit, the project team pulls the bar charts out of the bottom drawer. The site team politely reviews the meticulously designed and printed reports that the planner brought with him before putting them all away as the planner departs in the corporate Cavalier (Tummala & Burchett, 1999). Think about the function of purchasing software. Someone makes the purchase of some trout. The purchasing department receives the request, enters it into the central purchasing system, and then sends an order out by postal mail and a copy order to the accounts department (Mitroff et al., 1987). There will be any trout if there is no order. The invoice will be paid if the accounts department isn't informed of the order, and eventually the supplier will ask for their trout back.

The purchasing software has communicated information and played a part, but it has not served as an external model of reality. It is in the primary purchasing line (Miyamoto, 2011). If it were taken away, another system, such as a manual one, would have to be put in its place. Any program that manages a machine is comparable to accounting software. With projects, there is a nagging feeling that everything would still go according to plan if not for the plans, cash-flow curves, labor histograms, and gorgeous, colorful critical-path diagram they drew on the plotter in the design department. The deliverable would be made available in some way. The worst part is that they cannot even demonstrate that their preparation paid off (Angell & Klassen, 1999). Since the project was only completed once, the planning may have increased the project's duration and expense. It is impossible to demonstrate that project planning is anything other than unnecessary. These are some of the causes behind the feeling that something is off with project management software. Software for managing programs can vary (Wagar, 1998). People at a company where all work is planned, resources are allocated, and tasks are assigned use their computers to determine what they are expected to complete this week. Although their terminal is still an island, messages in bottles are constantly coming and going from it. The messages are transmitted via a cable or over local area networks to the mainframe. The software keeps track of plans, project modifications, assignments, and other things being added to the system on other islands (Spillan & Hough, 2003). It is aware of what is happening in other areas of the business. Each user examines their portion of the plan to determine what they or they should be doing, and they may then report back on what they did to influence other people's plans. The software is no longer an external model of the project. It plays a vital role in modeling and conveying that model across the company. Now, it's highly unlikely that their local privatized Electricity Board will state, "We're cooking with gas." This has been accomplished by some organizations now using gas for cooking. Humans do not just roam around picking up tasks and working on them sporadically. They put the program-management tool in the spotlight and communicated with one another about what was happening with the system. It is a method for sending messages in bottles between the various islands in one sense (Kreiner, 1995).

Of course, this is not inexpensive. Planning practically everyone and everything is necessary for such a system to function, which requires time and effort. Huge additional benefits may result from such an investment, which has all the spin-off advantages of a single-project strategy (Meredith, 1998). The thought that "it's a valuable tool" should take the place of that nagging sense is the more appropriate one. Also, the expectations raised by "program management" are considerably more likely to be fulfilled. What more is there to ask?

ACTIVITY11.

In 2006, Microsoft made the competitive move and released Zune, its version of the futuristic, one-buttoned, every-song-in-their-pocket iPod. The onscreen colors were punchy and the interface was type-led with a beautiful minimalist font. It was a bold move to challenge Apple, but in the world of product, success is not always about being first.

It could be argued that the Zune-only features, such as wirelessly sending a song from one Zune to another (an innovative feature in the mid-aughts) were just as good as the iPod-exclusive features, making Microsoft's product a seemingly strong contender. But instead, it was a failure.

There was a project management failure in this project of Microsoft. Identify and provide solutions to this management failure of the Microsoft.

SUMMARY

Project Management is directing and managing individuals directly or indirectly impacting the project. Project managers must accomplish the goal within the specified limits and ensure its success. Time, scope, and money are fundamental restrictions in any project, despite each project having unique constraints. If one has a solid understanding of a project's basics, one can execute it within limits. Project management is vital for the successful and timely execution of projects according to expectations. After reviewing the project's requirements and viability, the most crucial stage in project management is deciding to begin. The project must be continuously monitored and directed from beginning to end. A deliverable accomplishes its objectives within the specified budget and timeline. There are formidable obstacles that project managers must overcome to achieve this aim, which makes it more difficult than it seems. Therefore, planning, acquiring, and utilizing resources effectively and designing the work plans to guide the project from beginning to end are necessary.

Program management manages related projects to achieve specific strategic goals and benefits. A program typically involves several interdependent projects designed to deliver a specific outcome. Program management involves various activities, including defining program goals and objectives, identifying, and managing stakeholders, developing a program plan, managing program finances, and reporting progress. Effective program management requires strong leadership, communication, and collaboration skills and an understanding of project management principles and techniques. Program management is often used in large organizations, government agencies, and non-profit organizations to manage multiple projects related to a common goal.

REVIEW QUESTIONS

1. Define and explain some fundamental concepts of project management.
2. What is program management, and how does it differ from project management
3. Define projects and explain various projects in which project management is being used.
4. What are the key activities in program management, and how do they contribute to achieving program goals?
5. What are the types of project management? Explain in detail.
6. Describe various roles in project management.
7. What skills are necessary for effective program management, and how can these skills be developed?
8. Explain various phases of project management.

MULTIPLE CHOICE QUESTIONS

1. **What is the primary goal of program management?**
   a. To manage individual projects
   b. To achieve specific strategic goals and benefits
   c. To develop project plans
   d. To monitor project progress

2. **A process that involves continuously improving and detailing a plan as more detail becomes available is termed as**
   a. project analysis
   b. project enhancing
   c. progressive deliberation
   d. progressive elaboration

3. **A project is:**
   a. A temporary endeavor was undertaken to create a unique product, service, or result.
   b. An organizational function performs the ongoing execution of activities that produce the same product or provide a repetitive service.
   c. A function of operations focusing on sustaining business that may have a one-time configuration or ongoing processes.
   d. A seemingly impossible challenge that, when approached systematically, makes it appear doable, if only temporarily.

4. **Which of the following is not a key activity in program management**
   a. Defining program goals and objectives
   b. Managing program finances.
   c. They are managing individual project schedules.
   d. Identifying and managing stakeholders.

5. **Project management is:**
   a. The centralized coordination of operations and programs to achieve the program's strategic objectives and benefits.
   b. The centralized coordination of processes and programs to achieve the program's strategic goals and benefits.
   c. Applying knowledge, skills, tools, and techniques to project activities to meet the project requirements.
   d. The centralized, coordinated program management to achieve the program's strategic objectives and benefits.

6. Which of the following skills is important for effective program management?

a. Technical expertise in a specific field
b. Ability to micromanage individual projects
c. Strong communication and collaboration skills
d. Focus solely on program-level outcomes

Answers to Multiple Choice Questions

1. (b); 2. (d); 3. (a); 4. (c); 5. (c); 6. (c)

REFERENCES

1. Aapaoja, A., & Haapasalo, H., (2014). A framework for stakeholder identification and classification in construction projects. *Open Journal of Business and Management, 1*, 6–9.
2. Alam, M., Gale, A., Brown, M., & Khan, A. I., (2010). The importance of human skills in project management professional development. *International Journal of Managing Projects in Business, 3*(3), 495–516.
3. Angell, L. C., & Klassen, R. D., (1999). Integrating environmental issues into the mainstream: An agenda for research in operations management. *Journal of Operations Management, 17*(5), 575–598.
4. Artto, K. A., & Dietrich, P. H., (2007). Strategic business management through multiple projects. In: Morris, P. W. G., & Pinto, J., K., (eds.), *The Wiley Guide to Project Program & Portfolio Management* (Vol. 1, pp. 1–33). New Jersey: John Wiley & Sons Inc.
5. Ashurst, C., Cragg, P., & Herring, P., (2012). The role of IT competences in gaining value from e-business: An SME case study. *International Small Business Journal, 30*(6), 640–658.
6. Bartl, M., Jawecki, G., Bilgram, V., & Wiegandt, P., (2013). The BMW group co-creation lab: From co-creation projects to programs. *Discontinuous Innovation: Learning to Manage the Unexpected, 1*, 179–203.
7. Bartlett, J., (2017). *The Essentials of Managing Risk for Projects and Programs* (Vol. 1, pp. 3–9). Taylor & Francis.
8. Bibarsov, K. R., Khokholova, G. I., & Okladnikova, D. R., (2017). *Conceptual Basics and Mechanism of Innovation Project Management, 1*, 1–5.
9. Blichfeldt, B. S., & Eskerod, P., (2008). Project portfolio management–there's more to it than what management enacts. *International Journal of Project Management, 26*(4), 357–365.

10. Blumberg, B., Cooper, D., & Schindler, P., (2014). *E-Book: Business Research Methods* (Vol. 1, pp. 6–8). McGraw Hill.
11. Bond-Barnard, T. J., Fletcher, L., & Steyn, H., (2018). Linking trust and collaboration in project teams to project management success. *International Journal of Managing Projects in Business, 11*(2), 432–457.
12. Brass Island, P. M. B., (2011). Ethical compliance by the accountant on the quality of financial reporting and performance of quoted companies in Nigeria. *Asian Journal of Business Management, 3*(3), 152–160.
13. Chang, J., & Rieple, A., (2013). Assessing students' entrepreneurial skills development in live projects. *Journal of Small Business and Enterprise Development, 20*(1), 225–241.
14. Clarke, N., (2010). Projects are emotional: How project managers' emotional awareness can influence decisions and behaviors in projects. *International Journal of Managing Projects in Business, 3*(4), 604–624.
15. Clough, R. H., Sears, G. A., & Sears, S. K., (2000). *Construction Project Management* (Vol. 1, pp. 4–9). John Wiley & Sons.
16. Cobb, A. T., (2011). *Leading Project Teams: The Basics of Project Management and Team Leadership* (2nd edn., pp. 6, 7). Sage.
17. Cobo-Benita, J. R., Rodríguez-Segura, E., Ortiz-Marcos, I., & Ballesteros-Sánchez, L., (2016). Innovation projects performance: Analyzing the impact of organizational characteristics. *Journal of Business Research, 69*(4), 1357–1360.
18. Cooke-Davies, T. J., (2003). *Do "Business Change" Projects Really Change the Business?* (Vol. 1, pp. 6–9) PMI Global Congress.
19. Cwikla, M., & Jalocha, B., (2015). Unspread wings: Why cultural projects don't provide refreshing ideas for project management although they could? *International Journal of Managing Projects in Business, 8*(4), 626–648.
20. Easterby-Smith, M., Jaspersen, L. J., Thorpe, R., & Valizade, D., (2021). *Management and Business Research* (Vol. 1, pp. 2–6). Sage.
21. Edmondson, A. C., & Nembhard, I. M., (2009). Product development and learning in project teams: The challenges are the benefits. *Journal of Product Innovation Management, 26*(2), 123–138.
22. Ehret, M., (2004). Managing the trade-off between relationships and value networks. Towards a value-based approach of customer relationship management in business-to-business markets. *Industrial Marketing Management, 33*(6), 465–473.
23. El Khatib, M., Al Mulla, A., & Al Ketbi, W., (2022). The role of blockchain in e-governance and decision-making in project and program management. *Advances in Internet of Things, 12*(3), 88–109.
24. El Khatib, M., Alhosani, A., Alhosani, I., Al Matrooshi, O., & Salami, M., (2022). Simulation in project and program management: Utilization, challenges and opportunities. *American Journal of Industrial and Business Management, 12*(4), 731–749.

25. Engström, A., Johansson, A., Edh, M. N., Sollander, K., & Barry, D., (2023). Knowledge creation in projects: An interactive research approach for deeper business insight. *International Journal of Managing Projects in Business, 16*(1), 22–44.

26. Fabeil, N. F., Pazim, K. H., & Langgat, J., (2020). The impact of COVID-19 pandemic crisis on micro-enterprises: Entrepreneurs' perspective on business continuity and recovery strategy. *Journal of Economics and Business, 3*(2), 5–10.

27. Fatemi, K., & Lankenau, M. J., (2004). *False Claims on Public Projects: Don't Bet Your Business on It* (Vol. 1, pp. 6–10). AACE International Transactions, CD11.

28. Gransberg, D. D., Shane, J. S., Strong, K., & Del Puerto, C. L., (2013). Project complexity mapping in five dimensions for complex transportation projects. *Journal of Management in Engineering, 29*(4), 316–326.

29. Gurca, A., Bagherzadeh, M., Markovic, S., & Koporcic, N., (2021). Managing the challenges of business-to-business open innovation in complex projects: A multi-stage process model. *Industrial Marketing Management, 94*, 202–215.

30. Håkansson, H., & Snehota, I., (1989). No business is an island: The network concept of business strategy. *Scandinavian Journal of Management, 5*(3), 187–200.

31. Heravi, A., Coffey, V., & Trigunarsyah, B., (2015). Evaluating the level of stakeholder involvement during the project planning processes of building projects. *International Journal of Project Management, 33*(5), 985–997.

32. Iveroth, E., Westelius, A., Petri, C. J., Olve, N. G., Cöster, M., & Nilsson, F., (2013). How to differentiate by price: Proposal for a five-dimensional model. *European Management Journal, 31*(2), 109–123.

33. Kreiner, K., (1995). In search of relevance: Project management in drifting environments. *Scandinavian Journal of Management, 11*(4), 335–346.

34. Kujala, J., Nystén-Haarala, S., & Nuottila, J., (2015). Flexible contracting in project business. *International Journal of Managing Projects in Business, 8*(1), 92–106.

35. Labuschagne, C., & Brent, A. C., (2005). Sustainable project life cycle management: The need to integrate life cycles in the manufacturing sector. *International Journal of Project Management, 23*(2), 159–168.

36. Lee, K. H., (2009). Why and how to adopt green management into business organizations? The case study of Korean SMEs in manufacturing industry. *Management Decision, 47*(7), 1101–1121.

37. Levin, G., & Green, A. R., (2016). *Implementing Program Management: Templates and Forms Aligned with the Standard for Program Management, (2013) and Other Best Practices* (Vol. 1, pp. 3–9). CRC Press.

38. Loushine, T. W., Hoonakker, P. L., Carayon, P., & Smith, M. J., (2006). Quality and safety management in construction. *Total Quality Management and Business Excellence, 17*(9), 1171–1212.

39. Luehrman, T. A., (1998). Strategy as a portfolio of real options. *Harvard Business Review, 76*(1), 89–101.

40. Lussier, R. N., (1995). A nonfinancial business success versus failure prediction mo. *Journal of Small Business Management, 33*(1), 1–8.
41. Lynch, M. M., & Roecker, J., (2007). *Project Managing e-Learning: A Handbook for Successful Design, Delivery and Management* (Vol. 1, pp. 2–8). Routledge.
42. Marnewick, C., (2016). Benefits of information system projects: The tale of two countries. *International Journal of Project Management, 34*(4), 748–760.
43. Martinsuo, M., (2020). The management of values in project business: Adjusting beliefs to transform project practices and outcomes. *Project Management Journal, 51*(4), 389–399.
44. Martinsuo, M., Klakegg, O. J., & Van, M. A., (2019). Delivering value in projects and project-based business. *International Journal of Project Management, 37*(5), 631–635.
45. Melton, T., Yates, J., & Iles-Smith, P., (2011). *Project Benefits Management: Linking Projects to the Business* (Vol. 1, pp. 1–6). Butterworth-Heinemann.
46. Meredith, J., (1998). Building operations management theory through case and field research. *Journal of Operations Management, 16*(4), 441–454.
47. Mirbagheri, F. A., & Khajavi, G., (2013). Impact of ERP implementation at Malaysian SMEs: Analysis of five dimensions benefit. *International Journal of Enterprise Computing and Business Systems, 2*(1), 6–10.
48. Mitroff, I. I., Shrivastava, P., & Udwadia, F. E., (1987). Effective crisis management. *Academy of Management Perspectives, 1*(4), 283–292.
49. Miyamoto, K., (2011). The 'growth triangle' and the labor market of Japanese-affiliated enterprises on Batam island. *Economic Journal of Hokkaido University, 40*, 1–14.
50. Morris, P. W., (2010). Research and the future of project management. *International Journal of Managing Projects in Business, 3*(1), 139–146.
51. Nair, R., & Chelliah, J., (2012). Understanding key impediments to small businesses in south pacific island nations: A case of Fiji. *Journal of Global Business Management, 8*(1), 175.
52. Newcombe, R., (2003). From client to project stakeholders: A stakeholder mapping approach. *Construction Management and Economics, 21*(8), 841–848.
53. Nicholas, J. M., (2004). *Project Management for Business and Engineering: Principles and Practice* (Vol. 1, pp. 4–10). Elsevier.
54. Null, G. L., (2017). *An Empirical Investigation of Lean Six Sigma Tool Selection in a Program Management Organization (Doctoral dissertation),* (Vol. 1, pp. 5–9).
55. Oertig, M., & Buergi, T., (2006). The challenges of managing cross□cultural virtual project teams. *Team Performance Management: An International Journal, 12*(1, 2), 23–30.
56. Pellegrinelli, S., (2008). Program management. In: *Thinking and Acting as a Great Program Manager* (Vol. 1, pp. 3–16). London: Palgrave Macmillan UK.
57. Reis, S. M., & Renzulli, J. S., (2018). The five dimensions of differentiation. *International Journal for Talent Development and Creativity, 6*(1), 87–94.

58. Reiss, G., & Rayner, P., (2012). *Portfolio and Program Management Demystified: Managing Multiple Projects Successfully* (Vol. 1, pp. 6–9). Routledge.

59. Reiss, G., (2002). *Portfolio and Program Management Demystified: Managing Multiple Projects Successfully* (Vol. 1, pp. 2–7). Routledge.

60. Reuvid, J., (2010). *Managing Business Risk: A Practical Guide to Protecting Your Business* (2nd edn., pp. 6–11). Kogan Page Publishers.

61. Risius, M., & Spohrer, K., (2017). A blockchain research framework: What we (don't) know, where we go from here, and how we will get there. *Business & Information Systems Engineering, 59*, 385–409.

62. Rohloff, M., (2009). Case study and maturity model for business process management implementation. In: *Business Process Management: 7th International Conference, BPM 2009, Ulm, Germany, September 8–10, 2009; Proceedings 7* (Vol. 1, pp. 128–142). Springer Berlin Heidelberg.

63. Rosemann, M., & Vom, B. J., (2014). The six core elements of business process management. In: *Handbook on Business Process Management 1: Introduction, Methods, and Information Systems* (Vol. 1, pp. 105–122). Berlin, Heidelberg: Springer Berlin Heidelberg.

64. Rosemann, M., Recker, J., Safrudin, N., & Marketsmueller, R., (2012). Program and project management. *A Handbook of Business Transformation Management Methodology, 1*, 217–244.

65. Rosenau, M. D., & Githens, G. D., (2011). *Successful Project Management: A Step-by-Step Approach with Practical Examples* (Vol. 1, pp. 1–10). John Wiley & Sons.

66. Sanchez, H., Robert, B., Bourgault, M., & Pellerin, R., (2009). Risk management applied to projects, programs, and portfolios. *International Journal of Managing Projects in Business, 2*(1), 14–35.

67. Scott-Young, C., & Samson, D., (2008). Project success and project team management: Evidence from capital projects in the process industries. *Journal of Operations Management, 26*(6), 749–766.

68. Sherman, H., & Chappell, D. S., (1998). Methodological challenges in evaluating business incubator outcomes. *Economic Development Quarterly, 12*(4), 313–321.

69. Simons, R., (1991). Strategic orientation and top management attention to control systems. *Strategic Management Journal, 12*(1), 49–62.

70. Sirkin, H. L., Keenan, P., & Jackson, A., (2005). The hard side of change management. *Harvard Business Review, 83*(10), 108.

71. Smith, M. D., & Telang, R., (2018). Data can enhance creative projects—Just look at Netflix. *Harvard Business Review, 23*(1), 4–8.

72. Somers, T. M., & Nelson, K. G., (2004). A taxonomy of players and activities across the ERP project life cycle. *Information & Management, 41*(3), 257–278.

73. Spillan, J., & Hough, M., (2003). Crisis planning in small businesses: Importance, impetus and indifference. *European Management Journal, 21*(3), 398–407.

74. Springer, M. L., (2019). *Project and Program Management: A Competency-Based Approach* (Vol. 1, pp. 1–10). Purdue University Press.

75. Tummala, V. R., & Burchett, J. F., (1999). Applying a risk management process (RMP) to manage cost risk for an EHV transmission line project. *International Journal of Project Management, 17*(4), 223–235.

76. Unlucan, D., (2010). Characteristics of SMEs in North Cyprus: A small island. *Problems and Perspectives in Management, 8*(3), 139–147.

77. Van, D. H. P., & Lepoeter, K., (1996). Managing design data: The five dimensions of CAD frameworks, configuration management, and product data management. *Proceedings of the IEEE, 84*(1), 42–56.

78. Van, D. M. A. P., (2002). Project management and business development: Integrating strategy, structure, processes and projects. *International Journal of Project Management, 20*(5), 401–411.

79. Vollmann, T. E., Cordon, C., & Heikkila, J., (2000). Teaching supply chain management to business executives. *Production and Operations Management, 9*(1), 81–90.

80. Walenta, T., (2016). Projects & programs are two different animals, don't underestimate the gap. *Procedia-Social and Behavioral Sciences, 226*(1), 365–371.

81. Whyte, J., Stasis, A., & Lindkvist, C., (2016). Managing change in the delivery of complex projects: Configuration management, asset information and 'big data.' *International Journal of Project Management, 34*(2), 339–351.

82. Winch, G. M., Morris, P., & Pinto, J., (2007). Managing project stakeholders. *The Wiley Guide to Project, Program, and Portfolio Management, 1*, 271–289.

83. Yang, M. G. M., Hong, P., & Modi, S. B., (2011). Impact of lean manufacturing and environmental management on business performance: An empirical study of manufacturing firms. *International Journal of Production Economics, 129*(2), 251–261.

84. Young, M., Young, R., & Romero, Z. J., (2014). Project, program and portfolio maturity: A case study of Australian Federal Government. *International Journal of Managing Projects in Business, 7*(2), 215–230.

85. Yu, S., Wang, J., & Guo, N., (2008). The application of project portfolio management in the government investment projects. In: *2008 International Seminar on Business and Information Management* (Vol. 2, pp. 513–516). IEEE.

86. Zighan, S., & El-Qasem, A., (2021). Lean thinking and higher education management: Revaluing the business school program management. *International Journal of Productivity and Performance Management, 70*(3), 675–703.

CHAPTER 2

PRINCIPLES OF PROJECT AND PROGRAM MANAGEMENT

UNIT INTRODUCTION

There are various types of cultures in companies and all of their help to achieve the strategic objectives that the firm must accomplish. This chapter will concentrate on the essential project and program management principles, focusing on continuous improvement in project management. Since, unlike numerous others, these principles are not limited to a single direction or function but affect the entire organization. This signifies that operations involving the organization must be described at the organizational level (Goedknegt & Silvius, 2012) (Figure 2.1).

Whenever it comes to performance, it is no longer sufficient to assume merely product-related quality. Still, as described by ISO, it must be comprehended that all the procedures and processes required to ensure the satisfaction of customers need to be decided in the organization's strategy and implemented across the business (Sarkisov et al., 2013).

A similar issue applies to the project and program management environment, as projects are tools for an organization to achieve its strategic objectives. The project management characterization of processes incorporates the entire organization since when a project must be produced, all departments and the company's leadership must be represented:

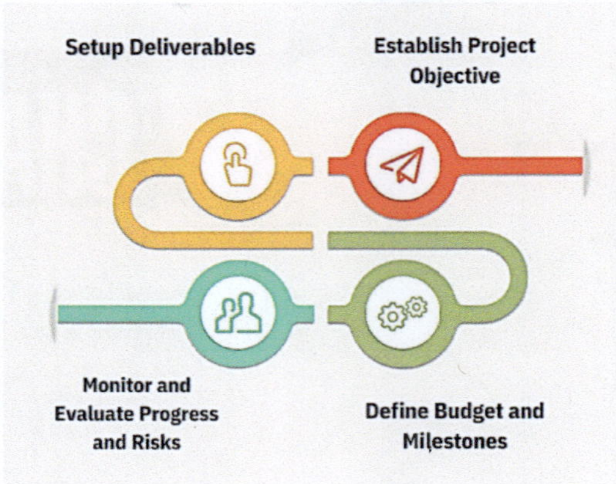

Figure 2.1. Schematic of the project and program management principles.

Source: Team Board, creative commons license.

Inside the project and program management framework, the senior management has to determine which projects should be produced and when (immediately, subsequently, etc.) and set their responsibilities (Ajelabi & Tang, 2010) (Figure 2.2).

- **Marketing:** most likely, the project will have to be designed to satisfy a corporate necessity, and this orientation (Marketing) will still have expectations that must be met, for which they will be the major project participants (Koskela & Howell, 2002).
- **Technical:** any direction or persons responsible for creating the item or service required by marketing.
- **Purchases:** This will oversee the bidding process to buy goods and services, in addition to all commercial aspects of projects.
- **Legal:** If someone works with agreements as suppliers or buyers, they must define and examine contractual clauses. Sales – whether an item or service is created to satisfy a company's needs, someone needs to be capable of selling it (Boehm & Ross, 1989).

Figure 2.2. Schematic of the principles of project and program management.

Source: Sara Williams, creative commons license.

Another exception would be Project Management, which is not generally assigned a specific position inside businesses; it can sometimes be found in functional areas, advertising, and sales. In certain instances, it is possible to witness a hybrid organization in which the Portfolio Management and the Project Management Office (PMO) management is the responsibility of top management or specific instructions. In contrast, project organizational management falls under the purview of many other instructions (Gareis, 2013). Any solution may be suitable when there are no templates specified and prepared to be used and can fulfill the needs of businesses efficiently and effectively. There are numerous project management guidelines and standards that, while not always direct, refer to just how organizations should be managed (Cicmil et al., 2006).

Learning Objectives

At the end of this chapter, readers will be able to learn:

- The principles of project management
- The cultural environment principle
- The project system principle
- The strategy and success principle
- The leadership and commitment principle
- The single point responsibility and tetrad trad-off principle

Key Terms

- Business
- Commitment
- Life Cycle
- Principles
- Project System
- Single point responsibility
- Strategy
- Tetrad Trade-off

2.1. THE PRINCIPLE OF CULTURAL ENVIRONMENT

To guarantee that the project delivery team can operate to the fullest extent given individual abilities, management needs to establish an informed and supportive cultural environment suitable for the research project (Saynisch, 2010) (Figure 2.3).

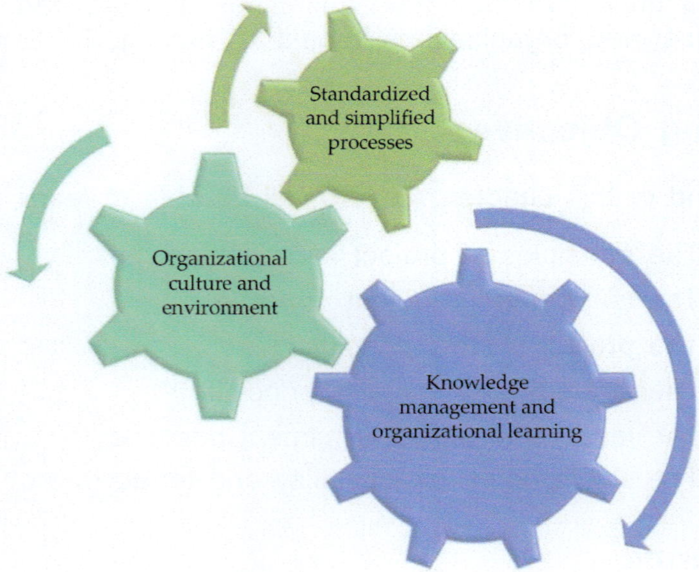

Figure 2.3. Illustration of the organizational culture and environment is an essential factor in project and program management.

Source: Mounir Anjum, creative commons license.

This cultural background significantly impacts a project delivery team's ability to create deliverables quickly and effectively (Silvius & Schipper, 2014). This cultural environment includes project relationships and ideas on the external and internal levels. Internally, the group leader's management strategy needs to be appropriate for the project's type and stage in the life cycle. Externally, the development's management must be encouraging, the effort must be funded appropriately, and there must be no impediments in the surrounding area (Talbot & Venkataraman, 2011).

The atmosphere that results promotes and maintains collaboration and integrity and shows that:

a. Everyone is aware of the project's primary goals and is striving towards those objectives, whatever they may be;
b. Everybody is clear and in agreement about who the client is;

c. When needed, the necessary degrees of competence or knowledge are accessible; and
d. Everybody desires the achievement of project objectives (Lycett et al., 2004).

2.2. THE PRINCIPLE OF PROJECT SYSTEM

A well-managed project is a complicated system where performance management moves forward in an organized timetable. It significantly depends on the appropriate action at the proper time (Zhang, 2007).

A well-managed project maximizes productivity during the implementation stages while maximizing performance during the planning stages. Implementation includes giving the product to the client for their care, possession, and control. The complicated structure being discussed is, in fact, a complex network of interconnected balancing and non-balancing cognitive feedback systems, each with distinct cause, consequence, and adverse reactions characteristics (Smyth & Morris, 2007). This complicated, random arrangement is sufficient to stump many brains. In other respects, numerous people struggle with "an inability to see the forest for the trees." However, the deliverable necessitates the project's leader to have "the capacity to see the forests as well as the individuals" (Figure 2.4).

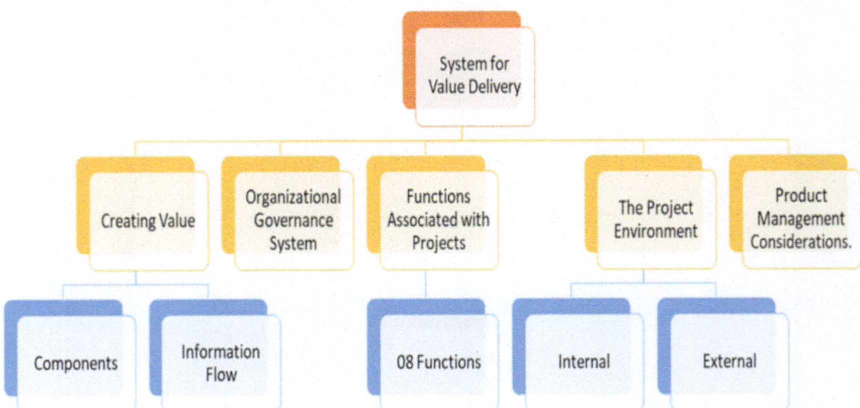

Figure 2.4. Diagram representing the project system principle in project management.

Source: Atul Gaur, creative commons license.

Thus, project management is dominated by high decision-making processes that consume substantial work, as judgments on one system component might significantly affect other sections (Engwall & Jerbrant, 2003).

2.3. THE STRATEGY PRINCIPLE

A targeted set of chronological and continuous processes must be used to implement a strategy that involves planning first and then acting (Zhong-Mei, 2006).

The word "project management" actually serves as the origin of the project's average lifespan in its simplest form. By definition, a project has a beginning and end with some action in between. It is fundamental for the management to "plan before doing." Thus, the four distinct phases of Start, Plan, Do, and Finish comprises the most basic project life span procedure. These four timeframes can, of course, be divided into various phases, each with its intermediate objectives and executive control checkpoints (or gates), which can also be considered emergency escape ramps. These can be created to meet the control needs of every project in any area for project management. They are especially significant from the perspective of portfolio management for projects. As Figure 2.2 in Part 1 of this work suggests, this process is equally relevant at every level and branching of the construction project. It applies when using a rapid development plan or an iterative methodology (Powers & Dickson, 1973) (Figure 2.5).

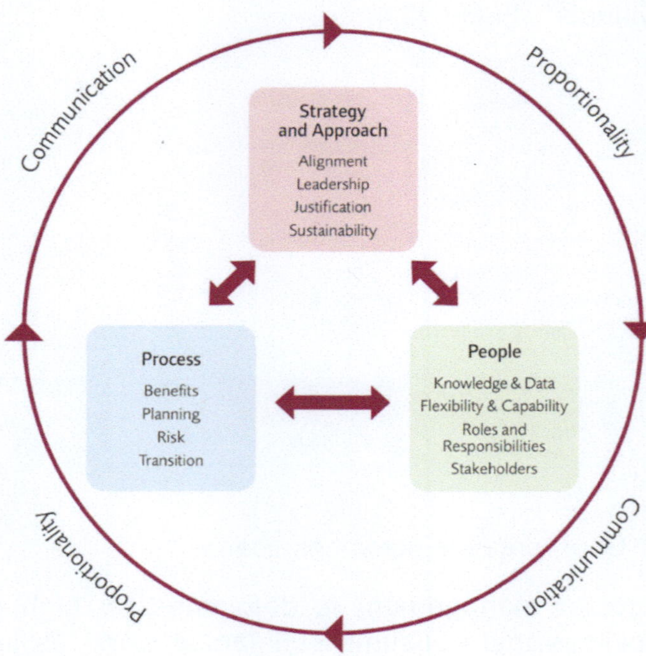

Figure 2.5. Explanation of the role of strategy in project and program management.

Source: Scottish Government, creative commons license.

It is impossible to overstate the significance of this life cycle process and its impact on project management. Projects and non-projects can only be distinguished by this brief life-to-death atmosphere and the following implications (Ofori, 2008).

2.4. THE PRINCIPLE OF SUCCESS

As a foundation for project and program management decision-making and post-project evaluation, the process and product measurements of project success must be developed from the start of the project.

Delivering the finished product is the ultimate purpose of project management; alternatively, this management expense is unnecessary. The project's supporters must, first and primarily, determine the project accomplishment in terms of the desirability of the project's achievements, including breadth, reliability, applicability to customer needs, performance, affordability, overall advantages to the organization, and so on (Mir & Pinnington, 2014).

Furthermore, the internal procedures of the project should be used to determine success, including schedule, cost, implementation efficiency, etc. It can also be necessary to explain when victory will be chosen. Furthermore, all of the project's supporters must agree on how these success criteria should be defined because it will be impossible to assess the project's overall performance (Ika, 2009).

It should be evident that during the project process, these performance indicators should be confirmed and strengthened. As a logical extension, it should be appropriate to abort the project or put it on hold for re-evaluation if the success measures are not clearly in line with the business objectives at any stage (Schindler & Eppler, 2003).

2.5. THE PRINCIPLE OF COMMITMENT

Before such a program can be viable, there needs to be an appropriate engagement between the helpful resource and the project management team.

The project's owner or sponsor is the one who supplies the materials (cash, products, services, and general guidance). The project team is in charge of developing the most efficient strategies, plans, and safeguards for putting all essential abilities to use and turning those capabilities into the desired deliverable or result. A fair engagement is one in which all participants actively undertake the challenge and are adequately informed about the project, including the general goals, the technologies, the processes required, and the dangers involved (Buvik & Tvedt, 2017) (Figure 2.6).

Figure 2.6. Illustration of the role of leadership and commitment in project and program management.

Source: ISO.org, creative commons license.

For the project to succeed, both parties' qualifications should include expertise, necessary technological—related skills, and competence. Every project's ownership must comprehend that there needs to be a distribution of the associated risks, even with competent management control measures.

2.6. THE PRINCIPLE OF MANAGEMENT

Innovative and cost-effective policies and guidelines need to exist to operate the project commitments (Guo, 2003) successfully.

This principle is an extension of the strategy principle. What will be done, however, when determined by the strategic premise? The Managerial Function specifies who will perform it and how it will be done. The project's assumptions, reasoning, and benchmark background in each key variable that serve as a foundation for direction correction and performance evaluation are all included in this organizational process's characteristics. Defined roles and duties, authoritative transmission, step methods to complete, timeliness, budget, etc., and monitoring modifications to the product's scope and project scope are all characteristics of strong guidelines and policies (Ward & Chapman, 2003).

2.7. THE PRINCIPLE OF SINGLE-POINT RESPONSIBILITY

There must be a digital communication signal with the project's sponsor and the manager (or the team leader) about any decisions that impact the product specifications, reliability, and delivery schedule, including total cost (Figure 2.7).

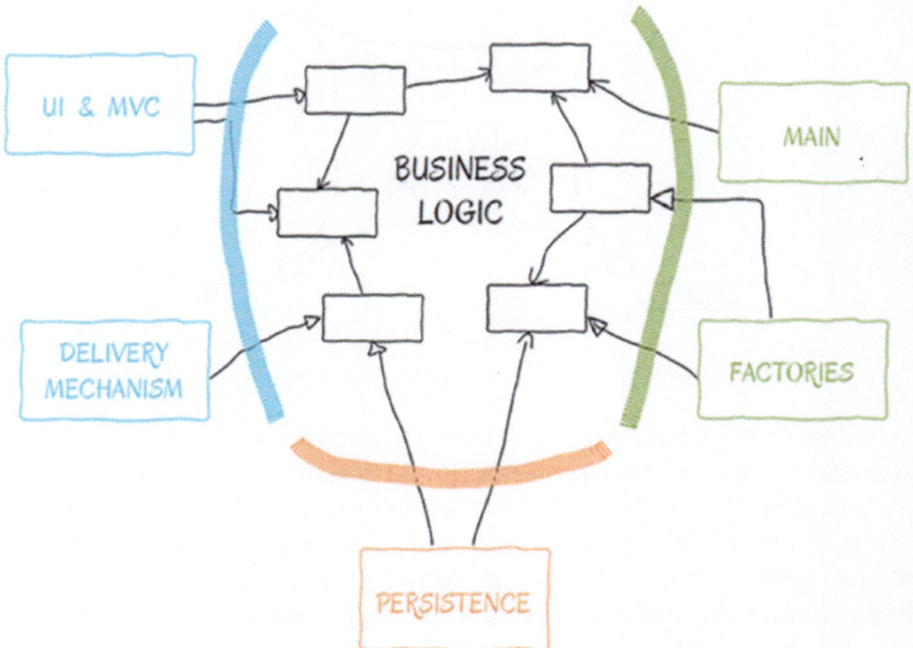

Figure 2.7. Illustration of the single-point responsibility principle.

Source: Patkos Csaba, creative commons license.

This principle extends the management principle and is essential for successfully and efficiently administrating project commitments. For instance, the owner of the final product, if represented by multiple individuals, must speak with one voice thru a primary spokesperson who has accessibility to the sponsor's resources. Likewise, the project delivery team must have a principal representation (Khanzadi et al., 2019).

This only holds for choices that impact the manufacturer's quality level and, consequently, the project's total expenses and timeliness. Free and open communication is required to manage various project operations in all dimensions. The efficient flow of data through the system of project communication channels, which is imperative to incorporate all parts of the project, should not be hindered by this concept (Atkinson, 1999).

2.8. THE PRINCIPLE OF TETRAD TRADE-OFF

The project management process's fundamental factors, including production area, quality grading, time, and the overall proportion of households, must be dependable and achievable (Dinnella et al., 2022) (Figure 2.8).

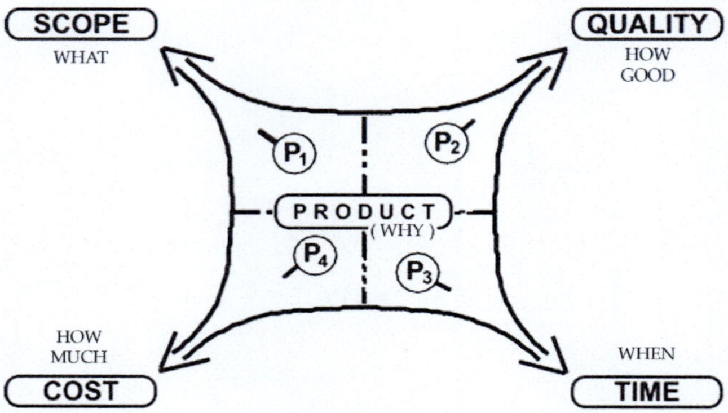

Figure 2.8. Diagram of tetrad trade-off principle.

Source: Max Wideman, creative commons license.

This rule builds from both the Commitment Principle and the Success Principle. Assessments of internal organizational outcomes include the critical parameters of scope baseline, performance rating, moment, and overall cost at finalization, collectively known as the field of view, reliability, duration, and expense in both. If these factors are not coherent and realistic, neither the commitment nor the Key Success Indicators are likely to be reached. The interrelationships of such four distinct factors are comparable to that of a flexible four-sided frame. One side can be fixed, and another can be moved, but doing so will affect the remaining two sides (Farashah et al., 2019).

2.9. EXPLICIT PRINCIPLES OF PROJECT AND PROGRAM MANAGEMENT

2.9.1. Customer Focus

Businesses must comprehend their current and future buyers' necessities to meet their demands and exceed expectations. By their fundamental nature, organizations rely on their customers, whether they belong internally or externally to an organization (Cicmil & Hodgson, 2006).

There is no mention of customer satisfaction among the three primary objectives: time, money, and needs (PMI, 2012; ISO, 2012). Instead, other criteria, like the ICB, describe the project's success as satisfying customers and the three primary goals (cost, time, and requirements) (IPMA, 2006). An example is the Sydney Opera House, which is a massive failure according to PMBOK views because it took so long and cost much more than expected. Still, from the ICB view, this is one of the significant successes in the nation's history because it came to represent the entire nation (Hodgson, 2002).

Remember

The principle goes against what are the indications from some standard, like the PMBOK and ISO 21500, which defines the success of projects.

2.9.2. Leadership

The establishment of an atmosphere in which employees may be intimately engaged in attaining the organization's objectives is an important concept that must guide all companies (but is unfortunately too often disregarded). It is important to remember that people's participation is a significant source of their motivation. Companies should place people with strong leadership qualities in positions of authority because it is only through leadership that organizations can be managed. It must be kept in mind that not everyone can rise to positions of power solely because they have performed their tasks correctly. Must be recognized need to create two different career opportunities within organizations: the first one, based on conventional resources management and strategy, and the other, dedicated to experts, through which they can advance in their roles without actually requiring managerial duties. Too often, businesses face challenges due to leaders who cannot perform their duties; this necessitates the existence of a framework for recognizing leadership qualities, which is regrettably not existent in all organizations (Handzic & Durmic, 2015).

The leadership of an organization can be well-defined through the:

a. Quality policy establishment and self-improvement (such as performance standards)
b. Definition of the infrastructure and resources to ensure the achievement of the objectives
c. Description of an organizational structure conducive to achieving the objectives
d. Empowerment and motivation of the staff to improve the processes
e. Planning of future preventive actions

2.9.3. Involvement of People

Individuals at every level are the essence of the organization. So as previously noted in the topic of leadership, their effective decision-making allows them to put their abilities to work for the business. Along with this idea, it is necessary to describe the responsibilities of individuals in a specific and straightforward manner so that they may implement the authorities and take the commitments that have been allocated to them (Ajmal & Koskinen, 2008).

2.9.4. Process Approach

The essential processes for all organizational operations constantly support the organization and are the foundation of the identical organizations' sustainability and value creation. The critical consideration is the necessity of organizing resources and tasks as procedures if the outcomes are productive.

The organization must establish processes and effectively convey the operation to all relevant parties while defining the linked processes so that it may be comprehended as a relationship. The methods are distinctive, making it impossible to develop answers that can adjust to any situation. In this context, it is critical to study the past to enhance outcomes in the future, a basic principle that will be taken into account by the people who follow, but it is also considered necessary:

1. identification of the appropriate processes.
2. identification of the responsible for the process, establishing their authority and responsibility.

2.9.5. System Approach to Management

Recognizing and characterizing the interconnected operations as a system enables the organization's effectiveness and efficacy in attaining its goals. It is also emphasized that a systemic management strategy provides synchronization and interoperability of scheduled organizational procedures and a precise specification of their interconnections.

There should be a clear separation of responsibilities and powers between the project organization and other participants for the project's operations. These could be identified and documented.

The project organization should guarantee that effective communications protocols are developed and that information is transmitted within the construction process, including between the program, others sure to boost, and the organization (Van Marrewijk et al., 2008).

2.9.6. Continuous Improvement

Organizations should strive for continual and everlasting development for working efficiency with almost all of their energy and capabilities to advance and progress. This continual development method is founded on the PDCA principle (Plan, Do Check, Act).

Organizations should develop a method (process) to capture and analyze information collected throughout project operations to gain insight from prior experience. Another critical role throughout this environment is the administration of learning lessons and knowledge of history. These two categories of understanding are the company's resources, and managing them is the objective of organizational learning (Bassi, 2014; Bassi, 2014; Bassi, 2015).

To discover any chances for development, mechanisms for consciousness, audit committees, and, if appropriate, the external audit should be offered. In this context, the project organization is in charge of conducting an ongoing study to increase the efficiency and effectiveness of the operations over which it has authority.

2.9.7. Data-Based Decision-Making

Decisions must be taken solely and entirely based on the evaluation of information, but the assurance that the knowledge is proper is more crucial. Much emphasis should be placed on the 'validation' of the data; making decisions based on inaccurate information will only lead to poor choices.

In a project environment, productivity and effectiveness should be evaluated to determine the project's state. The organization must analyze and interpret effectiveness and progress assessments to enhance practical investment decisions and assess the project's management plan. In this context, it is critical to record information and judgment, together with their outcomes, so they can be leveraged to think critically in similar or distinct contexts (Pinto et al., 2009).

2.9.8. Mutual Benefit Relationship with Suppliers

An organization and its vendors are inextricably linked, and a mutually beneficial relationship enhances the ability to create value. The project organization should collaborate with its vendors to define plans for making the necessary deliveries. To take full advantage of both parties' skills, quality requirements should indeed be produced collaboratively by the provider and the client. In this connection, the project organization should also examine a supplier's capacity to meet its processing and production needs (Alderman et al., 2005).

Thus, the distributors must become collaborators of the organization, but this is a fundamental premise that is regrettably ignored by many organizations, even though they fail to acknowledge that their success is contingent on their suppliers' ability to give them what they genuinely need by having provided all of the knowledge that they require thru working on their more comprehensive description.

2.10. IMPLICIT PRINCIPLES OF PROJECT AND PROGRAM MANAGEMENT

2.10.1. Stakeholder Satisfaction

Stakeholder satisfaction can be attained in a variety of ways. Many principles and conventions have varied perspectives on it. According to the PMBOK, the sponsors/client is satisfied if the project was carried out on schedule, within budget, and following the specifications.

However, the ICB and ISO 10006 state that the project's ultimate objective is to satisfy both the client and stakeholder, potentially overlooking individuals who may have been affected by the project's progress.

An organization must specify how initiatives and operations can be regarded as successful. If the outcomes are unsatisfactory, a process is developed that evaluates the causes and creates corrective steps for present or future activities (Taylor & Chi, 2006).

2.10.2. Culture of Quality and Project Management

Cultures connected to project management and quality management should be defined within organizations to satisfy customers through adequate characterization of the processes that regulate this organization.

These cultural differences run throughout the corporation, affecting all orientations and departments.

To accomplish the stated objectives for which it was founded, the entire firm, beginning with senior executives, must engage in the goodness of these cultures. These cultural groups are established by defining rules, procedures, processes, and tools based on the organization's activities and through adequate staff development and knowledge transfer communications (Kadefors, 2004) (Figure 2.9).

Figure 2.9. Schematic of components of quality culture in project management.

Source: Testify, creative commons license.

2.10.3. Communication – Information Certification

Communication is the vital component that keeps all companies running. Individuals cannot exist without connections, and organizations cannot grow without communications. On the other hand, businesses must establish a communication infrastructure and the accompanying procedures to ensure that data is managed efficiently. The organization must determine its information needs and implement a formalized data management system, including identifying external and internal sources of information. A sufficient level of data security must be ensured, considering the information's confidence, availability, and reliability. It is critical to remember that communication is a crucial element in the process of motivating others. People are more driven to produce positive results when they absorb information as part of the work they must develop (De Bakker et al., 2010).

2.10.4. Strategy Definition

Organizations must develop approaches for accomplishing their objectives. Project management methodologies should be established as a component of the project process. The project's entire life cycle must be specified through the definition of mechanisms that facilitate development projects. In the case of businesses that manage many projects concurrently, it is critical to set the appropriate criteria and indicators to execute tasks with varying characteristics. The project management strategy plan must be developed; guidelines must be defined to allow the project team to establish the project schedule. Establishing and educating employees on technological and logical tools for project management is essential. In this scenario, the literature may only be used as a point of reference because organizations cannot find ready-made solutions but just sources of information. After all, each organization is unique (Bannerman, 2008).

2.10.5. Maturity Model

By definition, the organization cannot seem stationary; instead, it must be proactive and adapt over time to seize potential opportunities. After identifying the methodological framework on which they are founded, companies must also establish the reference model about which they wish to aim. In this regard, there are several accurate models of real maturity, all of which include the final piece in the ongoing improvement of procedures (Bassi, 2011). Businesses should not seek this high-performance model; what matters is that the instruments that characterize the systems that support them are always compatible with anticipations and capable of achieving high levels of achievement (Crawford & Bryce, 2003).

2.10.6. Resource Management

The integrity and success of a project, such as the same organization, depends on the people engaged, not simply the firm (policies, procedures, and processes). As a result, additional consideration should be given to human resource organizational activities operations. These procedures must have a common purpose of creating an environment where staff may participate effectively and productively in all project or organization operations.

Personnel must be selected based on an accurate and fair explanation of the position and function and their competency in terms of previous experiences. Whenever choosing an individual for a role of obligation, whether the person walks from outside or within the organizational structure, priority must be given to leadership skills. These processes must also organize and coordinate resources appropriately to determine each user's motivating elements and maintain a high level of enthusiasm. We must always recall that individuals are an organization's capital, and we must understand how to utilize them.

2.10.7. Organizational Structure

For their competency, the organization and the project manager must guarantee that the organization structure always reacts to the needs of the company, the number of the workforce, the local environment, and the procedures employed. Frequent revision of organizational structures should be offered, and if they are not more suitable for the needs, they must be modified. In this context, it is necessary to be careful with how these reorganizations can affect people in terms of demotivation. The most crucial thing to accomplish is to effectively and quickly convey the reasons for this transformation by articulating/discussing, and sometimes co-creating the concept of the new arrangement.

2.10.8. Motivation

When duties are assigned to individuals, their self-interests, social connections, abilities, and limitations must all be considered. Personal attributes and experiences can help select the correct definition and distribute responsibilities between members of the organization. When an individual is assigned a new role, they must understand and embrace it.

As previously stated, special consideration must be given to the management of people's motives in employee management. Organizations must constantly have motivated employees and ensure that the degree of motivation has always been high. They recognize that a person leaving a company due to a lack of enthusiasm is a mistake that the entire organization should work on to enhances management processes.

2.10.9. Team Building

One of a company's first tasks is to provide a work environment where employees may form strong bonds of collaboration through team development. Understand that the company's strength is greater than the total of the individuals' forces (Blanchard, 1997).

All program and organizational leaders must create a work atmosphere that promotes excellence, successful collaboration, confidence, and tolerance inside the workforce and with all other persons involved in a particular working environment. A decision-making process that includes consensus, structured resolving disputes, good communication, open and productive communication, and joint dedication to customer loyalty should be established and fostered. Corporations must also display consistent behaviors to support team development rather than evaluate employees based on personal aspirations. Performance targets should be assigned to assess the individual's ability to contribute to the group.

2.10.10. Historical Information and Lessons Learned

The organization should specify the knowledge it requires from projects and establish a procedure for recognizing, gathering, maintaining, modifying, and retrieving information. The company should make sure that pertinent info is used for different purposes. The handling of historical data is the foundation of continual improvement. The organization must create, develop, and allow access to all individuals to an effective and productive framework for collecting and utilizing this information. Understand that the content to be controlled falls into two categories (Hwang & Low, 2012):

i. Historical information – documents retrieved from projects/activities managed by the organization;
ii. Lessons learned – what the organization and people have learned during the activities.

ACTIVITY 2.1.

Consider you are a project manager of a small construction project. Develop a project management plan by applying all the principles of project management.

SUMMARY

Therefore, management can be "the transfer of skills, tools, and procedures to project operations to achieve project requirements." And project management principles serve as a general operating manual. They cannot offer you all the explanations or tell you precisely what you should do, but they may provide guidance. The project management principles include the cultural environment principle, the project system principle, the strategy principle, the success principle, the commitment, and management principle, the single point responsibility, and tetrad trade-off principle, and the implicit and explicit principles.

REVIEW QUESTIONS

1. Briefly describe the principles of project management.
2. Describe the cultural environment principle of project management.
3. Define and explain the project system principle of project management
4. What are the strategy and success principles of project management.
5. Describe the management and commitment principles of project management.

MULTIPLE CHOICE QUESTIONS

1. A sound project management system provides for defining the interface between the project team and the organization in all the following areas except _______.

a. Authority

b. Development of project team members

c. Integration of the project into the organization

d. Allocation of resources

2. Which of the following is an advantage of a functional project management organization?

a. Maximum flexibility in the use of staff

b. Good integration across functional units

c. Shorter project duration

d. The strong motivation of project team members

3. A project management system provides a framework for launching and implementing project activities within a ______ organization.

a. Sponsor

b. Parent

c. Balanced
d. Matrix

4. Matrix management violates the management principle of _______.

a. Span of control
b. Parity principle
c. Unity of command
d. Empowerment

5. The project structure that is ranked as least effective is _______ organization.

a. Functional
b. Balanced matrix
c. Weak matrix
d. Project

Answers to Multiple Choice Questions

1. (b); 2. (a); 3. (b); 4. (c); 5. (a)

REFERENCES

1. Ajelabi, I., & Tang, Y., (2010). The adoption of benchmarking principles for project management performance improvement. *International Journal of Managing Public Sector Information and Communication Technologies (IJMPICT), 1*(2), 1–8.
2. Ajmal, M. M., & Koskinen, K. U., (2008). Knowledge transfer in project-based organizations: An organizational culture perspective. *Project Management Journal, 39*(1), 7–15.
3. Alderman, N., Ivory, C., McLoughlin, I., & Vaughan, R., (2005). Sense-making as a process within complex service-led projects. *International Journal of Project Management, 23*(5), 380–385.
4. Atkinson, R., (1999). Project management: Cost, time, and quality, two best guesses and a phenomenon, it's time to accept other success criteria. *International Journal of Project Management, 17*(6), 337–342.
5. Bannerman, P. L., (2008). Risk and risk management in software projects: A reassessment. *Journal of Systems and Software, 81*(12), 2118–2133.
6. Bassi, A., (2014). Human and organizational knowledge in a project management context. *Modern Management Review, 19*(21), 7–19.
7. Bassi, A., (2014). Project management human and organizational learning. In: *MakeLearn Conference* (Vol. 1, pp. 4–15).

8. Bassi, A., (2015). General management principles in ISO norms in a project management context. In: *IFKAD 2015: 10th International Forum on Knowledge Asset Dynamics: Culture, Innovation, and Entrepreneurship: Connecting the Knowledge Dots* (Vol. 1, pp. 237–247).

9. Bassi, S., (2011). Undergraduate nursing students' perceptions of service-learning through a school-based community project. *Nursing Education Perspectives, 32*(3), 162–167.

10. Blanchard, K. H., O'Connor, M. J., & Ballard, J., (1997). *Managing by Values* (Vol. 1, pp. 111–125). Berrett-Koehler Publishers.

11. Boehm, B. W., & Ross, R., (1989). Theory-W software project management principles and examples. *IEEE Transactions on Software Engineering, 15*(7), 902–916.

12. Brown, C. J., (2008). A comprehensive organizational model for the effective management of project management. *South African Journal of Business Management, 39*(3), 1–10.

13. Buvik, M. P., & Tvedt, S. D., (2017). The influence of project commitment and team commitment on the relationship between trust and knowledge sharing in project teams. *Project Management Journal, 48*(2), 5–21.

14. Cicmil, S., Williams, T., Thomas, J., & Hodgson, D., (2006). Rethinking project management: Researching the actuality of projects. *International Journal of Project Management, 24*(8), 675–686.

15. Crawford, P., & Bryce, P., (2003). Project monitoring and evaluation: A method for enhancing the efficiency and effectiveness of aid project implementation. *International Journal of Project Management, 21*(5), 363–373.

16. Davies, A. R., Doyle, M. A. T., Lansky, D., Rutt, W., Stevic, M. O., & Doyle, J. B., (1994). Outcomes assessment in clinical settings: A consensus statement on principles and best practices in project management. *The Joint Commission Journal on Quality Improvement, 20*(1), 6–16.

17. De Bakker, K., Boonstra, A., & Wortmann, H., (2010). Does risk management contribute to IT project success? A meta-analysis of empirical evidence. *International Journal of Project Management, 28*(5), 493–503.

18. Dinnella, C., Pierguidi, L., Spinelli, S., Borgogno, M., Toschi, T. G., Predieri, S., & Monteleone, E., (2022). Remote testing: Sensory test during the COVID-19 pandemic and beyond. *Food Quality and Preference, 96*, 10–20.

19. Engwall, M., & Jerbrant, A., (2003). The resource allocation syndrome: The prime challenge of multi-project management. *International Journal of Project Management, 21*(6), 403–409.

20. Farashah, A. D., Thomas, J., & Blomquist, T., (2019). Exploring the value of project management certification in the selection and recruiting. *International Journal of Project Management, 37*(1), 14–26.

21. Gareis, R., (2013). Rethinking project initiation and project management by considering principles of sustainable development. In: *Sustainability Integration for Effective Project Management* (Vol. 1, pp. 129–143).
22. Goedknegt, D., & Silvius, A. J. G., (2012). The implementation of sustainability principles in project management. In: *Proceedings of the 26th IPMA World Congress* (Vol. 1, pp. 875–882).
23. Guo, W., (2003). A principle-tactics-based approach for guiding student project management. *WSEAS Transactions on Computers, 2*(1), 48–52.
24. Handzic, M., & Durmic, N., (2015). Knowledge management, intellectual capital and project management: Connecting the dots. *Electronic Journal of Knowledge Management, 13*(1), 51.
25. Hodgson, D., (2002). Disciplining the professional: The case of project management. *Journal of Management Studies, 39*(6), 803–821.
26. Hwang, B. G., & Low, L. K., (2012). Construction project change management in Singapore: Status, importance, and impact. *International Journal of Project Management, 30*(7), 817–826.
27. Ika, L. A., (2009). Project success as a topic in project management journals. *Project Management Journal, 40*(4), 6–19.
28. Kadefors, A., (2004). Trust in project relationships—Inside the black box. *International Journal of Project Management, 22*(3), 175–182.
29. Khanzadi, M., Shahbazi, M. M., Arashpour, M., & Ghosh, S., (2019). The fewer agents, the more schedule reliability: An examination of single-point responsibility model in design management. *International Journal of Civil Engineering, 17*(8), 1307–1316.
30. Koskela, L. J., & Howell, G., (2002). The underlying theory of project management is obsolete. In: *Proceedings of the PMI Research Conference* (Vol. 1, pp. 293–302).
31. Lycett, M., Rassau, A., & Danson, J., (2004). Program management: A critical review. *International Journal of Project Management, 22*(4), 289–299.
32. Mir, F. A., & Pinnington, A. H., (2014). Exploring the value of project management: Linking project management performance and project success. *International Journal of Project Management, 32*(2), 202–217.
33. Ofori, G., (2008). Leadership for the future construction industry: Agenda for authentic leadership. *International Journal of Project Management, 26*(6), 620–630.
34. Pinto, J. K., Slevin, D. P., & English, B., (2009). Trust in projects: An empirical assessment of owner/contractor relationships. *International Journal of Project Management, 27*(6), 638–648.
35. Powers, R. F., & Dickson, G. W., (1973). MisProject management: Myths, opinions, and reality. *California Management Review, 15*(3), 147–156.
36. Sarkisov, P. D., Stoyanova, O. V., & Dli, M. I., (2013). Principles of project management in the field of nano industry. *Theoretical Foundations of Chemical Engineering, 47*(1), 31–35.

37. Saynisch, M., (2010). Beyond frontiers of traditional project management: An approach to evolutionary, self-organizational principles and the complexity theory—Results of the research program. *Project Management Journal, 41*(2), 21–37.
38. Schindler, M., & Eppler, M. J., (2003). Harvesting project knowledge: A review of project learning methods and success factors. *International Journal of Project Management, 21*(3), 219–228.
39. Silvius, A. J., & Schipper, R. P., (2014). Sustainability in project management: A literature review and impact analysis. *Social Business, 4*(1), 63–96.
40. Smyth, H. J., & Morris, P. W., (2007). An epistemological evaluation of research into projects and their management: Methodological issues. *International Journal of Project Management, 25*(4), 423–436.
41. Talbot, J., & Venkataraman, R., (2011). Integration of sustainability principles into project baselines using a comprehensive indicator set. *International Business & Economics Research Journal (IBER), 10*(9), 29–40.
42. Taylor, R. S., & Chi, M. T., (2006). Simulation versus text: Acquisition of implicit and explicit information. *Journal of Educational Computing Research, 35*(3), 289–313.
43. Van, M. A., Clegg, S. R., Pitsis, T. S., & Veenswijk, M., (2008). Managing public–private megaprojects: Paradoxes, complexity, and project design. *International Journal of Project Management, 26*(6), 591–600.
44. Ward, S., & Chapman, C., (2003). Transforming project risk management into project uncertainty management. *International Journal of Project Management, 21*(2), 97–105.
45. Zhang, H., (2007). A redefinition of the project risk process: Using vulnerability to open up the event-consequence link. *International Journal of Project Management, 25*(7), 694–701.
46. Zhong-Mei, D. E. N. G., (2006). Construction-agent system project management pattern study based on principle-agent theory. *Journal of Chongqing Jiaotong University (Natural Science), 25*(2), 128.

CHAPTER 3

KEY ROLE PLAYERS IN PROJECT AND PROGRAM MANAGEMENT

UNIT INTRODUCTION

The topic of "who does what" hardly ever comes up in most business-as-usual companies. Employees can take action on their initiative or according to previously established procedures. Although for a program or project to be successful, it is important to assess everyone's involvement and the initiative's importance to the organization before they begin.

Although there are connections between the permanent organization and the organization needed for the project or program, each has its unique traits in regard to structure, staff, management style, systems, culture, and strategy. Obviously, the two types of organizations will differ from one another. Tensions between them that are inevitable and normal become a manifestation of this (Figure 3.1) (Rodrigues & Bowers, 1996).

Every project and program has three main roles: the owner, the project or program manager, and the member of the team (Figure 3.2) (Morris et al., 2006). The team member is capable, appreciates their work, and completes their duties. As the project or program manager, they want the work to be completed so that they may provide a project deliverable or a program outcome. The owner is driven, has a resourceful mindset, and desires a result or outcome.

Learning Objectives

At the end of this chapter, readers will be able to learn the following:

- Role of project or program owner in setting the agenda
- Role and responsibilities of project or program manager
- Efforts of team members in projects or programs
- Different approaches to organizing programs and projects
- The environment of the project and program within which it will exist

Key Terms

- Agenda
- Committee
- Management Plans
- Matrix Structure
- Program
- Project
- Stakeholders
- Suppliers

3.1. PROJECT OR PROGRAM OWNER SETS THE AGENDA

It is obvious from the normal course of events that the management department is in charge of planning and supervising operations (Assaf & Al-Hejji, 2006). In the past, general management has created policies and procedures that give employees autonomy when doing their duties.

In established groups like management teams, committees, and departmental meetings, the status of this activity is discussed. The organizational structure outlines who is in charge of what, who oversees what, and so forth. Too frequently, attempts are tailored to fit a certain project or program into these established practices and standards (Munns & Bjeirmi, 1996) (Table 3.1).

Table 3.1. Significant Differences between Permanent and Project or Program Organization

Permanent Organization	Variable	Project/Program organization
Vertical Hierarchic Oscillating	Structure	Horizontal Coordinated Flowing
Activity-oriented Entrepreneurial	Personal/management style	Result-oriented Concluding
Year planning Departmental budgets It could be better	Systems	Project planning Subproject budgets Good is good enough
Avoid precedents Routine Club spirit	Culture	Adhoc reactions Situational Team spirit
Continuity	Strategy	Temporary

Source: Rudy Kor, Creative Commons License.

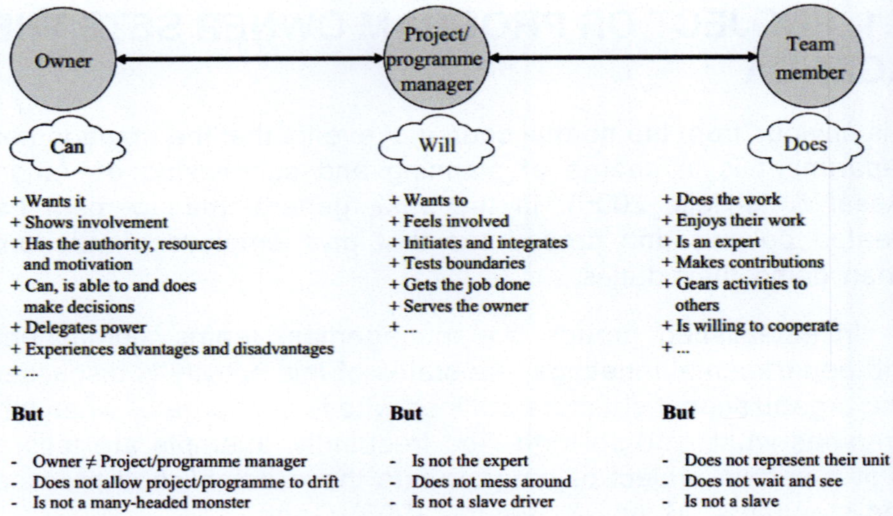

Figure 3.1. Representation of three key role players.

Source: Gert Wijnen, creative commons license.

As program and projects are transient events, it is not easy to rely on already-established structures, practices, regulations, and conventional managing bodies (Iyer & Jha, 2005; El-Gohary et al., 2006). This implies, among other things, that the tasks and functions of the owner must be interpreted uniquely for each assignment. One of the organization's current management corporations, such as a leadership team, steering committee, or policy board, tends to be given the duty of a special assignment.

The justification for this is "We meet regularly anyway," which sounds plausible. Project owners must carefully balance the benefits of utilizing current leadership and other systems against the drawbacks (Cleland, 2007). An existing group's composition is doubtful to be planned for their involvement in the particular project.

Hence, they should carefully assess whether it makes perfect sense for the project or program manager to report to an existing structure or if it would be preferable to designate a distinct individual for this particular job to increase clarity and involvement.

Owners are required to put in greater effort when working on projects and programs (Bonner et al., 2002). However, many managers view these projects as time-consuming planning challenges that conflict with their current schedules. Because of this, they do not put enough time and effort into developing the owner role.

Owners of the projects are required to be involved throughout the duration of the project. To ensure that the appropriate resources (people, money, tools, and other means) are available, they must first identify the outcome of a project or the program's goals. And as the assignment progresses, the owner's position assumes even greater significance as they are needed to oversee the program or project by making timely decisions and decisions that are essential to its effective advancement.

The task management must be made available by the owner for the project or program manager (Assaf & Al-Hejji, 2006). Also, the owner is responsible for making sure that the work is either continued at the designated times or stopped and changed. It will be clear that the owner's involvement will and should continue throughout the project and that their responsibility goes beyond just the financial component.

Whether to choose a group or an individual as the owner remains if the decision is made not to assign the position to an existing organization. A single project owner is preferred whenever possible because managerial unanimity is necessary (De Wit, 1988).

Owners and project or program managers must frequently consult with one another; this consultation cannot wait until the next steering group committee or management-team meeting.

The best candidate for the position of the owner is a person with a stake in seeing the issue resolved or who desires to take advantage of the opportunity presented. It need not be the person who started the project or program; rather, it should be the person who will be affected by the results.

In other words, it's someone who can accept the highs and lows of the program or project, who can picture how their decisions will turn out, and who can make the best use of the deliverables or outcomes.

A responsible owner is willing to act and take risks because they are emotionally invested in the task. When things go difficult, these are those who do not pass the buck to someone else. When their shared task is in jeopardy, boards, and management teams will not be as dedicated. Everyone might anticipate that one of their co-workers will step in to save them.

A project or program owner is expected to:

i. stay involved throughout the project or program;
ii. guarantee that the project or program manager is able to handle the job;
iii. stay involved throughout the project or program (Baccarini, 1999);
iv. make decisions and have the final say;
v. want the issue to be resolved or seize the opportunity (Ibbs & Kwak, 2000);

vi. accept the profits and costs connected with the deliverable or outcome;

vii. be emotionally invested in the project or program and be prepared to take risks (Lim & Mohamed, 1999).

3.2. PROJECT OR PROGRAM MANAGER MAKES IT ALL HAPPEN

There must be someone willing to take ownership of achieving the agreed-upon deliverable or outcome for every project and program (Nielsen et al., 2018). This project or program manager, who may be a manager, team leader, project leader, chairman, or program director, must be able to use the power that has been granted to them. The ability to organize all non-managerial operations and direct their execution in accordance with the management plans created should be made possible by this authority.

It's critical that they have pleasure in leading, coaching, and managing a team. Project or program managers need to be able to direct their emphasis away from individuals and towards a topic, behavior, or issue to lead people effectively.

Remember

A project manager is a professional in the field of project management.

They must also be able to boost team members' self-confidence and foresee when to take the lead and when to delegate to others. Lack of communication skills and knowledge gaps can be greatly compensated for by consistent behavior and a pleasant attitude towards people (Andersen, 2016).

Project and program managers have challenging jobs. It entails juggling between technical proficiency and interpersonal management, uncertainty, and perfection. Additionally, there are various attitudes and abilities that must be matched (Figure 3.3) (Aubry et al., 2010).

Their duties, accountability, and level of authority are largely based on the function that has been assigned to them by the organization. That might be the essential materials (Kerzner, 2017).

They are not given access to them, and they have little to no control over the project's workers. This is what a "chairman" does. They can only be referred to as a "manager" if they control the person hired for their project or program, have their budget, adhere to their particular quality standards, and use their information systems (Cowie, 2003).

The project or programme manager opts for:		
Personal power	← Versus →	Informal power
Belief that something can be made	← Versus →	Belief in natural development
Autocratic	← Versus →	Delegation
Independent ego	← Versus →	Serving ego
Patience	← Versus →	Impatience
Supportive	← Versus →	Steering
Rigid	← Versus →	Flexible
Manager	← Versus →	Leading
Facts-oriented	← Versus →	Feelings-oriented
Concrete	← Versus →	Abstract
Perfection	← Versus →	Ambiguity
Generalities	← Versus →	Details
Action-focused	← Versus →	Reflective
Complex	← Versus →	Simple
Today	← Versus →	Future
Verbal	← Versus →	Written
Good method	← Versus →	Good person

Figure 3.2. Image of the project or program manager balances behaviors or skills cost.

Source: Covey, creative commons license.

Despite their position, it is their responsibility to start the actions. They must also make sure that coordination between the many parties involved preventing operating in opposition to one another, particularly with the project owner (Levitt, 2011). Making sure that management plans are in place with the required margins to enable planning and progress oversight of the endeavor or programs is one of their primary responsibilities. These plans may be created by them; alternatively, the line manager may create them. It should clearly state who is in charge of tracking progress and how in the latter scenario. If everything is in order, one task is left: keeping track of things themselves or making sure someone else does it. They will create their timetables and budgets and track progress on a small project; on a larger program, they might have assistance that did this.

They ought to be someone who enjoys and gets along with others. They must have the ability and willingness to persuade others, including their coworkers, superiors, potential clients, and people outside their environment. It entails using their position of power and being able to interact with others (Murch, 2001). Their mindset as project leaders must be goal-oriented, which means that they must deliver the service, product, etc. As project managers, they should have a mindset focused on altering the environment, behavior, and so forth. Activities in their regular employment are focused on continuity, but in a special assignment, everything is focused on a predetermined deliverable or result. They must have faith in the outcome; else, others will see that they are only doing what is necessary. They must be emotionally invested in the job they are doing in order to believe that it has value and that it may be realized.

In addition to having strong moral judgment, a project or program manager needs to be knowledgeable about the organization(s) in which the program or project is, for the most part, conducted (El-Sabaa, 2001). To use them effectively for their project or program, they must have knowledge of the formal and informal division of responsibilities, responsibility, and authority. Only then can they decide whether anything needs to be handled formally or can be handled informally?

They must be able to communicate their plan for handling the assignment to their team as well as the owner of the project or program in advance (Rasdorf et al., 2010). Those concerned will know what has to be done and how to execute it if they comprehend this.

As professional or technical knowledge is in high demand, they will likely handle the majority of the non-managerial work on small projects. To assess contributions at both the project and program levels in large programs and projects, it could be adequate for them to merely have a cursory awareness of the language used by the different disciplines (Pitagorsky, 1998).

The responsibilities of the project or program manager, as well as the authority they are given, are frequently very ambiguous. They must have the authority to delegate tasks to their team members within the parameters of the established management plans if they are to uphold the obligations they have been given. They should be able to implement corrective action within their plans and agreements, at the absolute least.

Project or program managers are expected to:

- ensure that plans are adjusted;
- draw up the relevant decision documents;
- initiate activities or efforts at each phase or stage;
- draw up management plans for the program or project (Peisach & Kroecker, 2008);
- influence the environment and anticipate any changes in external factors;
- ensure that these plans contain adequate margins;
- describe the intended project deliverable or the goals of the program (Nicholas & Steyn, 2020);
- make it clear who will monitor progress and how they will do so;
- Recognize that one of their responsibilities is to monitor the connections within their project or program;
- act as coordinator for the various parties involved (Shao, 2018).

3.2.1. Leadership Role of Project Manager

A project manager is, first, and foremost, a leader; the group needs guidance throughout the project, and the project leader directs the group to realize the vision the proposal has generated. The project manager accomplishes this by enabling, trying to coordinate, and inspiring the team to achieve the project's objectives. This is the core responsibility of the project manager, and their performance as a project manager will be determined by their capacity to influences, encourage, help guide, and start communicating. Leadership is a crucial job that entails cooperating with and then through others to accomplish the project's goals. The achievement of the project's objectives will be determined by the manager's capacity for leadership.

The primary purpose of such a role is to ensure that the project team and participants understand the project's goals. It is not uncommon for the company to begin moving its focus away from the end goal through the execution of the project; this is where the project manager must communicate and inspire the group to the eventual goal. The communicator, administrator, and motivational responsibilities are all components of the leadership position (Neuhauser, 2007).

3.2.2. Coordination Role of Project and Program Manager

Coordination is merging the goals and actions of the people and organizations participating in development. The functional departments inside the organizations, such as financial, personnel management, and purchasing, as well as the development's recipients and collaborators, must work together for the advantage of the project. This duty is required of project managers to ensure that all these individuals work toward the same objective. Without collaboration, these groups will lose sight of their function in the project and follow their interests at the expense of the initiative if the project leaders do not advise them of what is anticipated of them.

The necessity for coordinating relies on the amount to which their operations must be coordinated with those of other organizations and the type of communication requirements. When conditions in the project environment change and there is a significant amount of interdependence between the actions of the various groups, a more excellent standard of coordination is required. In this instance, one system demands the output of some other subgroup to finish a task.

Communication is the most efficient tool for achieving true collaboration. The project manager is responsible for ensuring that all organizations obtain information at the appropriate time; the higher the uncertainty and complexity surrounding the project objectives, the larger the need for information exchange.

The project manager must determine the optimum method for coordinating formal and informal communications. The technique must balance the project's capability for collaboration with its demand for coordination; if the requirement for coordination exceeds the project's ability to coordinate, the project manager must enhance the resources to assist him in coordinating.

3.2.3. Role of Project and Program Manager as a Motivator

Development projects are exceedingly complex and demanding on the project's personnel; professional project managers should act as a collective motivator when circumstances go rough. Working with individuals is not always easy due to such entitled to participate because each person's circumstances are distinctive.

The project manager's job as a motivator for a developmental team to take the actions necessary to complete a task within the project constraints is finding the components that act as a motivator.

The characteristics of infrastructure project settings, maximum security concerns, international travel, constrained lodgings, and other problems—as well as other considerations- have a role in the low motivation of the team. The project team is essential; poor performance might arise from dissatisfied employees and high turnover due to a lack of motivation. If individuals are not motivated, a project will fail even if it can produce the best policies and contains all the required resources. Construction companies operate as transformation catalysts to get the consumers, donors, planning committee, and management to work together and accomplish the project's goals. They facilitate collaboration among all construction stakeholders.

3.3. SKILLS OF PROJECT AND PROGRAM MANAGERS

3.3.1. Management Skills

The skills needed by project managers have evolved with the progress of development projects. Previously, the concentration was on technical capabilities, and project managers were selected based on their expertise and competence in the technical field in which the project was concerned.

In recent years, the nature of development projects has shifted significantly; they are no longer merely unidimensional methods centered on a single solution. Today's development projects use multidimensional methodologies that incorporate a range of approaches, such as rights-based, gender, and partnerships (Cowie, 2003).

Figure 3.3. Illustration of project manager's essential skills.

Source: Prabir Panda, creative commons license.

Project managers involve more stakeholders, and behavioral skills are becoming as crucial as technical knowledge. To be a successful project manager in this new phase, one may need to grasp effective management instead of being a technical expert. Projects are getting so complicated that the project manager can no longer continue as a technical specialist in all parts of the project. Instead of just providing specialized instruction, construction companies should devote more time to planning, organizing, directing, and supervising the project (Chipulu et al., 2012).

Project management is simultaneously a science and an art; it is scientific knowledge because it requires quantitative analysis such as rankings, charts, and financial information, and it is an art since it deals with a qualitative approach such as attempting to negotiate, conflict management, ideological, interactional, and organizational factors. To fulfill management duties and undertake different roles, project managers must be knowledgeable in both the science and art of project management. Process, problem-solving skills, negotiation, and thinking skills are the five management skills required for success (Goodwin, 1993; Fisher, 2011).

3.3.2. Process Skills

The project manager must be capable of employing management strategies, protocols, and instruments. They must be able to comprehend a financial statement, read a statistical study of the status of the project data, and grasp the proper use of various management approaches. In accumulation to the preceding, the project manager must be skilled in using information and communication technologies to be more efficient in their profession (Henneman, 1999).

Interacting with tools and procedures requires process strategies. They use specialist experience, expertise in managing projects, and the project's unique techniques for carrying out project operations. These abilities are needed to successfully collaborate with the development team, identify risks, and conduct trade amongst budgetary, time, scope, and quality challenges.

Because project managers do not execute the actual task of the project, managers do not require the same technical skill level as those performing the task. This is not to argue that the project manager does not require specialized knowledge; instead, the more skill the project manager has in the development's processing facility, the further successful he will be in directing the project. Operational expertise is required to spot possible difficulties and improve the project manager's ability to coordinate all project components.The project managers must keep a broad perception and not allow their technical expertise to lead to micromanagement or project work. They must focus on project management, delegating technical tasks to perform the assigned, and limiting their technological engagement to reviewing team performance (MacLachlan et al., 2003).

TIPS

Techniques such as breaking problems down into manageable parts, identifying root causes of problems, analyzing strengths, weaknesses, opportunities & threats, must be mastered in order to solve problems.

3.3.3. Problem-Solving Skills

All projects are susceptible to issues and difficulties not anticipated in the development's risk or scope description and must be handled effectively. A precise characterization of the situation discovered early enough to provide time to respond is required for problem-solving. In many circumstances, the initial problem is a symptom of a more significant issue (Napier et al., 2009) (Figure 3.4). Skills in problem-solving employ several strategies, and by utilizing these approach-es, the program manager can begin to address challenges that would otherwise appear massive, overpowering, and overly complex (Keil et al., 2013).

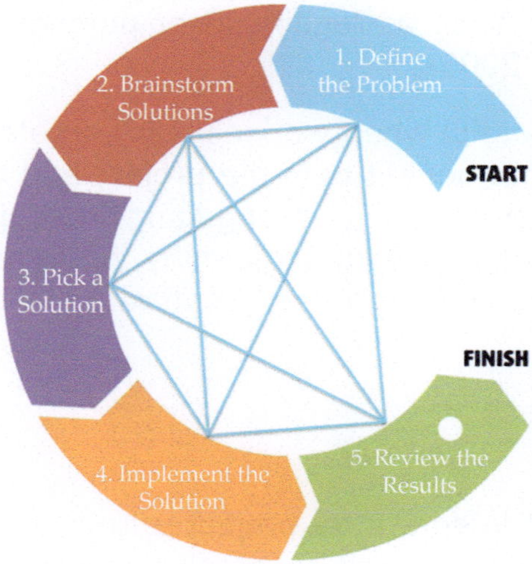

Figure 3.4. Schematic of the problem-solving process.

Source: Humor that works, creative commons license.

Furthermore, the project manager must be capable of synthesizing and analytical reasoning. A project manager must be able to leverage data, gathering and organizing diverse data into a meaningful whole. A project manager must be able to recognize configurations in data and derive meaning from disparate pieces of data. The analysis is the ability to divide a whole into constituent parts, similar to how work is decomposed into a breakdown structure (WBS.)

3.3.4. Negotiation Skills

Project managers spend significant time bargaining for personnel, technology, or other assistance, and their chances of succeeding are considerably lowered if they lack excellent negotiation abilities. A considerable amount of negotiating occurs inside the Organization to obtain the resources needed for the project, capabilities that other project managers also desire.

The process of reaching mutually agreeable arrangements between people or groups is known as negotiation. Based on the project's structure and the level of authority granted to the project manager, they may be capable of negotiating on behalf of the corporation. Negotiation typically entails attempting to make an exchange when interested parties request changes or changes to the construction process and its mineral wealth; negotiating process also entails trying to deal with manufacturers or professionals able to bid for a specific good or service; this region may necessitate the help and support of specialized staff such as legitimate or purchasing department delegates (Yaoyuenyong et al., 2005).

Negotiation skills are also helpful when working with targeted beneficiaries and developing arrangements that benefit both the project and the beneficiary. Beneficiaries often have other priorities, and engaging in project tasks may not be one of them. The project manager must identify the appropriate way to develop a shared understanding and align the beneficiary's interests with the program's (El-Sabaa, 2001).

3.3.5. Conceptual Skills

The capacity to coordinate and integrate all project efforts needs the project manager to see the project as a whole and simply the sum of its components, as well as the capacity to understand how all elements interact and are dependent on each other.

This skill is essential because it can predict how a change in one component of a project will influence the overall effort. The greater the project's size and complexity, the greater the demand for this type of ability. This talent assists the program manager in maintaining a clear vision of the project's final purpose and understanding its dependencies and connections with the project's surroundings (Zulch, 2014). The capability to comprehend the "big picture" is conceptual skills. Project managers have good theoretical skills to understand how different parts of the project environment or ecosystem interact and affect each other. They comprehend the interconnections among projects, international agencies, donor organizations, recipients, and their environments and how modifications in one element of the surroundings affect the project. Intellectual abilities are required to deal effectively with project policies and gain suitable senior executives' support.

3.3.6. Interpersonal Skills

Although technical competence is vital, project leaders are not required to be experts in the specialized area of the project. Indeed, the project manager should be a professional rather than a specialist. This is because experts tend to be very narrow in their views. Experts in the safekeeping of a project are less inclined to be interested in substitute standpoints. Professionals tend to believe that their approach is correct and, thus, the only option. In contrast, a generalist is significantly more open to team members' thoughts and suggestions. Overall, generalist initiatives provide far superior outcomes than equivalent projects led by experts in a single technical field (Lovell, 1993).

The best project management abilities in the universe will not substitute for a legal technicality resulting from a lack of awareness of the firm culture, regulations, personality, or geopolitics. The project manager tries to negotiate with many individuals and must be familiar with their characteristics, wants, and cravings. The more he understands about the Organization, the best prepared that manager is to avoid mistakes and obtain what is required for the program. Every Organization has its philosophy, and different departments frequently have distinct personalities. Recognizing these environments and characteristics can aid a project manager's performance.

Understanding individuals and their perceptions and treating humans are indispensable for developing communication skills. They represent a project manager's dimensions to lead a development team efficiently and foster teamwork among the construction stakeholders and other organizations with which the development team communicates.

For effective processing in a project context, they are essential. Communication, team building, mentoring, inspiring, training, managing, attempting to persuade, negotiating, and supporting people participating in the project are central to personal communication.

The project manager must be sensitive to cultural diversity when working with varied individuals and their perspectives, values, and behaviors. This is especially true for international projects that bring together individuals from various cultural backgrounds. Interpersonal help build positive relationships and a productive workplace by fostering confidence and trust among project team members. Management, communication, conduct, and negotiation are crucial interpersonal skills needed to manage developments (Lovell, 1993).

3.3.7. Leadership Skills

Project managers should impact others' conduct and have strong leadership qualities. Since project managers rely on other individuals to do the work, they need to be able to exercise leadership. The effectiveness of the project leader is primarily a result of management. In smaller initiatives, effective leadership can prevail despite incompetent administration. The project manager can establish a distinct vision and give guidance thanks to this capacity.

3.3.8. Communication Skills

The second most crucial ability, and one to which they will devote most of their time over the project's duration. Respectable communication involves verbal and nonverbal communication, allowing a project manager to present project data in a manner that all stakeholder groups understand and understand.

This ability is helpful in any undertaking but is particularly difficult in project management. Project managers are predicted to spend 80% of their time having conversations: with the project team, the customers, company executives, and higher management. Communication is only effective when both the sender and the recipient comprehend the same data as a consequence of it. A person communicates their thoughts and ideas effectively by getting the point across. When unproductive, the opinions and views transmitted do not always represent what is proposed, resulting in a communication interruption and creating bottlenecks that impede project objectives.

3.3.9. Behavioral Skills

Behavioral skills are the abilities that allow the project manager to collaborate with individuals and encourage those associated with the project. Behavioral skills often referred to as interpersonal, are required in development projects because of the vast and diverse number of people with whom the project interacts. It is the capacity to foster collaboration among the development team, external project participants, and the project organization that is referred to as behavioral or people skills. These abilities necessitate a grasp of views and attitudes, which aid in the attitude of both individuals and groups (Paton et al., 2010).

3.4. INFLUENCE AND POWER OF THE PROJECT AND PROGRAM MANAGERS

An organization bestows responsibility on project leaders; this authority gives a measure of interest in the project and its participants, which the project manager can exploit to create its power.

Power refers to the capacity to persuade the project team to do things they would not typically do. A project manager can wield five sorts of power (Peck & Norman, 1999):

- Coercive power is a pessimistic view of authority that employs punishment or monetary treatment to persuade others to do something. A project manager can threaten to terminate a team member if they do not complete a task or modifies their conduct. This strategy is usually employed as a last option after all other kinds of persuasion have succeeded, and it must always be done in collaboration with top operations. This should never be used as only one persuasion element because it negatively impacts the team's enthusiasm.
- Reward power entails using encouragements such as income, prestige, advancements, acknowledgment, or special job assignments; these

are employed as compensation for desirable comportment or task. The project manager can use various incentives depending on the available project resources and organizational policies.

- Expert power is the application of knowledge and skills to affect a team's compliance with instructions. Suppose the team perceives the project manager as an authority in their field, and the project manager has proved this competence. In that case, the company will be more inclined to comply with the project manager's instructions or ideas regarding how work should be performed (Catsambis et al., 2012).
- Legitimate power is grounded on authority and leverages the capabilities given to the project manager by the association to make judgments deprived of consulting the project team. Inappropriate use of this power can result in the project's catastrophe because this category of authority includes the project manager's function, location, and management's backing.
- The referent POWER depends on the manager's charm, the project manager's strategic orientation, and how they have established a positive too close to calls of confidence with the squad. This is the best authority to affect another team since it must be gained before it can be utilized (Aure, 2013).

3.5. PLACING ROLES, RESPONSIBILITIES, AND SKILLS TOGETHER

Project and program managers must accomplish project objectives using their knowledge, skills, and practical experience. They must employ various accountabilities (enabler, communication, and management) and aptitudes throughout the project management phase (management and interactive, Goetsch, 2008).

Each of these jobs and abilities is crucial to oversee a project correctly. Competent managers are anticipated to and must perform any unique, or a mixture, of these responsibilities, depending on the circumstance and the stage of the project's life cycle. The characters of leadership during the implementation stage, integrator during the planning process, supervisors during the project execution, and administration during the closing process should all receive comparatively more attention from construction projects. Though each of these positions has certain unique traits, it should be understood that other characteristics are shared and overlap with those of different roles. Successful project managers need to be able to adapt their duties to the project's scale, sophistication, and surroundings, as well as the people's cultural backgrounds and the company's core culture (Díez et al., 2011).

3.6. TEAM MEMBERS DO THE WORK

A team should feel accountable for accomplishing the project deliverable, pursuing the program goals, and for each other's contributions. Only then is a team truly a team. The outcomes of individual efforts in a team are more than the sum of their parts. They should only act as a leader of project or program managers when it is essential (Rosemann et al., 2012). Team members must be given enough freedom to consult one another and make judgments that are appropriate for the circumstances. The decision-maker may be the specialist in certain cases, the majority may decide in others, and occasionally they should make a choice themselves.

Remember

Until recently, the American construction industry lacked any level of standardization, with individual States determining the eligibility requirements within their jurisdiction. However, several trade associations based in the United States have made strides in creating a commonly accepted set of qualifications and tests to determine a project manager's competency.

Regardless of how the team is structured, team members are accountable for applying their knowledge to complete the tasks within the constraints of the management plans and for reporting to the project or program manager, whether or not they are asked to (Cash & Fox II, 1992).

Effective team members are distinguished from ineffective ones primarily by their enthusiasm, social intelligence, and active participation in the project or program, in addition to their professional competence (Chen & Partington, 2006). The first guideline for teamwork is self-management. It is key to having latitude; take the initiative and know when to seek help from co-workers or the project or program manager (Reiss, 2002). Members of a productive team will value being assigned tasks and responsibilities that are appropriate for their degree of expertise as well as authority. They will need to develop coping mechanisms for the "employee's dilemma," which requires them to acknowledge the differences in roles and responsibilities between themselves and their project or program management (Turner & Speiser, 1992).

Team members have also invested in the project or program's aims and aspirations and their professional objectives. Regardless of the project or program's nature, it is crucial that they give their all to the task the team needs to complete. They must share authority and responsibilities with others and possess strong communication skills. It's also crucial to be willing to offer and accept assistance (Levitt, 2011). Working under a mostly informal structure, team members must bring a task to a successful completion.

This information will not be appreciated by many team members. Nonetheless, they must possess a certain level of proficiency in reading management plans and be willing to work with constrained resources to perform well in a team. In addition to their project or program manager, team members may find themselves reporting to multiple bosses (Miterev et al., 2016). There are probably not many team members who do not work part-time in the organization that serves as their home base (the division, section, group, unit, or department). Their operational boss in this situation determines what they do, but their functional boss determines how (Levene & Braganza, 1996).

In a permanent organization, the functional boss will also be in charge of developing their knowledge and monitoring each team member's well-being, including holidays, rewards, and the coordination of their performance evaluation.

Those who work on projects and programs must be able to function even when these three supervisors are not the same individual. While team members may be required by the organizational structure to report hierarchically to their department chief on both assignments, they may be held accountable to project leader A for the operational activities in one project and to program manager B for those in another (Evaristo & Van Fenema, 1999).

Further complicating matters, they might get functional support from an outside consultant for project A while getting it from a coworker in a different department for program B.

Team members are expected to:

- complete the tasks in accordance with the predetermined plans and inform the project program manager of any updates;
- be willing to both give and receive help from others;
- contribute their expertise (Brown, 2014);
- be able to work with more than one boss at any one time.
- to manage the "employee's paradox"—to regard the manager as their equal while also acknowledging the differences in their duties, responsibilities, and authority;
- communicate and share power and responsibility with others;
- be able to function in settings with a more lax power structure and balance (Miller et al., 2000);

3.7. DIFFERENT APPROACHES TO ORGANIZING PROJECTS AND PROGRAMS

Program and project management tasks, responsibilities, and authority can be assigned to participants in various ways. A "dependent project or program organization" is created when all responsibilities are turned over to the administration of the permanent organization (bottom right of Figure 3.5)

(Pellegrinelli, 2002). On the other hand, using an "independent organization," it is possible to assign each task to a different project manager (top left of Figure 3.5) (Sanchez et al., 2009). The variations in between involve splitting power

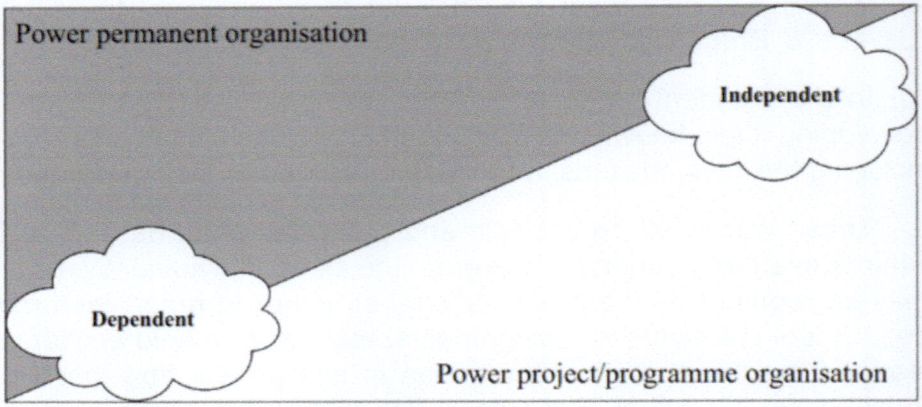

Figure 3.5. Image of organization forms for projects and programs within a permanent organization.

Source: Kerzner, creative commons license.

(authority and responsibilities) between the management of the permanent organisation, and the project manager. The connection between a persistent organization and the one created to carry out the project or program is not formalized, just as there is no standard model for constructing organizations.

3.7.1. Coordination Structure

A program or project organization that is reliant on the primary organization can be identified by a variety of structures (Pellegrinelli, 2011). They include the structures for cooperation and consultation. The project or program manager in the coordination structure is a part-time manager, and team members contribute to the assignment from within their organization.

They have little or no control over the individuals carrying out the assignment. The managers of the permanent organization or organizations continue to hold this authority (Aubry et al., 2007).

They keep tabs on everyone's development and inform them of the projected project or program progress. Because the formal authority granted to them is insufficient, only the managers of the permanent organization or the project owner are allowed to direct or amend.

3.7.2. Matrix Structure

There are two alternate kinds of a matrix-style organization: one in which the managers conduct the consultations (they contribute nothing to the task other than to gather and assign work for their staff), and the other in which those involved discuss with one another (Lycett et al., 2004).

Whatever option is chosen, the project or Plan Company, and frequently the project or program's cost, are not subject to the permanent organization's control.

3.7.3. Independent Structure

They are given resources when working with an independent project or program organization (Gray, 1997). In some circumstances, individuals and the team are in a position to complete the assignment successfully. In others, team members operate with their quality, information, and other management systems, have access to their financial resources and are hired for a set period.

3.7.4. Which Structure Is Most Suitable for Which Situation?

If the permanent organization's acceptance of the project or program's output over direct management is what is most important, then the reliant structure is the most appropriate (Pellegrinelli, 1997). Resources like budgets are challenging to link back to the project since they appear as internal posts in the departmental accounting systems.

This indicates that the project or program director has no control over expenditures or budgets because spending decisions are made by department heads. Even though they have limited direct power, if they are familiar with the departments' procedures and are widely accepted by the people concerned, their informal influence can be significant (Winter et al., 2006).

Maintaining communication with and among the departments of the organizations assisting with the job is, therefore, a crucial task for them. Because so much is done informally, they must remind everyone frequently involved that they are working with a team working on a particular project if they want to foster goodwill.

The standalone structure best suits significant projects and programs focusing on the final product. Given that they are in charge of all the resources necessary to complete a project or program successfully, the expenses are clear, and those responsible are held accountable.

3.8. PROJECT AND PROGRAM ENVIRONMENT

Every project and every operation should be managed to fit the context where it will exist or where its output or conclusion must be incorporated (Artto et al., 2009). A project deliverable's physical environment is one of many important elements. The underlying technology and available resources may also be crucial elements. However, as the players have the most control over most variables, this chapter mainly focuses on them. Projects or programs may include a variety of stakeholders (Figure 3.6) (Elonen & Artto, 2003; Yeong & Lim, 2010). In a previous section of this chapter, they talked about individuals who are most directly involved: the owners, managers, and team members of projects and programs. They shall now address those who are less directly involved, albeit this does not always does not lessen their significance. Individuals who work in the project or program's affected environment frequently play a crucial role in the achievement or failure of a project or program, even if it's simply because they're the ones who must use the deliverables or outcomes or because these tasks require outside funding.

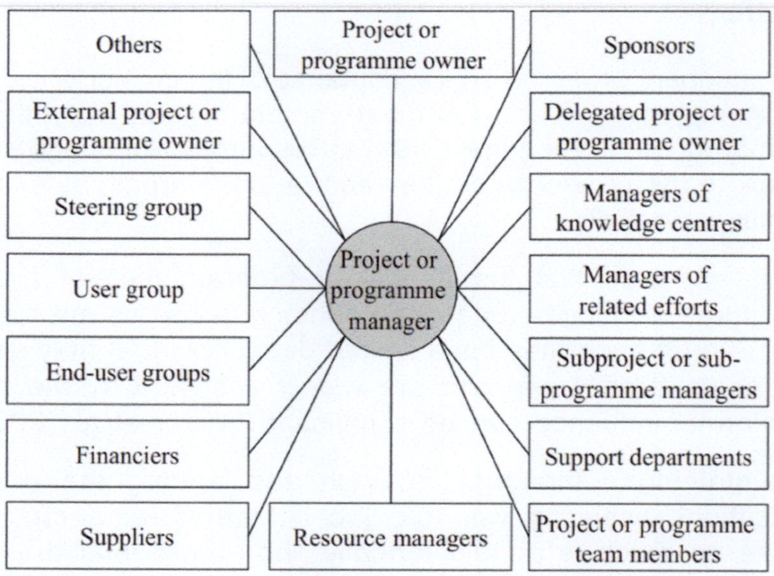

Figure 3.6. Illustration of stakeholders involved in projects and programs.

Source: Rudy Kor, creative commons license.

Its impact may be so pervasive that it becomes a part of any physical or legal limitations (Aritua et al., 2009). Those engaged in co-financing, supplying, or whose passive acceptance is necessary may have a less significant influence.

Its relevant environment includes everyone and everything that might have an impact on the project or program. No matter how well a task is planned or how enthusiastic and professional the approach is, there will inevitably be something or someone from this environment that throws the strategy off course. People stop being supportive, want to be more involved, and suddenly want something different. The major responsibility for influencing and continuously monitoring these environmental aspects is on the project and program manager and owner (Martinsuo & Hoverfält, 2018).

The internal and external participants in a project or program are depicted in Figure 3.7 (Zdanytė & Neverauskas, 2011). Four types exist. Sometimes it is difficult to predict in advance whether a particular player will act inwardly or externally.

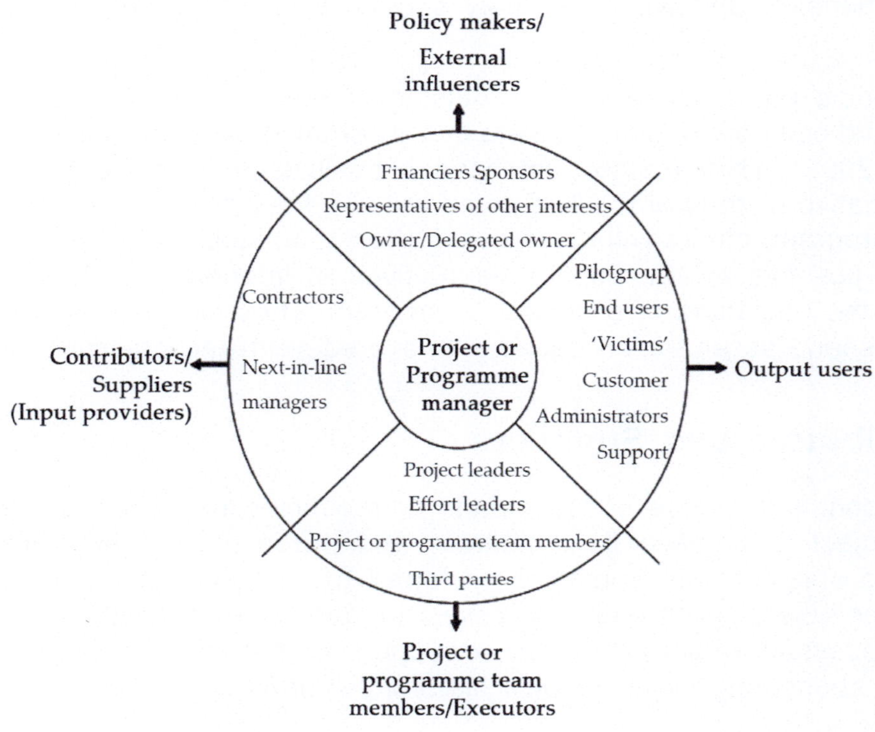

Figure 3.7. Representation of four categories of internal and external players.

Source: Gert Wijnen, creative commons license.

3.8.1. Policy Makers and External Influencers

The program or project owner, who ultimately has the most influence over policy, directly contributes to the project's or program's justification (Kabeyi, 2019). In other words, they contribute to deciding the assignment's "what" or the desired result. Occasionally someone else is given the responsibility of being the project or program owner. This person has the power to act in place of the actual project or program owner and is empowered to take all necessary actions within the confines of agreed-upon parameters. The three groups of persons who have the power to affect policy are financiers, sponsors, and those who speak for other interests.

Financiers are essential if access to financial resources is necessary (and when is this not the case in initiatives and programs?). They supply the materials required. Money is a crucial resource since it is used to buy supplies like raw materials, machinery, and labor.

In particular, external sponsors are crucial for projects and programs. They are the ones who can make sure that the initiative or program will be supported whenever possible. They can broadcast their support for these special missions over all the networks they participate in (Partington et al., 2005). They defend the initiative whenever and whenever they see fit, whether or not they are asked to.

The individuals representing various outside interests in the assignment comprise the third category of policymakers and external influencers (Wideman, 1995; Jaafari, 2003). They do not just have a positive or negative attitude towards the initiative or program. While some will use their power to sabotage the project or program, others will make every effort to ensure it is successful. It's not always possible to see the representatives of interested parties and their intents at the beginning of a project or program. They can unexpectedly appear on the scene as an action squad with a predetermined objective.

3.8.2. Contributors and Suppliers

Because they contribute some of the means or resources necessary for the program or project to achieve its objectives and produce its deliverables, contributors and suppliers are sometimes referred to as input providers. The next-in-line supervisors are frequently asked to permit their employees to carry out the necessary project activities or support the delivery. They are not included in the sponsoring organization's hierarchy (Wirth, 1992).

Sister enterprises and independent third parties can also be viewed as belonging to this group; some of them may not, in an operational sense, fall under the supervision of the program and project owner or manager, but they nevertheless fall into this category (Pretorius & Steyn, 2005).

For every project or program, the engagement of suppliers can differ significantly. Vendors or input providers fall between the two extremes of "partner" and "anonymous" on the involvement scale. At one end of another scale are "universal" and "particular," respectively. Figure 3.8 illustrates how combining these two scales can separate the relevant parties into four different categories (Vukomanović et al., 2016). A particular organization that provides input to the project or program may fall under more than one of these categories at any time.

Everyone can purchase what is offered in the corner store (Lycet et al., 2004). Nobody cares what the customer intends to do with their purchase, and most buyers do not give a damn about who manufactured the item. Any program or organization can benefit from this form of participation because it is the simplest and involves the least effort.

The situation with contractors is more complicated. Contractors are known specifically for each project or program, whether from the building sector, the installation sector, computerization, reorganization, or policy (Blomquist & Müller, 2006) (Figure 3.8).

Supply \ Involvement	Anonymous	Partner
Universal	Corner shop	Contractor
Specific	Research institute	Architect

Figure 3.8. Categorization of input providers.

Source: Carroll, creative commons license.

Then, if all goes as planned, they deliver exactly what was agreed upon. Although several equally qualified contractors may offer universally relevant components for a program or project, great care must be taken to identify the best.

Research institutes' prominence and independence are frequently used to justify including them in projects and programs (Pitsis et al., 2014). While it was previously impossible to describe the output in detail, it is typically a matter of achieving the best contribution to the assignment. The supplier's standing must then serve as a guarantee, particularly with regard to independence. The best course of action must be taken about the deliverable or the goals, not what one of the involved parties believes to be the best.

For architects (designers, policymakers, and engineers), "co-makers" is more difficult than for contractors. Architects are frequently tasked with defining the desired outcome regarding objectives, external interfaces, requirements, or desires; however, they are also frequently tasked with coming up with solutions that best achieve the objectives established for the specific outcome or deliverable specifications.

3.8.3. Project or Program Team Members

All individuals who, at least operationally, report to the program or project manager are considered part of the program and project team. This group also includes people who are the project or program manager's functional subordinates and those who have a hierarchy obligation to report to them. Project managers and other program effort leaders are frequently viewed as executors in larger programs (Ojiako et al., 2011).

ACTIVITY 3.1.

Define roles of project management team as a project manager of a small accounting firm. Moreover, prepare a skills chart of the project management team to accommodate each member effortlessly in the project.

Also, access their roles, responsibilities, and skills that are well suited to the firm's need as a project manager, and identify those roles, responsibilities, and skills that are required in a project manager to enhance the performance of the project.

3.8.4. Output Users

Several stakeholders use the results of projects, and this is even truer with programs (Thiry, 2002). There are subtle variances in their engagement, which might vary from, 'At last, I am going to obtain what I have been waiting for' to, 'All the work I have been focusing on for so long will be ruined when they have to use this project result.' As a result, these users include both happy beneficiaries and irate, dissatisfied "victims." They are frequently also middlemen organizations that might speak for the beneficiaries or the victims. The project and program owner frequently uses the pilot group as a body to ensure the usability of the results on behalf of the users. This organization, designated to protect users' interests, may act as its representative right from starting a project or program (Pellegrinelli et al., 2007). The marketing division will represent any sizable user groups that are typically anonymous due to their size. In other situations, a panel of users or residents may be consulted.

The latter two kinds of output users are those that support or sustain the project's or program's outcomes. They might even be the owners occasionally. The administrators are the ones who must constantly be aware of the precise outcome, its location, and its owner. Supporters of a project are those whose responsibility it is to take preventative or corrective action to preserve the results. When the outcomes or deliverables are no longer needed, a dedicated group may be established to shut them down or disassemble them. Anyone working on a specific project or program has the ability to be a part of multiple groups at once. For instance, a supplier might provide items without fully understanding their intended use, but on the other hand, their contribution and the way it is used might be essential to the project or program's success. This "partner's" involvement is essential to the program's success because it cannot be achieved without it. At various points throughout the project or program, each participant will and can exert influence. Some people will focus on influencing the course positively or negatively, such as by smoothing, blocking, directing participants to the ropes, interfering, causing distractions, misdirecting, etc. Others would rather focus on the product or the results: use, abuse, destruction, improvement, etc.

SUMMARY

In project and program management, there are three key role players. The project/program manager is responsible for planning, executing, and delivering the project or program successfully. They are in charge of overseeing the project or program team and ensuring that all tasks are completed on time, within budget, and to the required quality standards. The project/program sponsor is the person or group that provides the funding and resources for the project or program. They are responsible for setting the strategic direction and goals for the project and for ensuring that it aligns with the organization's overall objectives. The team members consist of individuals who are responsible for completing the tasks required to deliver the project or program successfully. This chapter also explains different approaches to organizing projects and programs.

REVIEW QUESTIONS

1. Identify and explain the various responsibilities of a project and program owner?
2. Identify and explain the various responsibilities of a project and program manager?
3. What is expected of team members in any project or program?
4. Explain different approaches to organizing projects and programs?

MULTIPLE CHOICE QUESTIONS

1. Which of the following statements best describes the role of the project and program manager?

a. Implement business goals
b. Create the measurable KPIs for the project
c. Lead the team in achieving project objectives
d. Carry out directives from the project sponsor

2. How is the success of a Project or Program Manager measured?

a. By achieving the project objectives
b. By building the right product
c. By completing the project on time
d. By developing the talents of the team

3. Select the process that assigns a project or program manager to a project.

a. Develop a business case
b. Develop a project charter
c. Develop Project Management Plan
d. Develop Strategic Plan

4. Which of the following is an approach to organizing projects and programs?

a. Coordination structure

b. Market structure

c. Independent structure

d. All of the above

5. Which of the following are a true statement regarding the project and program management role

a. The role of a project manager must be filled by someone who is certified as a project manager

b. The role of a project manager is the same as the role of the business analyst

c. The role of the project manager is tailored to fit the Organization.

d. The role of the project manager is limited to initiating, planning, executing, monitoring, controlling, and closing a project.

Answers to Multiple Choice Questions

1. (c); 2. (a); 3. (c); 4. (d); 5. (a)

REFERENCES

1. Andersen, E. S., (2016). Do project managers have different perspectives on project management? *International Journal of Project Management, 34*(1), 58–65.
2. Aritua, B., Smith, N. J., & Bower, D., (2009). Construction client multi-projects–A complex adaptive systems perspective. *International Journal of Project Management, 27*(1), 72–79.
3. Artto, K., Martinsuo, M., Gemünden, H. G., & Murtoaro, J., (2009). Foundations of program management: A bibliometric view. *International Journal of Project Management, 27*(1), 1–18.
4. Assaf, S. A., & Al-Hejji, S., (2006). Causes of delay in large construction projects. *International Journal of Project Management, 24*(4), 349–357.
5. Aubry, M., Hobbs, B., & Thuillier, D., (2007). A new framework for understanding organizational project management through the PMO. *International Journal of Project Management, 25*(4), 328–336.
6. Aubry, M., Müller, R., Hobbs, B., & Blomquist, T., (2010). Project management offices in transition. *International Journal of Project Management, 28*(8), 766–778.
7. Baccarini, D., (1999). The logical framework method for defining project success. *Project Management Journal, 30*(4), 25–32.
8. Blomquist, T., & Müller, R., (2006). Practices, roles, and responsibilities of middle managers in program and portfolio management. *Project Management Journal, 37*(1), 52–66.

9. Bonner, J. M., Ruekert, R. W., & Walker, Jr. O. C., (2002). Upper management control of new product development projects and project performance. *Journal of Product Innovation Management: An International Publication of the Product Development & Management Association, 19*(3), 233–245.
10. Brown, J. T., (2014). *The Handbook of Program Management: How to Facilitate Project Success with Optimal Program Management* (Vol. 1, pp. 5–9). McGraw-Hill.
11. Cash, C. H., & Fox, II. R., (1992). Elements of successful project management. *Journal of Systems Management, 43*(9), 10.
12. Chen, P., & Partington, D., (2006). Three conceptual levels of construction project management work. *International Journal of Project Management, 24*(5), 412–421.
13. Cleland, D. I., (2007). *Project Management: Strategic Design and Implementation* (Vol. 1, pp. 6–9). McGraw-Hill Education.
14. Cowie, G., (2003). The importance of people skills for project managers. *Industrial and Commercial Training, 35*(6), 256–258.
15. De Wit, A., (1988). Measurement of project success. *International Journal of Project Management, 6*(3), 164–170.
16. El-Gohary, N. M., Osman, H., & El-Diraby, T. E., (2006). Stakeholder management for public private partnerships. *International Journal of Project Management, 24*(7), 595–604.
17. Elonen, S., & Artto, K. A., (2003). Problems in managing internal development projects in multi-project environments. *International Journal of Project Management, 21*(6), 395–402.
18. El-Sabaa, S., (2001). The skills and career path of an effective project manager. *International Journal of Project Management, 19*(1), 1–7.
19. Evaristo, R., & Van, F. P. C., (1999). A typology of project management: Emergence and evolution of new forms. *International Journal of Project Management, 17*(5), 275–281.
20. Gray, R. J., (1997). Alternative approaches to program management. *International Journal of Project Management, 15*(1), 5–9.
21. Ibbs, C. W., & Kwak, Y. H., (2000). Assessing project management maturity. *Project Management Journal, 31*(1), 32–43.
22. Iyer, K. C., & Jha, K. N., (2005). Factors affecting cost performance: Evidence from Indian construction projects. *International Journal of Project Management, 23*(4), 283–295.
23. Jaafari, A., (2003). Project management in the age of complexity and change. *Project Management Journal, 34*(4), 47–57.
24. Kabeyi, M. J. B., (2019). Evolution of project management, monitoring and evaluation, with historical events and projects that have shaped the development of project management as a profession. *Int. J. Sci. Res., 8*(12), 63–79.

25. Kerzner, H., (2017). *Project Management: A Systems Approach to Planning, Scheduling, and Controlling* (Vol. 1, pp. 3–9). John Wiley & Sons.
26. Levene, R. J., & Braganza, A., (1996). Controlling the work scope in organizational transformation: A program management approach. *International Journal of Project Management, 14*(6), 331–339.
27. Levitt, R. E., (2011). Towards project management 2.0. *Engineering Project Organization Journal, 1*(3), 197–210.
28. Lim, C. S., & Mohamed, M. Z., (1999). Criteria of project success: An exploratory re-examination. *International Journal of Project Management, 17*(4), 243–248.
29. Lycett, M., Rassau, A., & Danson, J., (2004). Programmeme management: A critical review. *International Journal of Project Management, 22*(4), 289–299.
30. Martinsuo, M., & Hoverfält, P., (2018). Change program management: Toward a capability for managing value-oriented, integrated multi-project change in its context. *International Journal of Project Management, 36*(1), 134–146.
31. Miller, D. M., Fields, R., Kumar, A., & Ortiz, R., (2000). Leadership and organizational vision in managing a multiethnic and multicultural project team. *Journal of Management in Engineering, 16*(6), 18–22.
32. Miterev, M., Engwall, M., & Jerbrant, A., (2016). Exploring program management competences for various program types. *International Journal of Project Management, 34*(3), 545–557.
33. Morris, P. W., Crawford, L., Hodgson, D., Shepherd, M. M., & Thomas, J., (2006). Exploring the role of formal bodies of knowledge in defining a profession–The case of project management. *International Journal of Project Management, 24*(8), 710–721.
34. Munns, A. K., & Bjeirmi, B. F., (1996). The role of project management in achieving project success. *International Journal of Project Management, 14*(2), 81–87.
35. Murch, R., (2001). *Project Management: Best Practices for IT Professionals* (Vol. 1, pp. 1–5). Prentice Hall Professional.
36. Nicholas, J. M., & Steyn, H., (2020). *Project Management for Engineering, Business and Technology* (Vol. 1, pp. 3–10). Routledge.
37. Nielsen, J. V., Klakk, H., Bugge, A., Andreasen, M. L., & Skovgaard, T., (2018). Implementation of triple the time spent on physical education in pre-school to 6th grade: A qualitative study from the program managers' perspective. *Evaluation and Program Planning, 70*(1), 51–60.
38. Ojiako, U., Ashleigh, M., Chipulu, M., & Maguire, S., (2011). Learning and teaching challenges in project management. *International Journal of Project Management, 29*(3), 268–278.
39. Partington, D., Pellegrinelli, S., & Young, M., (2005). Attributes and levels of program management competence: An interpretive study. *International Journal of Project Management, 23*(2), 87–95.

40. Peisach, J., & Kroecker, T. S., (2008). *Project Manager and Program Manager* (Vol. 1, pp. 37–39). What's the difference.
41. Pellegrinelli, S., (1997). Program management: Organizing project-based change. *International Journal of Project Management, 15*(3), 141–149.
42. Pellegrinelli, S., (2002). Shaping context: The role and challenge for programs. *International Journal of Project Management, 20*(3), 229–233.
43. Pellegrinelli, S., (2011). What's in a name: Project or program? *International Journal of Project Management, 29*(2), 232–240.
44. Pellegrinelli, S., Partington, D., Hemingway, C., Mohdzain, Z., & Shah, M., (2007). The importance of context in program management: An empirical review of program practices. *International Journal of Project Management, 25*(1), 41–55.
45. Pitagorsky, G., (1998). The project manager/functional manager partnership. *Project Management Journal, 29*(4), 7–16.
46. Pitsis, T. S., Sankaran, S., Gudergan, S., & Clegg, S. R., (2014). Governing projects under complexity: Theory and practice in project management. *International Journal of Project Management, 32*(8), 1285–1290.
47. Pretorius, C. J., & Steyn, H., (2005). Knowledge management in project environments. *South African Journal of Business Management, 36*(3), 41–50.
48. Rasdorf, W., Grasso, B., & Bridgers, M., (2010). Public versus private perceptions on hiring an external program manager. *Journal of Construction Engineering and Management, 136*(2), 219–226.
49. Reiss, G., (2002). *Portfolio and Program Management Demystified: Managing Multiple Projects Successfully* (Vol. 1, pp. 2–5). Routledge.
50. Rodrigues, A., & Bowers, J., (1996). The role of system dynamics in project management. *International Journal of Project Management, 14*(4), 213–220.
51. Rosemann, M., Recker, J., Safrudin, N., & Marketsmueller, R., (2012). Program and project management. *A Handbook of Business Transformation Management Methodology, 1*, 217–244.
52. Sanchez, H., Robert, B., Bourgault, M., & Pellerin, R., (2009). Risk management applied to projects, programs, and portfolios. *International Journal of Managing Projects in Business, 2*(1), 14–35.
53. Shao, J., (2018). The moderating effect of program context on the relationship between program managers' leadership competences and program success. *International Journal of Project Management, 36*(1), 108–120.
54. Thiry, M., (2002). Combining value and project management into an effective program management model. *International Journal of Project Management, 20*(3), 221–227.
55. Turner, J. R., & Speiser, A., (1992). Program management and its information systems requirements. *International Journal of Project Management, 10*(4), 196–206.

56. Vukomanović, M., Young, M., & Huynink, S., (2016). IPMA ICB 4.0—A global standard for project, program and portfolio management competences. *International Journal of Project Management, 34*(8), 1703–1705.

57. Wideman, R. M., (1995). Criteria for a project-management body of knowledge. *International Journal of Project Management, 13*(2), 71–75.

58. Winter, M., Andersen, E. S., Elvin, R., & Levene, R., (2006). Focusing on business projects as an area for future research: An exploratory discussion of four different perspectives. *International Journal of Project Management, 24*(8), 699–709.

59. Wirth, I., (1992). Project-management education: Current issues and future trends. *International Journal of Project Management, 10*(1), 49–54.

60. Yeong, A., & Lim, T. T., (2010). Integrating knowledge management with project management for project success. *Journal of Project, Program & Portfolio Management, 1*(2), 8–19.

61. Zdanytė, K., & Neverauskas, B., (2011). The theoretical substation of project management challenges. *Economics & Management, 1*, 16–20.

CHAPTER 4

APPROACH TO MANAGING PROJECT AND PROGRAM

UNIT INTRODUCTION

A project is a particular outcome or objective individually decided upon and has to be realized with constrained resources through a special combination of actions. It is an invented idea. The term "project" is used by managers to refer to a particular set of distinct, transient, and goal-oriented activities (Pellegrinelli, 2011).

Project components include phases (non-managerial and content activities), management (planning as well as control activities), and decision-making procedures (Wideman, 2022). These tasks will be performed with constrained resources to achieve a particular deliverable. Not every task referred to as a project is one or should be handled that way. Only when a project satisfies specific prerequisites is a project management approach acceptable.

When considering a project approach, ensure the project contains a sufficient quantity of the qualities in the ideal project. These traits include:

i. A clearly defined beginning and completion
ii. Focused on a deliverable
iii. Outcome or product
iv. Special
v. Challenging

vi. Expensive

vii. Crucial to all involved

viii. Controllable from a single point

ix. Having just one client

x. Owner or principle (Winch et al., 2007)

A "program" is a special collection of predetermined objectives that must be approached with finite resources and a special assortment of hard tasks (Bushuyev & Wagner, 2014). There is no such thing as a program. Managers gathering together several particular, distinctive, temporary, goal-oriented activities that must be completed with restricted means call them a program. To do so, they should be willing to live with the repercussions of establishing guidelines and agreements that go against their custom. But more crucially, they should consent to operate following a management "technique" focused on programs.

After having opted to use the project and program management approach to complete a specific work as a project or program, one needs to be aware of the implications (Turkulainen et al., 2015). It would help if one recognized someone's ability and willingness to operate in a project-oriented manner. The vocabulary, the ground rules, and how to launch and oversee a project or program are covered in this chapter's discussion of the methodology. In the course, project and program management techniques (such as phasing, managing, and decision-making; Figure 4.1) cannot and must not be considered distinct from the other project management procedures of organizing and team building (Jaafari, 2007).

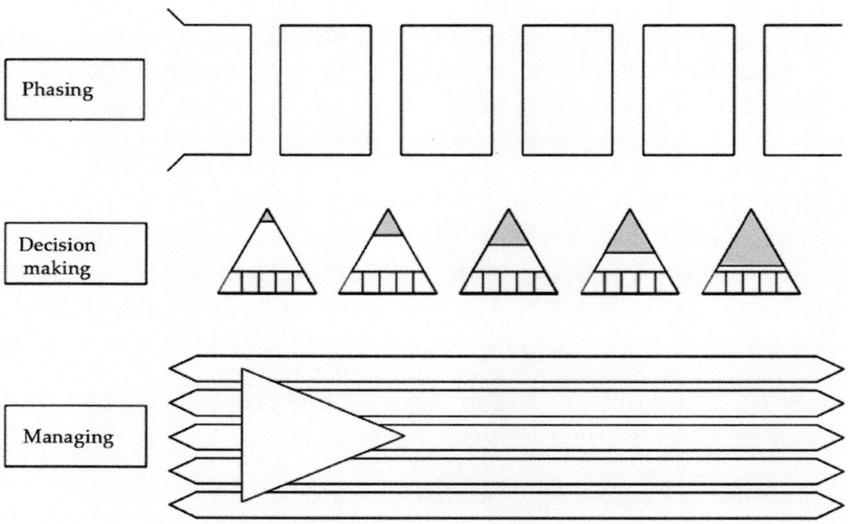

Figure 4.1. An illustration of the project management method integrating phasing, decision making, and managing.

Source: Micheal R. Kinney, creative commons license.

Learning Objectives

Readers will have the opportunity to learn the following by the chapter's conclusion:

- The fundamental concept of a project and program
- The rules and characteristics of project and program management
- Different phases or stages for project management
- The approach to managing project and program

Key Terms

- Characteristics
- Decision Making
- Deliverables
- MACIC
- Methodical Strategy
- Perspectives
- Research and Development

4.1. MANAGING PROJECT – THE APPROACH

4.1.1. Rules and Characteristics of Project Management

- Following are some of the rules for professional project management: Project members understand that ordinary activities must be handled differently from unique assignments. This implies agreeing on each project's objectives, products, and methodology.
- The duty for determining the project goals and the anticipated outcome or delivery is divided according to their respective responsibilities (the first is the owner's responsibility, while the second lies with the project manager) (Fernandes et al., 2018).
- As long as the outcome sought through the project is collaborative, everyone engaged may utilize it to pursue alternate objectives.
- There is just one designated owner—someone who will need to be able to handle major choices throughout the project. The owner makes sure that decision-making and project management are greatly accelerated and simplified (Thiry, 2007).
- Before anything else, the owner must specify the project's objectives, including the outcome, product, or deliverable. They must also ensure that the necessary resources (people, money, and materials) are available.
- The owner is accountable for ensuring the right things are done. A project manager's responsibility is to ensure that they are completed appropriately (Ann et al., 2007; Alfieri et al., 2012).
- The project owner and the manager should include the project team members as soon as feasible; the earlier they are made part of, the more dedicated they will be to seeing the project through to completion.
- Users, staff members who assist, and administrators must be involved in the project.
- The project manager and the project owner make sure the assignment complies with project requirements (unique, indeterminate, important to those involved, clear goals, and result-oriented) (Murray & Crandall, 2006).
- The project should be handled by concentrating on four factors: the important participants, the environment, the interactions, and the approach (Dingsøyr et al., 2018).

An increasing number of managers now recognize project management as an efficient and successful way to carry out unique projects (Trivedi & Singh, 2017). Regrettably, many people who attempt to manage projects frequently do it in a fragmented and ignorant manner.

The twelve common characteristics of the project management methodology are:

- Focusing on the objective while performing and thinking;
- Action after first contemplating (in broad strokes and finer specifics);
- Separating management (managing time, money, quality, release, and organization) from non-managerial or content tasks (Wideman, 2004);
- A methodical strategy for the start, completion, and handoff of a project;
- Creating a table of all non-managerial actions and the order in which they should be completed;
- Planning and obtaining clearance for the five project management views of time, quality, money, release, and organization while taking into consideration the risks associated with each of these perspectives margins, as well as a continuous "Check and Improve" process (Cavaleri et al., 2012);
- Deciding whether to halt or continue the project while also taking the project to begin documentation (the project brief or the business case) into consideration;
- Incorporating the results of a project's previous phase with a prediction of the non-managerial activities that must be carried out in the following phase/phases and, if required, modifying the strategies for the five project management standpoints in a decision document (Archer & Ghasemzadeh, 2007);
- The express allocation of duties, authority, and power;
- After each phase, make decisions (based on a decision document);
- Controlled management of modifications to the decision documents; and
- Incorporating interested parties at the correct time and on the right subjects (Vuorinen & Martinsuo, 2018).

4.1.2. Goals and Deliverables

It is crucial that all stakeholders involved in a project desire to produce the same output for it to be successful. Deliverables can also be results, products, services, solutions, or outputs (Görög, 2011).

The deliverable of the project should be a specified tangible or intangible item that is possible, measurable, and verifiable by the project owner.

Clarifying the challenges, problems, or goals is one of the first project tasks, which leads to a precise definition of the project output (Figure 4.2) (Pena & Parshall, 2012). The project manager must demonstrate empathy during this process, and the project owner must be forthcoming (also called the client, sponsor, principal, or the user). The project owner should be motivated to solve problems or recognize a golden opportunity. Good project owners go through both good and bad times. They are the ones who will utilize the deliverable and can foresee the effects of various decisions.

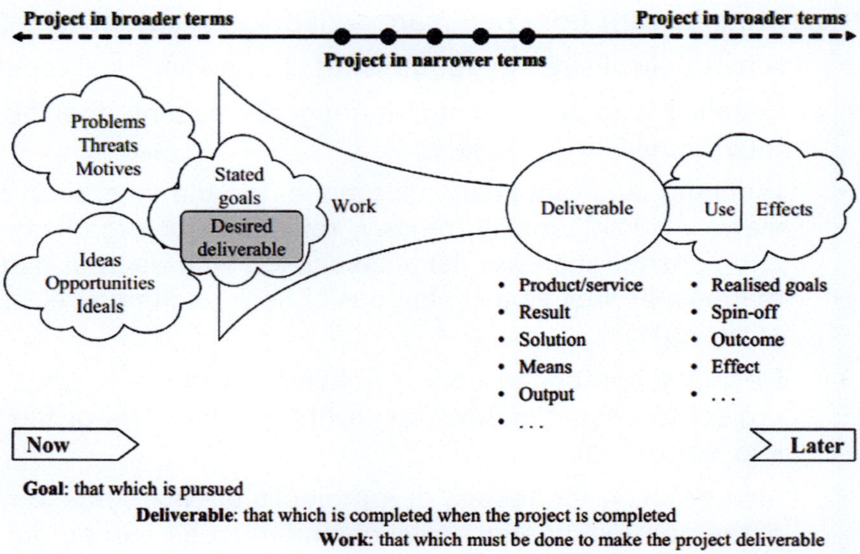

Figure 4.2. Image of a project oriented towards goals or problems, specifically towards one deliverable.

Source: Micheal R. Kinney, creative commons license.

The project owner should be eager to share information regarding the task (Ehsani et al., 2017). Also, they must be ready to articulate their objectives, desires, and ambitions. This strategy unnerves some owners, who believe project managers should follow instructions. Project managers must put in extra work on projects. They must be capable of committing to the project, have faith in it, and think it is doable.

The project manager acquires an understanding of the numerous elements influencing the assignment by looking at the environment in which it will be realized (Twigg, 2004). The technical (is the essential knowledge existing and available?) and social (would those engaged, such as members of staff, line managers, and society at large, allow the outcome to be created and used?) elements of a project are what determine its viability.

4.1.3. Phasing the Project

A record of the content or the phase activities that must be completed in a coherent arrangement is based on the description of the project deliverable. The tasks that must be carried out between the project's beginning and end must be determined. There are usually at least three phases: beginning, realizing/implementing, and, thirdly, utilizing (Figure 4.3) (Couillard, 1995).

The specifics of phasing differ depending on the project methodology. Several approaches modify the stages to correspond with the client organization's management cycle. A phase will represent this quarterly time frame in case the project owner and the steering board (management team) debate the project once each quarter. This is frequently called a 'management phase' and can be explained as the period during which the project manager is authorized to run the project (Bushuyev & Verenych, 2018).

Organizing work into stages in complicated projects and creating an inventory of the various operations is crucial. Every activity must be categorized under a certain phase (Figure 4.4) (Metzger & Boddie, 1996). As we will see later, phasing is essential for organizing and monitoring the real project's development.

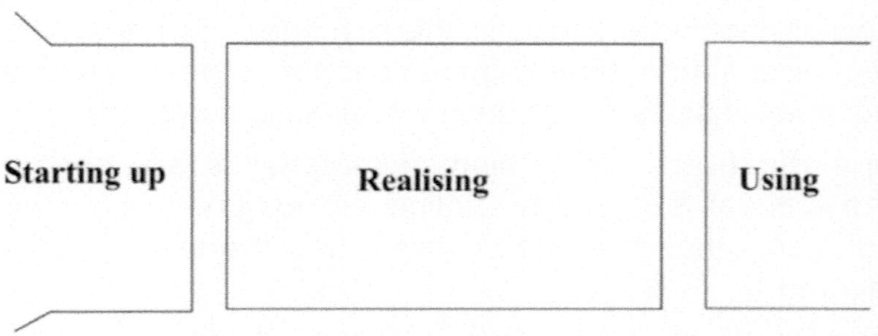

Figure 4.3. Representation of three basic phases of a project.

Source: Micheal R. Kinney, creative commons license.

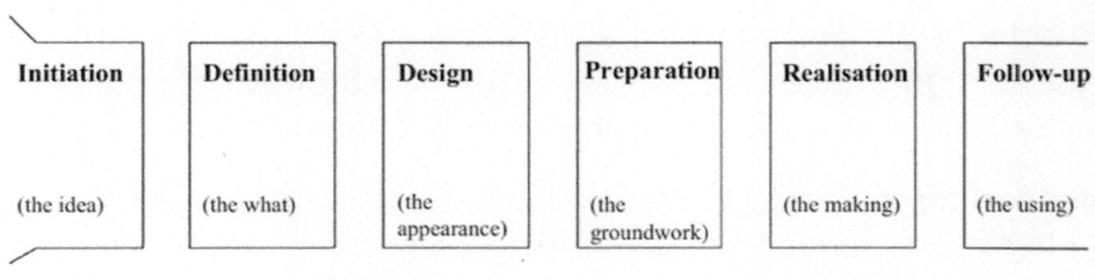

Figure 4.4. Illustration of phases of a project.

Source: Micheal R. Kinney, creative commons license.

By making progress apparent, phasing a project allows organizing decision-making and lowers ambiguity (Miterev et al., 2016). Phasing entails combining similar actions. Each phase needs to be given the same level of focus, not essentially in relation to time or materials needed, but most certainly in terms of importance. A reasonable time for the owner to decide whether to continue or end the project is during the transformation between each phase.

Even the most complicated projects may be broken down into duties and responsibilities that can be confidently planned and carried out in six parts (Khan et al., 2019).

The only phase of a project that lacks a solid start is the initiating phase. The project deliverable must be identified, and its implementation method must be decided upon after this phase (Cooke & Williams, 2013).

The project deliverable is defined in relation to external interfaces, operating and functional requirements, and design restrictions during the definitions phase. In this stage, the question of what the outcome will do or perform is answered.

Requirements for project deliverables might occasionally be categorized in several ways. The classification of needs for softer projects, including the creation of new policies, is as follows:

- **Effect Requirements:** What outcomes are anticipated from the project's success, and what conditions must be met? Examples include an efficient decision-making practice in the management panel about the policy outlined in a memo, unambiguous support in determining a point of view, and open disclosure of decision-making outcomes.
- **Content Specifications:** What kind of material is appropriate? For instance, the standards explicitly outline the judgments that must be made, the subjects that must be covered, and the level of detail that must be covered.
- **Design Specifications:** What do the specifications of a successful project mean for the memo's or policy document's design? For the sake of an example, a standard layout with no more than 25 pages and legible illustrations and figures could be necessary.

Once the selected solutions that will satisfy the project requirements are detailed during the design phase, the project starts to acquire real shape. The result should appear like a question that the design phase answers.

Everything needed for the project's realization is ready and accessible during the preparatory phase. Production plans, training plans, task instructions, and other operational and technological designs are created. Spending time in this phase will ensure that the execution can be done "by just clicking a button" without any problems (Winch et al., 2007).

The project is finally implemented during the realization phase; for instance, the organizational transformation procedure is run, or a fresh IT system is developed following the project specifications (Jiang et al., 2018).

The project's outcome is used, retained, maintained, and, if required, modified throughout the follow-up phase. Using, supporting, and sustaining the realized deliverable and the tools, aids, and resources related to it are among the content tasks in this phase. The project crew is accountable for planning but not executing this phase because it is not a fundamental project component. The project's owner is overseeing the completion of the follow-up stage. The goal of each project phase is summarized in Figure 4.5.

4.1.4. Managing the Project

Planning, accompanied by the progress control of any project, is an ongoing activity. Phasing the project assists find out which activities must be done (Martinsuo & Hoverfält, 2018) (Table 4.1).

Table 4.1. Specific Purpose of a Project's Phase

Phase	Purpose
Initiation	Consider what the project deliverable or result should and should not be; all those involved have the same picture
Definition	Consider exactly what the project deliverable should do
Design	Consider what the project deliverable should look like
Preparation	Consider what the project deliverable should look like, once made
Realization	The carrying out of the project deliverable; making it tangible
Follow-up	Using, supporting, maintaining, and dismantling the project deliverable

Source: Micheal R. Kinney, Creative Commons License.

Project management will make it possible to guarantee that everything will go according to schedule. It is crucial to take five management vantage points into account. Project time management, also known as project time, project quality management, project organization management, project money management, and project release management, are some of these points of view (Artto et al., 2009).

Every one of the five views must be understood in relation to the following:

i. What are the margins (or contingencies) needed to meet the management criteria (norm, standard, plan)?
ii. Who oversees progress monitoring, and how frequently?
iii. What steps should be taken to prepare data for a progress report?
iv. Who holds power to alter management plans? (within and beyond the defined boundaries).

- **Managing Time for Projects:** Have the project's commencement and completion dates, together with the necessary materials, man-hours, and other resources, been determined? It will be important to calculate the link between every activity, the scheduled dates, and the total lead time and lead times for each activity. Each activity must be given the required money, people, and other resources. Schedules must be obtained and delivered to all parties concerned to accomplish this. Is it evident how fantastic the outcome should be and how it will be verified? Quality management inside a project ensures that the project obeys the set quality standards by defining regulated, quantifiable criteria and performing predefined quality control tests. How effectively the project deliverable does meet the minimum requirements for quality?

Important project quality management and release management actions include defining the output quality criteria and ensuring these necessities can and will be appropriately controlled. Do formal processes exist for producing, sharing, publishing, and changing decision documents?

This includes determining what information must be handled, defining a coding scheme, deciding who should release and acquire each decision document, and determining how the documents would be exchanged and how, where, and with whom every decision document will be recorded and may be modified. Has a project management company created the essential frameworks for managing projects, ownership, team composition, task distribution, responsibility, and communication channels? Does everyone comprehend the numerous ways that decisions are made?

Important organization management tasks comprise making sure that responsibilities, tasks, and authority are delegated, describing formal communication channels as conferences, instituting both official and casual decision-making procedures, empowering individuals and groups inside the project to operate pragmatically, and constructing formal links for relationship and communication management between the project organization and its surroundings. Figure 4.6 provides a summary of each management perspective's goals (Liang, 2009). These five points of view need to be controlled in unison. For example, spending more time on time would be inappropriate if quality control was disregarded. Yet, investing more money in a project does not necessarily translate into faster turnaround times or better quality.

4.1.5. Decision Making

Throughout a project, judgments and selections must be made. Several stages of decision-making exist. For instance, a choice has to be made, and a decision on the project's start date and priority level must be made (Table 4.2).

Table 4.2. Different Purposes of Management Perspective

Management perspective	**Purpose**
Time	Ensuring that the project result is realized on time and that the content project activities are carried out by the people means and delegated in time allotted
Money	Ensuring that the project is profitable, that the cost do not exceed the budget and that the planned revenues of the project results can be achieved
Quality	Ensuring that the project deliverable is good enough
Release	Ensuring that the project deliverable is unequivocally recorded and approved
Organization	Ensuring that the project deliverable can be handed over to the owner and everyone knows the taskS, responsibilities, and authority

Source: Micheal R. Kinney, Creative Commons License.

Senior management often makes these choices since they are in charge of the organization's long-term growth and can thus assess if and how a particular project integrates into this picture.

The numerous choices that must be taken throughout each step, like whom to interview, what measuring method to employ, or how to keep those engaged informed, are still another factor. The project manager and the project team members decide on such matters.

The most crucial choices in this project management method are whether or not to continue the project after each phase (Fernandes et al., 2015). The project owner must make these choices, sometimes cooperating with senior management and other stakeholders.

They have access to choose (or baseline) materials to assist them in making these judgments methodically. Contracts, tenders, plans, proposals, task descriptions, milestones, offers, consolidation papers, and agreements related to the project are all included in this list.

Avoid repeating past judgments while deciding at the start of the following phase. These choices should not, however, needlessly interfere with the project's remaining life cycle. So, the type of choices the project owner must make depends on the project's stage (Figure 4.7) (Jugdev, 2012).

Using decision papers, one can incorporate and record the outcomes of the prior step or stages. The documents also outline what needs to be accomplished in the following phase, what further time and resources will be required, the monetary implications, how the project deliverable's quality will be guaranteed, unrestricted, and attuned, and what each person's tasks, duties, and levels of authority are. The decision document anticipates this way. The decision document's subjects become a contract as soon as the project owner has given his or her approval, serving as the foundation for the stages that follow (El Khatib et al., 2022).

Figure 4.5. Image of decisions to be made in a project.

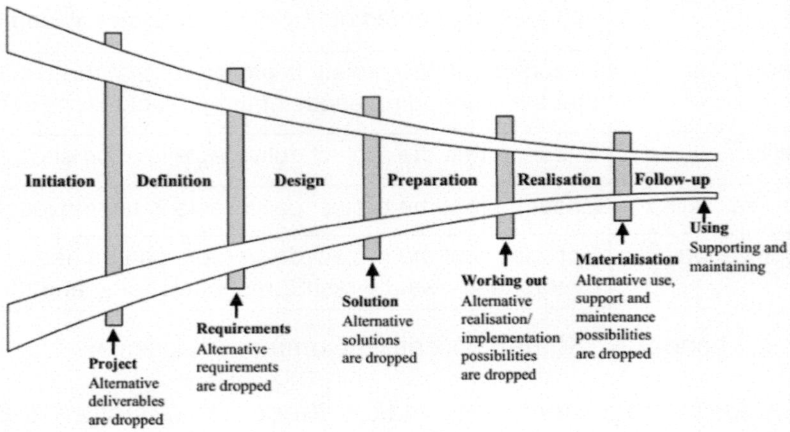

Source: Micheal R. Kinney, creative commons license.

Hence, a decision document serves as both the end of one phase and the beginning of another. This document serves as a contract between the project owner and the project manager, outlining the deliverable that must be met, the effort required to do so, and the management strategies for the pertinent viewpoints (Saynisch, 2010). The project manager may directly decide on matters that arise during the phase or stages that come within the bounds of this contract.

Any impending contract variations must be immediately communicated to the project owner. The decision documents must all be organized similarly and contain the following information to maintain consistency:

- A description of the project deliverable to the extent that this can be inferred from the project's activity during that phase.
- An explanation of the tasks to be completed. For the next phase and, more typically, for the following phases, each task should be specified in depth.
- An explanation of the management plans (covering money, time, quality, and organization) and the setup for progress reporting (including who monitors progress, how often, and in what ways) are provided in the item (Springer, 2019).

A decision document is an essential tool for communication. There is a steady exchange of thoughts at the end of each phase to help coordinate thoughts about what will and will not be realized in the project. This ensures that, in addition to the project team members, other stakeholders are participating in the project.

Frequent updates on the project's progress can help to maintain the project owner's engagement and sense of accountability. While transitioning from one phase to the next, at the absolute least, this should be done. Because they will have the decision papers at their disposal, the project owner will be better able to uphold their responsibility for the project.

When projects are handled correctly, there are huge inconvenience savings for all parties involved. Yet, a project cannot manage itself. Every project necessitates a temporary combination of human resources, requiring extra time and effort from all parties involved.

Every project has time, effort, and resource commitments from the project owner, project manager, and project team. This implies that a business can never deploy more projects than a specific amount at once.

4.2. PROJECT MANAGEMENT SUCCESS

Although there is no agreed-upon definition of a successful project, experts concur that a project manager's good decisions can lead to success (Gewanlal & Bekker, 2015).

Intending to advance current knowledge and methods, particularly in the field of construction management, this article discusses project management success. For most governments, customers, and communities, the success of building projects is a core concern, so it is essential never to cease looking for new methods to increase construction management performance (Gudienė et al., 2013).

Four components will be used to accomplish this goal. A thorough survey of the literature is provided in the first section, establishing several definitions and theories of successful project management through time. The success elements of project management are stated in a breakdown structure in the second section.

Project management competency, organizational components, and project management tools, techniques, methodologies, and approaches, make up the structure. In the third section, management of public, EU-funded water projects is used to describe the breakdown structure. In the fourth part, suggestions for further development are provided.

Project management is the process of planning, arranging, supervising, and regulating every aspect of a project while encouraging everyone involved to finish it safely and within the set timetable, budget, and performance parameters (Lukianov et al., 2019). According to the definition of project management, this discipline is focused on the brief components of project success, such as schedule, quality, and budget requirements. The "iron triangle" model was the first practical project management approach, but it has since been proven to account for just a percentage of the project's overall performance (De, 1988). From this point of view, it is simple to see how a project might be successful while project management fails and vice versa. A project could be productive regardless of the lousy management if it fulfilled lousy and prolonged goals. Short-term goals may not be accomplished when project management finishes. Still, long-term goals may be met because a wider variety of purposes, rather more extensive than the limited purposes that project management concentrates on, are met (Munns & Bjeirmi, 1996).

Various other approachesKrusebe employed in addition to the "iron triangle" to ensure project management success (Munns & Bjeirmi, 1996). The individual who bears the primary responsibility for the project's success is the project manager, as he is responsible for not only timing, budget, and quality management but also communication, integrations, scope, personnel management, risk, and contract administration. In light of this, it is unquestionably conceivable to expand the "iron triangle" to include theories that account for the management of stakeholders' contentment, advantages to the organization that controls the project, and long-term effects on the project environment (Maylor, 2001; Ribeiro et al., 2013).

How can the success of project management be accessed? The time, cost, quality, scope, resource, and activity criteria, as well as success measurement methods like PMPA – Project Management Performance Assessment or institutional maturity models like Project Excellence Model®, can be used to quantify project success. Considering that project management provides both tangible and intangible benefits, providing a concrete answer to measuring success is difficult (Westerveld, 2003; Thomas, 2014).

As previously mentioned, a good project may get completed without successful project management; however, profitable project management can increase the success rate of a project. Project management techniques and success are positively correlated (Papke-Shields et al., 2010). Project management success is among the elements of project success since it is nearly impossible without it.

4.2.1. Tools for Preventing Project Failure

Organizations were compelled to start depending more heavily on digital tools after the pandemic broke out in 2020. Leaders selected investing in the appropriate technologies as one of the three essential aspects contributing to actual performance in the PMI 2020 study (32%).

The areas expected to have the most gains over the next five years are technology advancement (49%) and digitalization (44%). The effects of the rapid increase in digitalization were evident. 2020 was predicted to break all records after a consistent annual rise in the proportion of enterprises reporting experiencing scope creep. Surprisingly, though, things began to improve by 2021. Organizations reporting scope creep decreased from 52% in 2018 to 34% in 2019. Similarly, after holding steady at roughly 12% for the preceding seven years, wasted investments decreased to 9.4% (Atkinson, 1999).

In 2021, gymnastics businesses—pioneers in digital advancement—faced 4% less scope creep than conventional businesses, according to PMI's 2021 Survey.

TIPS

In 2021, PMI made a distinction between gymnastic and traditional organizations, i.e., those that were agile and ready to embrace change and those that were not.

These figures are not shocking given that current project metamodern, like play, offer a wide range of practical features such as (Radujković, 2000):

a. Centralizing document sharing;
b. Monitoring teams and projects;
c. Enabling team communication;
d. Assessing progress;
e. Facilitating team communication; and
f. Organizing workload and personal tasks.

Utilizing digital resources is a quick and easy technique to increase project d productivity and efficiency. Software for managing projects will undoubtedly raise your likelihood of success because it will streamline management and put all necessary information at your fingertips without increasing your budget or adding to your workforce (Turner et al., 2009).

Project scope can be thought of as the project's foundation. It is among the initial management parts defined during a project's life cycle.

The project's scope outlines all of the available resources, needs, and goals of the project, in addition to a comprehensive timeframe for extended project deliverables. A firm scope keeps every person related to the project on the same level. It alerts all participants of the standards they agreed on before the commencement of before, preventing the project from spiraling out of control. As a result, the project scope is regarded as an essential part of the plan of project management, which serves as the foundation for every subsequent decision that will be made regarding the project (Radujković & Sjekavica, 2017).

4.2.2. Essential Factors for Project Success

Intelligent People: If you want your project to succeed, you'll need talented teammates. Any project can deviate from its original path at any time. The project workers and other project participants must show enthusiasm and dedication for this. The team should aim for success and set reasonable project goals. If the team members are lacking in any aspect, the project manager will have to face several issues in the journey toward a successful project. A project may fail due to ineffective leadership and an unorganized crew. The project is disorganized, making each team member allocate the appropriate task, and everyone gets along well (Yang et al., 2011).

Comprehensive Planning: The odds of a project's success are increased from the outset when there is a thorough plan. From the start, the staff and clients should be conscious of the project's objective. With careful planning, the team can stay organized and meet crucial deadlines (Feger & Thomas, 2012). Thoughtful planning has many advantages because a reasonable schedule can be defined in the project's initial step. It gives a specific deadline for creating cost estimates and aids in the detailed documentation of explicitly documenting things more accessible as the process develops. Planning establishes an alert system and specifies the resources needed. The alert system will provide a clear picture of if there is a void (Nahod & Radujković, 2013).

According to Learning Legacy: The scope and entanglement of building location and infrastructure for the London 2012 Olympics generated a program structure of almost 50 distinct projects, "Lessons Learned from the Lon 2012 Games Construction Project." The scope, specifications, and starting budgets for the entire program were determined in 2007 with meticulous planning, which aided in completing the London 2012 Olympics' physical infrastructure. To permit thorough evaluations and an integrated program overview, each project was also expected to produce specific information on the fiscal situation, Progress, and other issues, monthly. The program administration of this significant athletic event, which included numerous sub-projects, raised the norms of the centralized UK construction industry (Radujković & Sjekavica, 2017).

Open Communication: An available communication channel is significant for project success. When working under a deadline, the team must stay updated about every aspect of the project. Making promises one cannot fulfill is highly immoral. As a project manager, learn when to say no, and tell the truth regarding what you can supply and when you can deliver it (Besner & Hobbs, 2006).

Proper Risk Management: Projects frequently fail to meet their deadlines. Some projects fail spectacularly, while others fail terribly due to dangers that arise throughout the project. According to PMI's "Pulse of the Profession: The High Cost of Low Performance," organizations currently lose USD 109 million for every $1 billion invested in projects and programs. Create a risk journal with an implementation plan to address hazards that arise during the project. As the project manager, ensure that all parties know the backup plan. Hence, if something terrible happens, your team can deal with it promptly because of the set goal. This gives clients trust in the project's Progress and provides the team with confidence while dealing with project risks (Chou et al., 2013).

Strong Project Closure: To be successful, a project must have a firm conclusion. As the project manager, you must remain strong and affirm to the customer that all critical success criteria have been met. The project's supply, testing, and release permission must all be discussed and authorized.

According to various organizations, a project's success greatly depends upon the recruitment of certified and the previously mentioned aspects. Organizations with certified project managers see a significantly more remarkable performance in terms of the KPIs of quality, timing, scope, budget, and business advantages, according to PwC's "Insights and Trends: Current Portfolio, Program, and Project Management Practices." See the illustration below (Radujković & Sjekavica, 2017):

Project management best practices are taught through project management credentials, including the Prince2 Online Certification, CAPM Project Management Certification, PMP Online Training, MSP, and P3O. A good project manager can become an excellent one with the help of project management qualifications (Fortune et al., 2011).

4.3. PROJECT MONITORING AND CONTROLLING PROCESSES

When there are discrepancies between the outcomes of the procedures and the plan, corrective measures are made to alter the strategy rather than the manner it is being carried out.

To avoid future project work from being too disconnected from the strategy, the exercise's goal is to take into account what has been managed to learn from the implementation of the plan as well as to re-plan on the criterion of this new info.

The primary tenet of this project process is the assessment and contrast of actual observed values to those anticipated. To finish the building on time and within budget, corrective actions must be taken if there is a variation. The project management plan and performance reports, which include information gathered from the entire project, serve as the inputs. When progress markedly deviates from the expected path, which typically means going beyond a set specified tolerance, it is crucial to pinpoint the causative factors and take appropriate action.

Since reporting processes are time-sensitive, leaders must be able to respond appropriately as soon as variations are noticed. If the unique method is slow, they will not be able to manage the project; instead, they will have a record of how beyond regulation it was in the past. Depending on the scope, difficulty, and degree of involvement of the various management levels, the control process will change from project to project. Compared to longer-term, more stable projects, short initiatives susceptible to high uncertainty and risk will necessitate shorter report periods.

4.4. PROJECT CLOSURE PROCESSES

This signifies the project's deadlines' finalization and transmission to the final recipients, typically internal or external customers. This phase also involves administrative closing, which entails dismissing the project group's actions, finalizing all project information, and official execution any agreements (Momoh et al., 2010).

Documents relating to a project are typically archived so that they can be reassessed if the organization decides to undertake a project comparable to the one currently being worked on and in which the knowledge and expertise gained during the previous project could be of assistance. It is the responsibility of the project's closing phase, which should be managed appropriately, to guarantee that the project is brought to a controlled close. In reality, this entails the following (Jarczyk et al., 2018):

1. All of the project's deliverables are officially handed to others.
2. Every one of the moments that occurred throughout the project is recorded and saved.
3. All contracts that were created by the project are terminated legally.

Because once going to close the project is completed, the manager will monitor all data from the previous step closing to ensure that all tasks have been completed and the project has achieved its goals.

Because such a scope statement is evaluated against the project management plan, the project leader would examine this document to verify its finalization before declaring the project complete. This operation also sets guidelines for investigating and documenting the explanations for measures undertaken if a project is ended before it is finished.

Suppose external suppliers were employed on the project. In that case, this phase also includes confirmation that all jobs and milestones were satisfactory, administrative tasks such as closing open statements, updating records to reflect official outcomes, and cataloging this data for future usage. Typically, formal closure criteria are outlined in the contract's conditions and terms and incorporated into the planning process. This output is merely the buyer's legal statement that the agreement has been fulfilled.

A contract could be closed during any stage of a multi-stage project if its terms are only relevant to a particular phase. The contractual conditions and terms for agreements applicable to a given phase would outline the specific procedures for contract termination. If there are outstanding complaints at the end of the contract, the supplier relationship management procedure will specify how an action will be addressed.

Sometimes, a contract may need to be terminated sooner than anticipated. Any project agreement or contract must include a section detailing the parties' rights and responsibilities in the case of an immediate withdrawal. This unique form of procurement closure may result from (Townley & Trefry, 1991):

1. Agreement between both groups,
2. Nonpayment by one side, or
3. For the purchaser's comfort (as long as provision is made in the contract).

A contract might be terminated soon for the entirety of a specific piece. It is customary for the buyer to compensate the supplier according to the contract terms for any work-in-progress (WIP) performed. This is particularly significant if the project utilizes teaming agreements in which two or more businesses create a collaboration or partnership to complete the contract. The contract defines the buyer's and seller's respective roles and duties. Numerous specialists in outsourcing will have their partnering contract templates.

4.5. THE APPROACH TO MANAGING PROGRAM

4.5.1. Rules and Characteristics of Program Management

Following are some of the basic rules for professional program management:

- Individuals involved understand that "regular" jobs must be handled differently from special or "one-off" assignments (Christopher et al., 2011). An understanding must be developed of every program's objectives, methods, and strategy (unlike routine work, where this only has to be done sporadically).

- There is a separation between those in charge of setting and pursuing goals and those in charge of providing the results (the first is the responsibility of the program owner, while the second rests with the program manager) (Locander et al., 1979).
- Those engaged are free to utilize the program to pursue any number of objectives as long as they are compatible with the means necessary to accomplish the agreed-upon end and are a part of it.
- There is one program owner who must be allowed to judge crucial choices made throughout the program. This guarantees that management and decision-making are greatly sped up and simplified (Butler et al., 2020).
- The program owner must ensure that the objectives are met and, more importantly, that the intended result is specified in advance (Alve et al., 2016). Also, they must provide all essential resources, including employees, funding, supplies, and other tools.
- The program owner is in charge of ensuring the right things are done. After that, the program manager oversees their proper execution.
- The earlier the program team members are involved, the more dedicated they will be to seeing the program through to completion. The program owner and manager should include the program team as early as feasible.
- Users and maintenance personnel should be included in the program from the beginning (Kettl, 2006).
- The program manager and owner must make sure that their program meets the requirements of a program, including having a distinct assignment, being flexible, being essential to individuals participating, having clear goals, and being outcome-oriented.
- The program concentrates on the four program management processes: stakeholders, planning, teamwork, and method.
- Before starting work, the program manager must ensure that all parties agree with the program strategy (Bryzhko & Kosheleva, 2012). This entails paying attention to the objectives, backing up the tempo management strategies, and emphasizing viability, effectiveness, adaptability, and goal orientation.
- The sponsor should be prepared to decide whether to discontinue or continue the program at significant checkpoints, especially at the conclusion of certain stages (Krishna et al., 2004).

When a lot of related projects, efforts, or activities need to be carried out within or between organizations, such as when a company is momentarily pursuing a particular strategic goal or when a project grows too complicated to be managed, program management has frequently proven to be helpful. Yet, program management may also help reconcile objectives that are at odds with one another. For instance, increased railroad efficiency must be combined with increased railroad safety.

The use of program management is also appropriate for those special tasks requiring a complex web of interdependencies across several important initiatives. A different, more suitable management approach is required to complete this challenging job.

This approach to program management may be used for internal and external initiatives (carried out for external clients).

The following are the characteristics of this program management methodology that are shared by all of them:

i. Thinking and acting with the program goals, their impact, and outcome in mind (Mahadevan et al., 2011);
ii. Thinking first (from the big picture to the details), then acting; differentiating among content activities (non-managerial) and managerial ones (managing tempo, feasibility, efficiency, flexibility, and goal-orientation);
iii. Ensuring there is a systematic start-up, implementation, and shutdown (Bolisani & Bratianu, 2017).

In program management, only one thing can be anticipated completely: conditions will change. The powers will lose interest, new stakeholders will wish to become engaged, or third parties may realize results that render parts of the program's efforts irrelevant or unnecessary. There will be adjustments to the program and its surroundings (Pearson & Casassa-Mont, 2011). The pace of some program activities will be decreased while that of other program initiatives will be accelerated. Some goals will be eliminated, while others will be changed, expanded, and redefined.

All these changes can be handled only if the objectives sought and the related activities have been explicitly documented. Then, understand just how to react to given facts. For instance, being aware of when and how to respond to shifts in the power dynamic.

The management plan, if properly documented, will enable to judge the consequences and push through all the proposed and necessary changes relatively quickly.

The program management method consists of three main processes: programming, managing, and decision-making:

i. **Programming:** It involves the specification of the program's goals, the non-managerial efforts needed to achieve these, and the means needed. The key activity in programming is carrying out the specified efforts, which are logical and vital for pursuing the specified program goals.

ii. **Managing:** It entails planning and progress monitoring management plans (Vroom & Jago, 1988). The management plan for each management perspective is based on the goals to be pursued, the efforts needed, and the means available.

iii. **Decision-Making:** It is the final part of the process. The results of programming and managing are integrated with a program plan. The program plan must be unambiguous and consistent (Zwikael et al., 2006). Preparing a program plan involves drawing up plans and seeking, forming, and making decisions in response to these plans. Program plans must be drawn up at regular, predetermined intervals and the start and finish of each stage.

4.5.2. Programming: Not Just Thinking, But Doing

The ER goals are further defined or subdivided into MACIC or SMART goals in the program technique. An ER aim is a worthwhile but unachievable ideal representing an object's intended condition, quality, or attribute in a certain environment (Olsson, 2008). Examples of ER goals include improving committee consultation, finding a better building for accommodations in France, having receptionists treat clients with more courtesy, improving the city's transportation system in London, and increasing the market share for telephones in China. Measurable, Acceptable, Committing, Inspiring, and Communicated is abbreviated as MACIC. Specific, Measurable, Acceptable, Realizable, and Traceable is the abbreviation for SMART. This is done to enable programming, which entails listing, charting, grouping, and executing the necessary non-managerial tasks, to be capable of pursuing these broken-down goals.

Each measurable objective or sub goal is connected to one or more efforts so that it is obvious how much each effort contributes to each goal. Often, a diagram or goals/efforts network may be used to show the objectives and the efforts required to pursue them (GEN) (Rijamampianina & Carmichael, 2005).

Alternative objectives and activities are frequently linked, and vice versa, to provide a more comprehensive and easily defended or supported GEN (Imperial & Hennessey, 1996). With each variation, the program's purpose becomes increasingly obvious. Suppose the GEN is created in consultation with the most prominent program team members and the most significant champions of its goals. In that case, the dedication to goals, priorities, and boundaries can also drastically rise.

The aims, actions, and means those responsible for carrying out the program's defined efforts must be a part of the network (GEM). While building up a GEM, one must consider which resources are required and which are then available for each planned endeavor (the example in Figure 4.8) (Lemieux, 2004). In addition to people, resources may also include items like workspace, furniture, and equipment. These commodities can be characterized by their particular composition or quantity depending on what is required.

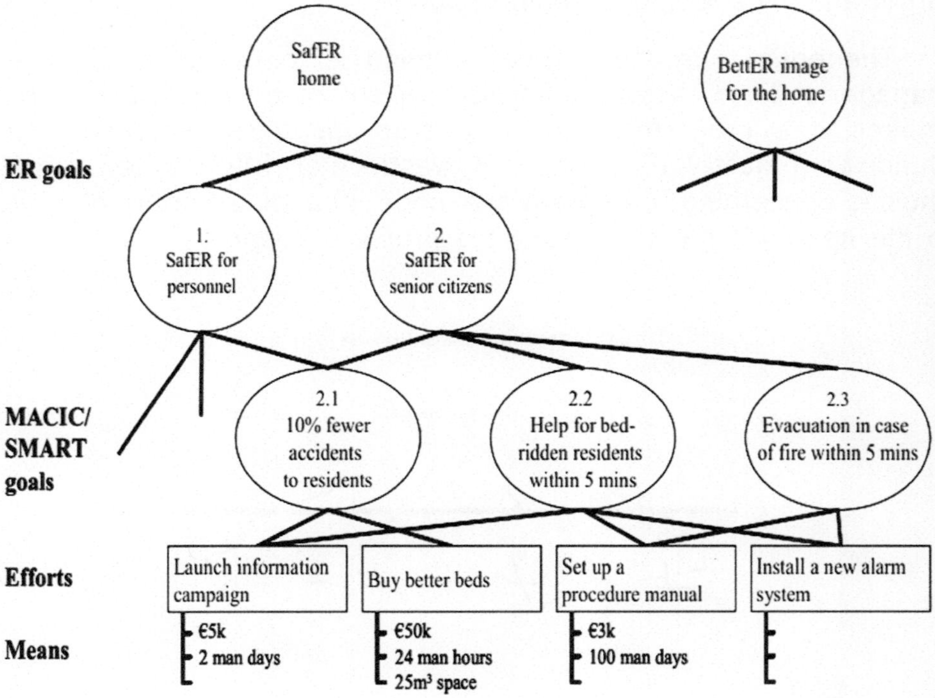

Figure 4.6. Image of goals/efforts/means network in program management.

Source: Micheal R. Kinney, creative commons license.

A GEM is an ideal tool for communication amongst all stakeholders participating in the program because it can frequently be replicated once finished on a single page of A4 (Martinsuo & Hoverfält, 2018).

Indicating, for instance, how much each effort helps to pursue a certain objective, a very well GEM can show which interfaces are deemed significant between the various activities. A GEM can be modified, expanded, or customized once it has been set up as needed (in a controlled manner, however). One of the fundamental frameworks for making decisions is the GEM (Bernon & Cullen, 2007). Naturally, a GEM is also a helpful and practical instrument for the program manager to show the logical and natural progression of the non-managerial activities that must be carried out with the corresponding defined resources.

It is typically required to group the numerous efforts into a program structure for the convenience of reference; this method is called clustering (Figure 4.9) (DeJoy, 2005).

Clustering can be carried out in several ways. Based on the parties engaged, clusters are occasionally formed; other times, it is simpler to classify the activities by discipline, funding source, target audience, or geographic region.

The entire purpose of programming is to complete all non-managerial tasks associated with the software. There are three phases in a program's life cycle: start-up, implementation, and shutdown (Figure 4.10) (Conradi & Westfechtel, 1998). When formal choices concerning a program are made, changing from one stage to the next is a natural but always practical event.

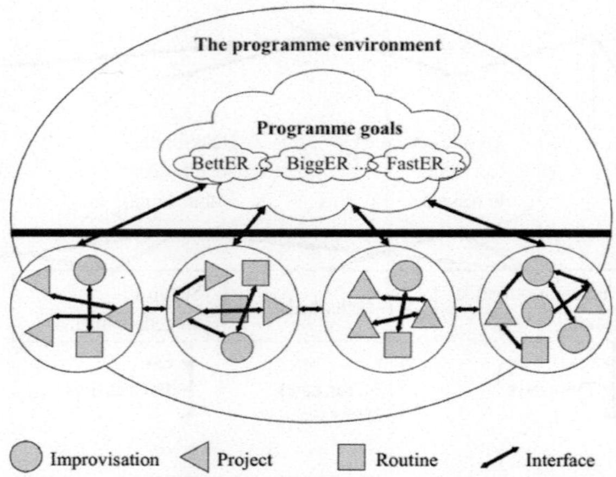

Figure 4.7. Representation of clustering a program.

Source: Micheal R. Kinney, creative commons license.

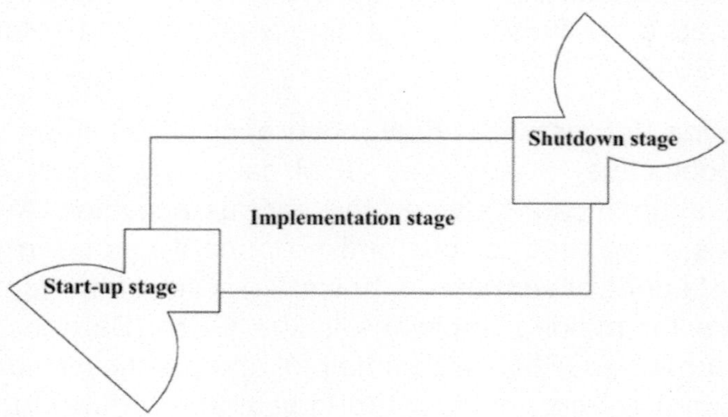

Figure 4.8. Representation of stages in a program life cycle.

Source: Micheal R. Kinney, creative commons license.

Program plans serve as a dividing line between the three stages, but they will be reviewed and amended as needed during each step.

The questions that are often answered during the start-up phase include the following:

i. Which stakeholders—individuals, organizations, or divisions of organizations—are engaged in the program's implementation? Who is not a party?

ii. Which objectives do the stakeholders want to pursue collectively, and which are the preceding?

iii. Which non-managerial initiatives should be included in the program, and which should not?

iv. Why were these initiatives incorporated into a program? Why haven't they been dealt with regularly, as straightforward labor tasks, or incorporated into a significant project?

Throughout the implementation phase, the program expands. The energy and resources used and the number of projects and other initiatives steadily rise. This level marks the maturity of the software.

Three options are available at the shutdown stage: halting, splitting or transferring (Keil, 1995).

A program must be stopped by properly finishing the tasks that still need to be done. If the program is split up into numerous new ones, the new programs must be developed concurrently with the termination of the old program. In this manner.

It is possible to turn the original program into one or more new ones, each with its life cycle. By dividing or moving a program, the program is essentially terminated. The appropriate parties are given all program outcomes and ongoing work for independent pursuit. Alternatively, all program activities might be combined into a brand-new, permanent organizational unit.

4.5.3. Managing Goal-Oriented Efforts

In addition to ensuring that all outcomes and intermediate results from previously documented efforts contribute as needed to the program, managing a program also involves managing and upholding all interfaces inside and between the program and its appropriate environment.

Instead of carrying out non-managerial initiatives, management focuses on providing the conditions that will enable them to be carried out (Garcia et al., 2007). To this end, management plans must be created to oversee the development of these (content) initiatives.

The primary program management responsibilities include general managerial tasks like encouraging and inspiring others and starting, organizing, and concluding routine program operations (Hedlund et al., 1990). When collaborating with project managers and department heads, this frequently necessitates that the program manager assumes the position of the (delegated) program sponsor.

In order to prioritize and assess various topics, a project manager requires views or criteria. These viewpoints may theoretically be changed for every new application. Integral management of the program is often made feasible by the five management perspectives of pace, feasibility, efficiency, and effectiveness (Barletta et al., 2020).

Figure 4.9. Image of management perspectives of program management.

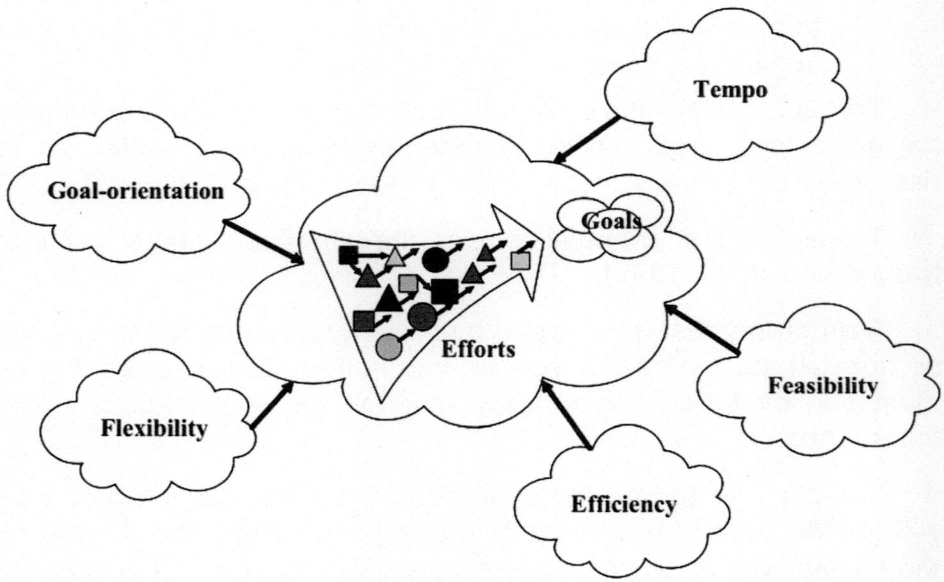

Source: Micheal R. Kinney, creative commons license.

Using these viewpoints, the program manager may assess the appropriateness of each non-managerial effort in light of the overall objectives and context of the program by comparing the different non-managerial efforts (Iversen et al., 2004).

These criteria also allow us to assess and compare the results of the program's various efforts, enabling us to decide whether or not to alter the program.

Below are the definitions of the five perspectives:

i. **Tempo:** From this vantage point, it is feasible to gauge and evaluate the program's development, and in particular, the time and tempo of a program effort required to deliver the intended result when necessary (Boehm & Ross, 1989). From a pace viewpoint, a particular effort will be more appealing the sooner it is finished.

ii. **Feasibility:** From the program management standpoint, feasibility gauges the likelihood that a particular endeavor will succeed or fall short of the desired contribution. The program activities with the best chance of advancing the goals must be given utmost attention (Boehm, 1999).

iii. **Efficiency:** Program management can use the efficiency perspective to compare the likely monetary worth of the program's efforts (Wideman, 2022). The more an effort contribution, the fewer resources are required to complete it, or the bigger the potential benefit or impact.

iv. **Flexibility:** The program management perspective of flexibility measures the effort's adaptability (Chen & Chen, 2009). Its adaptability is frequently seen in how quickly an endeavor may be adjusted or scaled back. It also becomes clear from the ease with which resources and capabilities may be moved from one endeavor to another. The majority of the program's resources must be properly controlled in efforts.

v. **Goal orientation**: This viewpoint assesses how much program activities may advance the objectives. Of certainly, efforts with a clear direction are better (Nidumolu & Subramani, 2003).

Each program will give a different amount of weight to the various views. While flexibility may be viewed as the most desirable quality in one program, feasibility may rank highly in another. One must assess the relative worth of each perspective to the others to run a program on this basis. This might be accomplished by giving each perspective a specific weighting factor.

Of course, a program's management viewpoints are all interconnected. An effort that is rigid and laborious, scoring poorly from the standpoint of pace but looks to be intensely goal-oriented and receives wide support may perform worse than an effort that is flexible and goal-oriented but receives limited support.

The program manager will be able to evaluate each non-managerial effort based on the viewpoints if the program's perspectives are given specific practicality and weighting criteria.

The second essential component of program management is progress control. Progress can be regulated only if timely, accurate, comprehensive, and, in crucial, forward-looking information on progress is obtained from the program's numerous contributors (Boland & Collopy, 2004). Also, all pertinent data from the program's environment must be current, accurate, comprehensive, and forward-looking.

4.5.4. Decision Making: Choosing Goals and Consequences

As the beginning of a program is typically hidden, it may seem straightforward at first glance, but looks can be deceiving. A program's start-up phase, which comprises figuring out the Objective, creating the organizational structure for the program, and looking for and logging requirements, is anything but simple (Locke et al., 1986). Conscious decisions on whether to continue, change, or terminate a program over its lifespan must be made to prevent it from being implemented mindlessly, needlessly, or incorrectly. Plans that call for a decision must be communicated to the program owner at predetermined intervals (Anderson, 1983). Its frequency will be higher at the beginning of the execution stage than in the middle, and it will rise again towards the end.

ACTIVITY 4.1.

Create a project plan for hypothetical project, including identifying project goals and objectives, defining scope, developing schedules and identifying resources.

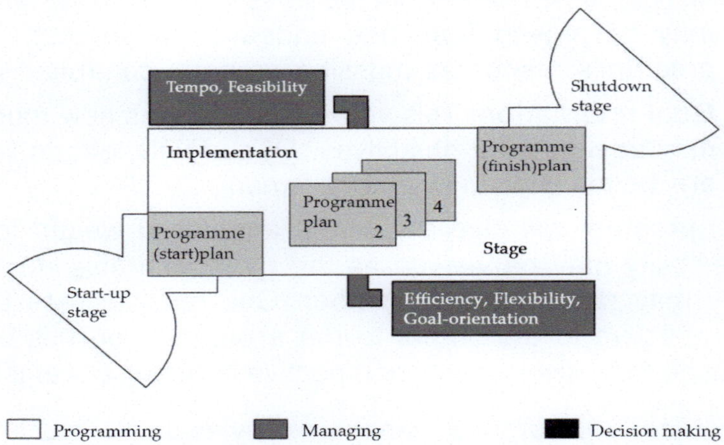

Figure 4.10. Illustration of program management integrating programming, management, and decision making.

Source: Micheal R. Kinney, creative commons license.

The program owner decides whether to accept or reject what has been accomplished thus far and whether to accept or reject the program manager's intentions for such efforts for the following phases by basing their judgment on the suggested program plan.

The five management perspectives will be involved, but plans for staff capacity, financial profit, loss, performance, and communication should also be included. This program management approach, in which planning, managing, and decision-making are interconnected, is schematically described in Figure 4.10(Brunsson, 1982).

SUMMARY

Planning, implementing, monitoring, and controlling a number of activities is a necessary component of trying to manage projects and programs to achieve certain goals within a predetermined time frame and budget. The major objective of managing projects and programs is to ensure that the project or program is finished on time, on schedule, and to the specified quality standards. It is crucial to have a clear knowledge of the desired outcomes and to create a comprehensive project plan that includes the important tasks, dates, resources, and deliverables to manage projects and programs efficiently. Overall, having a sound plan, having a team of qualified professionals who can execute the plan, and being committed to ongoing monitoring, evaluation, and improvement are all essential for successful project and program management. These factors will help to guarantee that the endeavor or program is on track to meet its goals.

REVIEW QUESTIONS

1. Write down five rules and characteristics of project management.
2. Write down five rules and characteristics of program management.
3. List and explain all the phases of a project and program.
4. List and differentiate five management perspectives in program management.

MULTIPLE CHOICE QUESTIONS

1. What is a project?

a. A temporary endeavor with a defined start and end date
b. A continuous operation within an organization
c. A long-term goal for an organization
d. All of the above

2. What is a program?

a. A temporary endeavor with a defined start and end date
b. A group of related projects managed in a coordinated way to achieve specific objectives
c. A long-term goal for an organization
d. None of the above

3. What is the primary goal of program management?

a. To complete the program on time, within budget, and to the required quality
b. To create a new product or service
c. To increase revenue for the organization
d. All of the above

4. What is the primary goal of project management?

a. To complete the project on time, within budget, and to the required quality

b. To create a new product or service

c. To increase revenue for the organization

d. None of the above

5. Which of the following is not a project management goal?

a. Avoiding customer complaints

b. Keeping overall costs within budget

c. Delivering the software to the customer at the agreed time

d. Maintaining a happy and well-functioning development team

Answers to Multiple Choice Questions

1. (a); 2. (b); 3. (a); 4. (a) 5. (A)

REFERENCES

1. Alfieri, A., Tolio, T., & Urgo, M., (2012). A two-stage stochastic programing project scheduling approach to production planning. *The International Journal of Advanced Manufacturing Technology, 62*(1), 279–290.
2. Alves, A., Sousa, R., Moreira, F., Carvalho, M. A., Cardoso, E., Pimenta, P., & Mesquita, D., (2016). Managing PBL difficulties in an industrial engineering and management program. *Journal of Industrial Engineering and Management, 9*(3), 586–611.
3. Anderson, P. A., (1983). Decision making by objection and the Cuban missile crisis. *Administrative Science Quarterly, 1*, 201–222.
4. Ann, T. W., Shen, Q., Kelly, J., & Hunter, K., (2007). An empirical study of the variables affecting construction project briefing/architectural programming. *International Journal of Project Management, 25*(2), 198–212.
5. Archer, N., & Ghasemzadeh, F., (2007). Project portfolio selection and management. In: Morris, P., & Pinto, J. K., (eds.), *The Wiley Guide to Project, Program & Portfolio Management* (Vol. 1, pp. 94–112).
6. Artto, K., Martinsuo, M., Gemünden, H. G., & Murtoaro, J., (2009). Foundations of program management: A bibliometric view. *International Journal of Project Management, 27*(1), 1–18.
7. Barletta, V. S., Caivano, D., Dimauro, G., Nannavecchia, A., & Scalera, M., (2020). Managing a smart city integrated model through smart program management. *Applied Sciences, 10*(2), 714.
8. Bernon, M., & Cullen, J., (2007). An integrated approach to managing reverse logistics. *International Journal of Logistics: Research and Applications, 10*(1), 41–56.

9. Boehm, B. W., & Ross, R., (1989). Theory-W software project management principles and examples. *IEEE Transactions on Software Engineering, 15*(7), 902–916.
10. Boehm, B., (1999). Managing software productivity and reuse. *Computer, 32*(9), 111–113.
11. Boland, R., & Collopy, F., (2004). *Managing as Designing* (Vol. 1, p. 298). Stanford, CA: Stanford business books.
12. Bolisani, E., & Bratianu, C., (2017). Knowledge strategy planning: An integrated approach to manage uncertainty, turbulence, and dynamics. *Journal of Knowledge Management, 1*, 5–10.
13. Brunsson, N., (1982). The irrationality of action and action rationality: Decisions, ideologies and organizational actions. *Journal of Management Studies, 19*(1), 29–44.
14. Bryzhko, V. G., & Kosheleva, L. A., (2012). The conceptual approach to managing the development of agricultural enterprises in the region. *World Applied Sciences Journal (Special Issue of Economics), 18*(1), 191–196.
15. Bushuyev, S., & Verenych, O., (2018). Organizational maturity and project: Program and portfolio success. In: *Developing Organizational Maturity for Effective Project Management* (Vol. 1, pp. 104–127). IGI Global.
16. Butler, C. W., Vijayasarathy, L. R., & Roberts, N., (2020). Managing software development projects for success: Aligning plan-and agility-based approaches to project complexity and project dynamism. *Project Management Journal, 51*(3), 262–277.
17. Cavaleri, S., Firestone, J., & Reed, F., (2012). Managing project problem-solving patterns. *International Journal of Managing Projects in Business, 5*(1), 125–145.
18. Chen, C. Y., & Chen, P. C., (2009). A holistic approach to managing software change impact. *Journal of Systems and Software, 82*(12), 2051–2067.
19. Chiocchio, F., Rabbat, F., & Lebel, P., (2015). Multi-level efficacy evidence of a combined interprofessional collaboration and project management training program for healthcare project teams. *Project Management Journal, 46*(4), 20–34.
20. Christopher, M., Mena, C., Khan, O., & Yurt, O., (2011). Approaches to managing global sourcing risk. *Supply Chain Management: An International Journal, 16*(2), 67–81.
21. Conradi, R., & Westfechtel, B., (1998). Version models for software configuration management. *ACM Computing Surveys (CSUR), 30*(2), 232–282.
22. Cooke, B., & Williams, P., (2013). *Construction Planning, Programming and Control* (Vol. 1, pp. 2–6). John Wiley & Sons.
23. Couillard, J., (1995). The role of project risk in determining project management approach. *Project Management Journal, 26*, 3–15.
24. D. Bushuyev, S., & Friedrich, W. R., (2014). IPMA delta and IPMA organizational competence baseline (OCB) New approaches in the field of project management maturity. *International Journal of Managing Projects in Business, 7*(2), 302–310.

25. DeJoy, D. M., (2005). Behavior change versus culture change: Divergent approaches to managing workplace safety. *Safety Science, 43*(2), 105–129.
26. Dingsøyr, T., Moe, N. B., & Seim, E. A., (2018). Coordinating knowledge work in multiteam programs: Findings from a large-scale agile development program. *Project Management Journal, 49*(6), 64–77.
27. Ehsani, E., Kazemi, N., Olugu, E. U., Grosse, E. H., & Schwindl, K., (2017). Applying fuzzy multi-objective linear programming to a project management decision with nonlinear fuzzy membership functions. *Neural Computing and Applications, 28*, 2193–2206.
28. El Khatib, M., Al Mulla, A., & Al Ketbi, W., (2022). The role of blockchain in e-governance and decision-making in project and program management. *Advances in Internet of Things, 12*(3), 88–109.
29. Fernandes, G., Moreira, S., Araújo, M., Pinto, E. B., & Machado, R. J., (2018). Project management practices for collaborative university-industry R&D: A hybrid approach. *Procedia Computer Science, 138*, 805–814.
30. Fernandes, G., Pinto, E. B., Machado, R. J., Araújo, M., & Pontes, A., (2015). A program and project management approach for collaborative university-industry R&D funded contracts. *Procedia Computer Science, 64*, 1065–1074.
31. Garcia, F., Serrano, M., Cruz-Lemus, J., Ruiz, F., Piattini, M., & ALARCOS Research Group, (2007). Managing software process measurement: A metamodel-based approach. *Information Sciences, 177*(12), 2570–2586.
32. Görög, M., (2011). Translating single project management knowledge to project programs. *Project Management Journal, 42*(2), 17–31.
33. Hedlund, G., Rolander, D., Bartlett, C. A., Doz, Y., & Hedlund, G., (1990). *Action in Heterarchies: New Approaches to Managing the MNC* (Vol. 1, pp. 15–46). Managing the global firm.
34. Imperial, M. T., & Hennessey, T. M., (1996). An ecosystem□based approach to managing estuaries: An assessment of the national estuary program. *Coastal Management, 24*(2), 115–139.
35. Iversen, J. H., Mathiassen, L., & Nielsen, P. A., (2004). Managing risk in software process improvement: An action research approach. *MIS Quarterly, 1*, 395–433.
36. Jaafari, A., (2007). Project and program diagnostics: A systemic approach. *International Journal of Project Management, 25*(8), 781–790.
37. Jiang, J. J., Klein, G., & Fernandez, W. D., (2018). From project management to program management: An invitation to investigate programs where IT plays a significant role. *Journal of the Association for Information Systems, 19*(1), 1–5.
38. Jugdev, K., (2012). Learning from lessons learned: Project management research program. *American Journal of Economics and Business Administration, 4*(1), 13.
39. Keil, M., (1995). Pulling the plug: Software project management and the problem of project escalation. *MIS Quarterly, 1*, 421–447.

40. Kettl, D. F., (2006). Managing boundaries in American administration: The collaboration imperative. *Public Administration Review, 66*(1), 10–19.
41. Khan, A., Waris, M., Ismail, I., Sajid, M. R., Ullah, M., & Usman, F., (2019). Deficiencies in project governance: An analysis of infrastructure development program. *Administrative Sciences, 9*(1), 7–9.
42. Krishna, S., Sahay, S., & Walsham, G., (2004). Managing cross-cultural issues in global software outsourcing. *Communications of the ACM, 47*(4), 62–66.
43. Lemieux, V. L., (2004). Two approaches to managing information risks. *Information Management, 38*(5), 56.
44. Liang, T. F., (2009). Fuzzy multi-objective project management decisions using two-phase fuzzy goal programming approach. *Computers & Industrial Engineering, 57*(4), 1407–1416.
45. Locander, W. B., Napier, H. A., & Scamell, R. W., (1979). A team approach to managing the development of a decision support system. *MIS Quarterly, 1*, 53–63.
46. Locke, E. A., Schweiger, D. M., & Latham, G. P., (1986). Participation in decision making: When should it be used? *Organizational Dynamics, 14*(3), 65–79.
47. Mahadevan, N., Dubey, A., & Karsai, G., (2011). Application of software health management techniques. In: *Proceedings of the 6th International Symposium on Software Engineering for Adaptive and Self-Managing Systems* (Vol. 1, pp. 1–10).
48. Martinsuo, M., & Hoverfält, P., (2018). Change program management: Toward a capability for managing value-oriented, integrated multi-project change in its context. *International Journal of Project Management, 36*(1), 134–146.
49. Metzger, P. W., & Boddie, J., (1996). *Managing a Programming Project Processes and People* (Vol. 1, pp. 2–6). Prentice-Hall, Inc.
50. Miterev, M., Engwall, M., & Jerbrant, A., (2016). Exploring program management competences for various program types. *International Journal of Project Management, 34*(3), 545–557.
51. Murray, M. J., & Crandall, R. E., (2006). IT offshore outsourcing requires a project management approach. *SAM Advanced Management Journal, 71*(1), 1–4.
52. Nidumolu, S. R., & Subramani, M. R., (2003). The matrix of control: Combining process and structure approaches to managing software development. *Journal of Management Information Systems, 20*(3), 159–196.
53. Olsson, R., (2008). Risk management in a multi-project environment: An approach to manage portfolio risks. *International Journal of Quality & Reliability Management,* 1, 5–8.
54. Pearson, S., & Casassa-Mont, M., (2011). Sticky policies: An approach for managing privacy across multiple parties. *Computer, 44*(9), 60–68.
55. Pellegrinelli, S., (2011). What's in a name: Project or program? *International Journal of Project Management, 29*(2), 232–240.

56. Pena, W. M., & Parshall, S. A., (2012). *Problem Seeking: An Architectural Programing Primer* (Vol. 1, pp. 5–6). John Wiley & Sons.
57. Rijamampianina, R., & Carmichael, T., (2005). A pragmatic and holistic approach to managing diversity. *Problems and Perspectives in Management*, (1), 109–117.
58. Saynisch, M., (2010). Beyond frontiers of traditional project management: An approach to evolutionary, self-organizational principles and the complexity theory—Results of the research program. *Project Management Journal, 41*(2), 21–37.
59. Springer, M. L., (2019). *Project and Program Management: A Competency-Based Approach* (Vol. 1, pp. 3–9). Purdue University Press.
60. Thiry, M., (2007). Program management: A strategic decision management process. *The Wiley Guide to Project, Program, and Portfolio Management, 1*, 113–143.
61. Trivedi, A., & Singh, A., (2017). A hybrid multi-objective decision model for emergency shelter location-relocation projects using fuzzy analytic hierarchy process and goal programing approach. *International Journal of Project Management, 35*(5), 827–840.
62. Turkulainen, V., Ruuska, I., Brady, T., & Artto, K., (2015). Managing project-to-project and project-to-organization interfaces in programs: Organizational integration in a global operations expansion program. *International Journal of Project Management, 33*(4), 816–827.
63. Twigg, J., (2004). *Disaster Risk Reduction: Mitigation and Preparedness in Development and Emergency Programing* (Vol. 1, pp. 6–9). Overseas Development Institute (ODI).
64. Vroom, V. H., & Jago, A. G., (1988). *The New Leadership: Managing Participation in Organizations* (Vol. 1, pp. 1–4). Prentice-Hall, Inc.
65. Vuorinen, L., & Martinsuo, M., (2018). Program integration in multi-project change programs: Agency in integration practice. *International Journal of Project Management, 36*(4), 583–599.
66. Waddell, D., (2005). Program management: The next step in the evolution of project management? *Problems and Perspectives in Management*, (3), 160–169.
67. Wideman, R. M., (2004). *A Management Framework: For Project, Program and Portfolio Integration* (Vol. 1, pp. 7–10). Trafford Publishing.
68. Wideman, R. M., (2022). *Project and Program Risk Management a Guide to Managing Project Risks and Opportunities* (Vol. 1, pp. 3–10). Project Management Institute, Inc.
69. Winch, G. M., Morris, P., & Pinto, J., (2007). Managing project stakeholders. *The Wiley Guide to Project, Program, and Portfolio Management, 1*, 271–289.

CHAPTER 5

PROGRAM AND PROJECT OFFICES

UNIT INTRODUCTION

The term "PMO" may refer to anything from a junior employee who assists a single project manager with administrative tasks (also known as a "project office") to a centralized team that supports and directs all the projects inside a large program (also known as a "program management office") to a group that manages a wide range of projects and programs (such as a portfolio management office or an enterprise program office) (Fernandes et al., 2020). PSO, where the "S" stands for support, should refer to a team solely offering administrative assistance; the abbreviation PMO should be utilized if the office also performs certain managerial duties.

The aims, duties, and structure of the PMO must reflect the uniqueness of each firm. Hence, the functions of PMOs and the estimated advantages they create vary from company to organization. To add to the ambiguity, the PMO team can be spread throughout the company; for example, some team members can monitor the strategic alignment of projects at the portfolio level, while others support individual project managers. As a result, perceptions of what a PMO is and does can differ depending on the observer's position within the business.

Learning Objectives

At the end of this chapter, readers will be able to learn the following:

1. A basic definition of the project and program management office
2. The necessity to make a project and program management office
3. Functions, role, and responsibility of PMO
4. Things that are critical for PMO success

Key Terms

- Finance
- Incident Log
- Maturity
- PMO
- Return-on-Investment
- Risk Registers

5.1. DEFINITION OF PMO

Although many books on PMOs omit it, it is customary to include a definition at a certain point in a book like this. Even when definitions are provided, there seems to be little agreement, and this ambiguity may be seen in the many offered definitions. The following definition can be considered:

A PMO is an organizational unit that offers various centralized services based on the organization's needs and conditions (Alexandrova et al., 2015). Still, all encompass management and direction components and are intended to improve the efficacy or performance of projects under its purview.

The following list of points concerning this definition should be noted.

i. This definition makes no assumptions about the structure or size of the unit. It might be a single individual, a part-time position for one individual, or a sizable department (Pellegrinelli & Bowman, 1994).

ii. The advantages of additional value the PMO is anticipated to offer would partly influence the services. They offer a lot more than simply administrative assistance (Too & Weaver, 2014).

Figure 5.1. Image of roles of PMO.

Source: Pngegg, creative commons license.

The delivery of services can be decentralized, even though the PMO's overall administration and control should be centralized (Baughn & Finzel, 2009). A single organization may have several PMOs, both at the organizational level and at the level of certain departments, each supported by a subordinate office to help with a specific program or project. Gaining beneficial outcomes for the organization is the main goal of setting up and running a PMO (Salameh, 2014).

Did you Know?

The first PMO was established in the early 1990s by NASA for its space projects.

This concept presupposes several projects, like those that may be managed globally by a program, several programs, or an overall portfolio of projects. Hence, it does not include any PMO-like organizations that assist specific projects; they may be better known as project offices.

5.2. WHY IMPLEMENT A PMO

Everyone does not run a PMO. Small organizations with few projects may believe there is no need to add another layer of possible expense and bureaucracy since they are expensive to set up and maintain (Bernstein, 2000).

Yet, PMOs are used in some capacity by most organizations that manage programs or several projects. According to research by Cranfield University, almost three-quarters of all big UK organizations claim to utilize them. Investigations in Europe point to a nearly comparable proportion.

Around 25% of big organizations without PMOs may still use certain PMO-like services; a separate business unit may not offer them (Rondinelli, 1983).

For instance, the corporate finance department may handle project accounting; the purchasing department may handle procurement, and operational line management may handle resourcing. Additionally, not all big businesses have a project-focused approach. Some people have such a strong commitment to "business as usual" practices and mentalities that they fail to see the benefit of managing change through separate initiatives.

Sometimes, one or two of the more experienced project managers kindly assume the position of the project office, advising and assisting other project managers and directing the entire portfolio (Pilkaitė & Chmieliauskas, 2015). Yet there is no denying that a well-run PMO, whether centered on a single program or linked to a full portfolio, may offer a variety of commercial advantages. When it comes to a program, it can:

- Ensure that common standards and language are used across the component projects to increase effectiveness (Darling & Whitty, 2016).
- That makes up the software, lowering the chance that projects won't meet their deadlines, budgets, or quality goals. To assist a project manager in completing a project initiation document, timeline, business case, communication strategy, etc., many PMOs maintain standard document templates and worked samples;
- Establishing a uniform standard of reporting on progress, risks, difficulties, etc., across a wide range of projects can serve to improve the efficacy of the governance process and aid in maintaining ongoing alignment between the program and the organization's strategy (Koria, 2009);
- By assisting struggling project managers with critical-path diagrams and other project management approaches, a researcher may support them with best practices. Managing contingency budgets, for instance, might help them supervise a successful risk management process while ensuring that any issues are discovered quickly enough for remedial action to be implemented;
- Possess and maintain all portfolio, project, and program management tools, including scheduling, collaboration, and document management software (Scanlin, 1998);
- boost the realization of business advantages by incorporating a benefit-realization emphasis into the individual projects' "time, cost specification" focus;
- the proper coordination of resource demands amongst all projects within the program will maximize the utilization of limited resources and avoid duplication of effort (Sanchez et al., 2009);
- Get "economies of scale" via centralizing project support tasks so that all projects under the program enjoy efficient assistance without needing individual "Barbaras" for each project.

These advantages are frequently quantifiable (Unger et al., 2012). According to PM Solutions, an American consulting business, organizations with a "mature" PMO may anticipate a 31% drop in project failure and a 17% decrease in project delivery costs, with corresponding improvements in delivery by schedule and budget.

The advantages may be greater when the PMO oversees a complete portfolio. The full implementation of a portfolio-level PMO inside the department will likely reduce total project costs by 8.6% in the 1st year and 15.8% over three years, according to an return-on-investment (ROI) study among several US-based IT departments.

5.3. THE ROLE OF PMO

Several studies have shown that there is currently no set of standard services that PMOs are required to provide. While many PMOs offer services like "project progress reporting," "supporting universal standards for project management," and giving a portion of "accounting and financial control," there doesn't seem to be a single service that all PMOs offer (Gassmann & Von Zedtwitz, 1998). The outcomes of one such research are shown in Figure 5.1 (Gareis, 2010). There are many distinct types of PMOs, which is somewhat reflected in the variance in the offered services. It also represents the preference of certain organizations to carry out particular tasks using their regular resources (Aubry et al., 2008). For instance, the organization's finance department may continue to provide "accounting and financial oversight" rather than being given that job. The International Centre for Project Management at Cranfield University has examined the connection between the scope and the services offered (Figure 5.2).

Figure 5.2. Illustration of services provided by PMO.

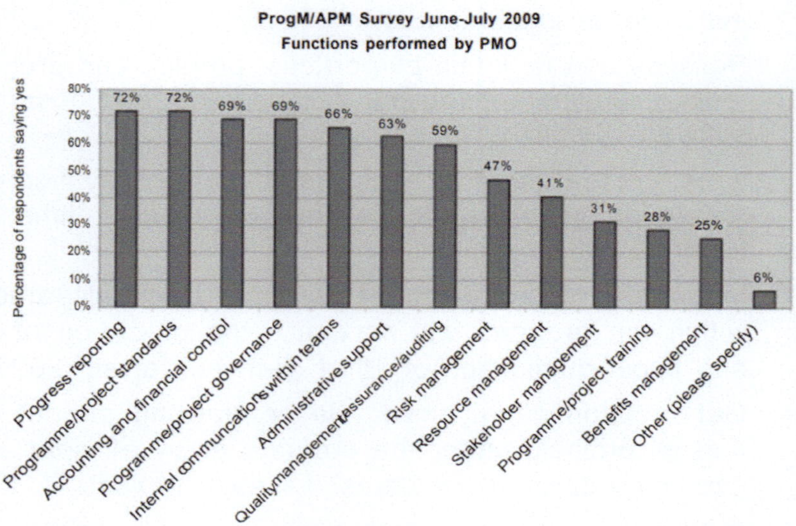

Source: Paul Rayner, creative commons license.

While the analysis confirms the lack of clarity regarding specific services, it also suggests that there is generally a hierarchy of services, ranging from more basic support services applicable to all types of PMOs to more complex services only applicable to PMOs that are managing portfolios or programs (Thiry & Deguire, 2007) (Figure 5.3).

The summary of this services hierarchy is provided below.

i. Most PMOs offer program managers and component project managers certain administrative assistance, like diary management, secretarial, and room-booking services, the same things Barbara used to offer to my software company all those years ago. They frequently offer a variety of essential services that are outlined in this chapter's introduction. They consist of the following:

a. Assembling and reporting information on the progress of individual projects before compiling it into a comprehensive report for the entire program, such as by producing and disseminating the monthly project and program status reports (Chen et al., 2019). It suggests that the PMO follows up with every project manager for their monthly progress information and may even report those that do not deliver;

b. Provide suitable standards, techniques, and tools for the program or portfolio. One of these options may be dictating how a pre-made methodology, like Prince2, is used throughout each project. Shared electronic workspaces, report templates, and standardized methods for creating project timelines or logging time spent are examples of common tools;

c. The control of project documents includes plans, schedules, risk registers, incident logs, etc. It can entail keeping an online archive of all relevant documentation (Pemsel & Wiewiora, 2013).

d. Researchers assist sponsors and individuals involved in governance by organizing project or program board meetings, distributing agendas and board materials, and taking minutes.

ii. Most of the services mentioned above, as well as several other more sophisticated and specialized ones, are often offered by PMOs supporting programs, including:

a. Giving knowledge in estimating, planning, communicating, and risk management to numerous project managers. To provide advice to the program manager and support the managers of the element project managers, a major PMO may hire specialists for all of these fields (Shen et al., 2006);

b. Giving knowledge in estimating, planning, communicating, and risk management to numerous project managers. To provide advice to the program manager and support the managers of the element project managers, a major PMO may hire specialists for all of these fields (Carvalho et al., 2018);

c. monitoring and evaluating component project performance, particularly concerning agreed-upon time, cost, and delivery targets;

d. Controlling the procedure for adding or removing items from the scope of projects and programs from the time a change is first requested until the updated project deliverables are finally accepted (Martinsuo & Hoverfält, 2018);

e. Keeping quality records and planning reviews ensures uniform program-level standards are followed throughout the program.

iii. In addition to those mentioned above, more advanced program-level PMOs will also offer extra consulting and advising services, such as:

a. Enhancing employee capabilities, including mentorship and training for project managers, sponsors, and other project/program governance participants;

b. Assessing the effectiveness of project managers. Normally, this entails utilizing an assessment methodology endorsed by the human resources department of the company (Aubry et al., 2009);

c. Project and program managers are hired, chosen, and assigned. These individuals may be considered to be PMO employees under some circumstances, which explains why some PMOs are rather large;

d. Recording, evaluating, and sharing the lessons learned from initiatives and programs (Laufer & Tucker, 1987). A high degree of project success is largely dependent on the spread of these lessons;

e. The researcher ensured the recognition, management, and assessment of benefits realization.

Did you Know?

The first PMO standard was published by Project Management Institute (PMI) in 2003.

iv. Full-service PMOs that are in charge of big project and program portfolios typically also offer supplemental strategic and governance services, like:

a. To guarantee that only the "correct" initiatives are executed, new projects and programs must be identified, chosen, and prioritized (Monteiro de Carvalho, 2013). It includes participation in business cases, benefits management, contingencies, etc.;

b. Obtaining and distributing resources across programs and initiatives;

c. Advising top management, including sponsors and members of the portfolio and program boards, and making suggestions to them. It can entail giving sponsors and board members the appropriate training (Teller et al., 2012);

d. Doing health checks on projects and programs, post-completion evaluations, and ensuring the right follow-up steps are made are all done. Such evaluations are an excellent way to find "lessons learned" that may be used in subsequent initiatives and programs;

e. The researcher monitors and evaluates PMO performance and its impact on project delivery and program benefit realization.

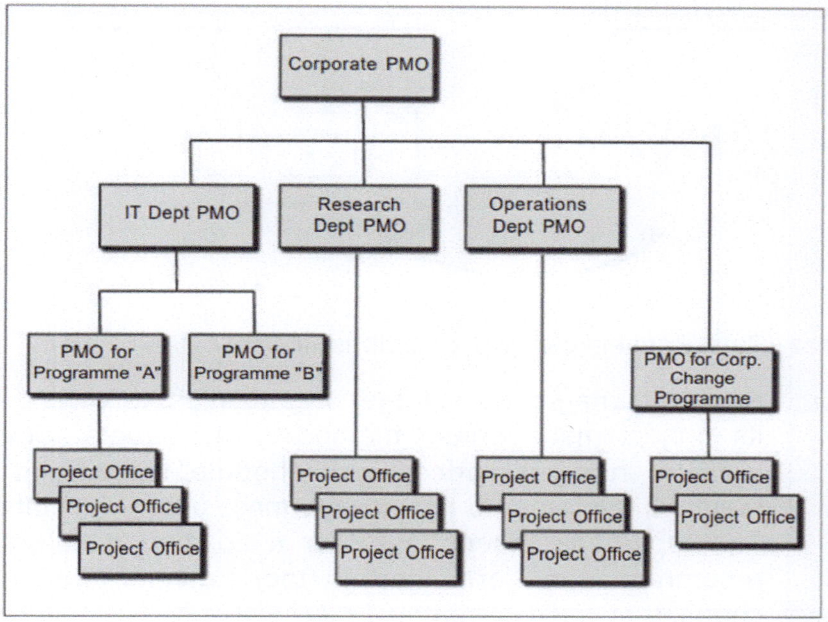

Figure 5.3. Representation of possible PMO structure in large organizations.

Source: Geoff Reiss, creative commons license.

5.4. MATURITY OF PMO

Despite the increased interest in PMOs over the past few years, relatively few are effective, particularly those functioning at the portfolio level (Bourne, 2016). According to a poll conducted by multinational consultants ESI, just 17% of organizations consider such PMOs to be "completely successful in tackling the most important business concerns." According to the same poll, 30% of PMOs had their existence significantly questioned in recent years. Some studies indicate that the average PMP has an extremely short lifespan, with most dying before age three.

According to Figure 5.4, which summarizes the five stages of a PMO's life cycle, many PMOs have short and miserable life cycles (Haukka & Lyytikäinen, 2020). The PMO life cycle is shown below.

Figure 5.4. Illustration of life-cycle of typical portfolio PMO.

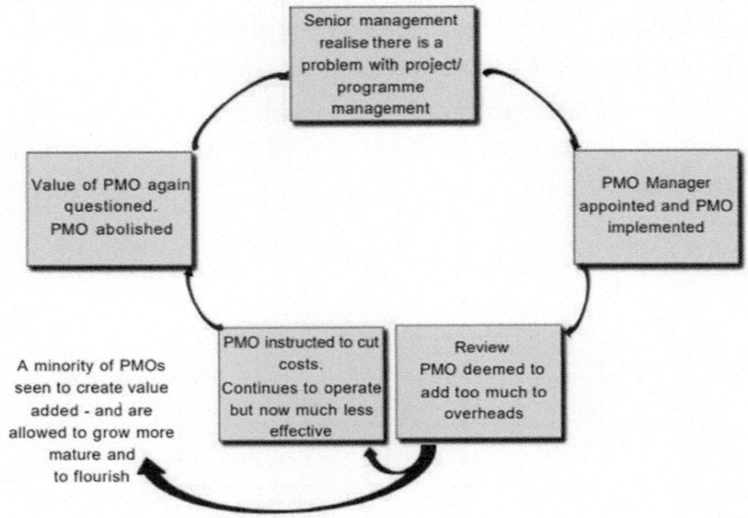

Source: Paul Rayner, creative commons license.

i. Senior management of the organization is aware that its project management method is inadequate. Several projects run past price and schedule limits, and the resultant systems do not always meet user expectations. The top management looks for a solution and, on the recommendation of a certain tool provider, frequently chooses to build a central PMO.

ii. A PMO manager is chosen, and they immediately begin implementing the PMO (Gasik, 2019).

iii. A corporate economy campaign is launched not long after all the expenditure of establishing the PMO. The finance department seeks objectives and concentrates on administrative costs that lack strong top management sponsorship. This category includes the PMO, which is scrutinized in depth. Since the office is still relatively young, few quantifiable advantages can be demonstrated to flow from the PMO. Furthermore, the top management, eager to see progress on its initiatives and programs, is now concentrating on other matters. Even if the PMO's expenses represent a small portion of the portfolio or program's overall worth, it would be susceptible if it may not justify that it has already generated substantial advantages.

iv. Staff members are let go as part of a cost-cutting directive for the PMO. The PMO is still in operation, but with fewer employees, it cannot accomplish its goals and now concentrates on providing basic administrative assistance (Pellegrinelli & Garagna, 2009).

v. The PMO's worth is being questioned once more. Management has finally decided that the PMO is unnecessary and that project managers must do without administrative help.

It appears that the entire life cycle lasts three years. The only benefit it offers PMO staff is that, in another 2 years, top management would recognize that the organization's approach to project management is inadequate, and the cycle will begin again.

The answer appears to rest in developing what is typically called a "mature" PMO that adds value to the organization and can provide evidence of this when needed. Table 5.1 summarizes this idea of maturity, with levels four or five considered "mature" (Owen, 2006). Due to the nature of business life, it is challenging to advance up this maturity ladder after top management's enthusiasm wanes.

Table 5.1. Summary of the Five Possible Levels of PMO Maturity

Maturity Description of PMO Status Level	
Level 1	Although there may not be any official tracking procedures, the organization's board of directors realizes that projects and programs are distinctive from "business as usual." It maintains an informal record of its investments.
Level 2	The company establishes a PMO to ensure that every project and program in its portfolio is managed according to a minimal set of standards for procedures and processes. Still, there can be no consistency or coordination.
Level 3	Each initiative can adapt within these procedures to fulfill the demand of particular initiatives thanks to the PMO's establishment of centrally managed programs and project processes.
Level 4	To forecast future performance, the PMO collects and keeps track of certain metrics for the entire portfolio of initiatives. It evaluates its ability to manage projects and programs and assigns priorities as necessary.
Level 5	To increase its capacity to forecast program, project, and portfolio outcomes over time and improve procedures, the PMO constantly enhances its management processes through proactive issue and technology management.

Source: Donnie Macnicol, Creative Commons License.

From the start, it is crucial to be clear about what the PMO will provide and ensure delivery from the start. When a program lasts for several years or longer, the life mentioned above cycle may also be applied to PMOs at the program level. Similar programs are typically reviewed with the same lack of perspective, attention to cost, and demands for the economy.

5.5. PMO SUCCESS

It seems that there are seven factors that, in general, are essential for PMO success and allow a PMO to escape the life cycle depicted in Figure 5.4 (Martinsuo & Hoverfält, 2018).

5.5.1. Fit the Needs of an Organization

Each organization has its structure, culture, challenges, and concerns (Hu et al., 2015). To be successful, a PMO must consider these criteria. The PMO must also help the organization's "governance" processes by promoting helpful initiatives and rejecting negative ones.

5.5.2. Assist with Project and Program Managers

The PMO must support the whole organization's requirements while offering program and project managers useful and efficient support. Often, this involves relieving such managers of rote tasks so they may focus on guiding their projects to success. Project managers are advised to spend 90 % of their time communicating; yet, if they are compelled to work long hours on administrative, accounting, or reporting responsibilities, none of them will even come close to meeting this recommendation.

5.5.3. A Valuable early Deliverable

A set of specialized guidelines with accompanying templates and examples to assist program and project managers in adhering to best practices and organizational standards could be a helpful early output from the PMO (Shao, 2018). Processes must be kept as straightforward and in line with those currently in place and known to add value, if possible.

5.5.4. Ensure Executive Support

PMOs can add significant value by determining which projects and programs have a low probability of delivering value or assisting the organization in delivering its objectives (Unger et al., 2012). However, such information is not always appreciated, and project management offices (PMOs) must occasionally contend with "political" opposition from projects, project sponsors, and other partners that could be affected. As a result, having strong executive support is necessary for the PMO to deal with challenges of this nature.

5.5.5. A Clear Statement of Vision

To obtain the executive team's support, the PMO needs a clear explanation of its vision that outlines how it will assist the organization (Hobbs et al., 2008).

5.5.6. Demonstrate Value Added

A proven way of maintaining executive support is for the PMO to be continually able to demonstrate the value that it brings. Examples of metrics that might be appropriate for doing this include:

i. Rates of projects and project success in terms of capital expense, time, operational expense, and benefits realized (Al-Zwainy & Al-Marsomi, 2023);
ii. Enhanced portfolio balance in terms of risk and phases of the program or project life cycle;
iii. Alignment with strategy and kind of investment;
iv. Improved support for strategic goals (Dai, 2002).

The lack of an existing baseline of data to give any metrics of such value added is a problem for newly founded PMOs. In these situations, surveys of project and program managers, sponsors, users, and stakeholders may help determine their satisfaction levels with the present arrangements. Thus, without detailed statistics on the success of projects and strategic progress, follow-up polls at six-month intervals must show the changes that have occurred.

The enhanced portfolio balance that strategically focused PMOs (like those at the portfolio level) produce is a significant source of corporate value (Jordan & Hackbart, 2005). It derives from creating the best possible combination of projects and programs to support the organization's goal and prevent redundancy when many departments simultaneously launch comparable projects and programs. A balanced portfolio would also guarantee efficient utilization of internal resources.

It's crucial to be clear about the advantages that every program and project is meant to bring to help balance portfolios. To halt low-value initiatives immediately could call for strengthening business justifications and introducing a formal sign-off process.

5.5.7. Presents the Clear Picture to Management

Ensuring the PMO offers important, accurate, easy-to-understand information that aids senior management in making decisions is another method to sustain executive support. Creating and updating a "management dashboard," which offers a high-level perspective of the progress of the project, program, or portfolio, is a regularly utilized strategy (Jones & Lucey, 2009). Color coding may highlight what works well instead of what is not, giving a quick overview.

ACTIVITY 5.1.

Create a PMO implementation plan for a hypothetical company. The plan should include the type of PMO to be established, the primary responsibilities of PMO, and a road map for implementation.

5.5.8. Link into the Wider Organization

The PMO must also communicate with various stakeholders and integrate with the larger corporate organization (Yeong & Lim, 2010). Hence, the other departments and groups must be aware of the PMO's goals, the support it can offer, and what it expects of them.

5.5.9. Manage PMO Implementation

There may be significant changes due to implementing a PMO, including those who oversee the impacted projects and programs, the users and stakeholders they impact, and senior management whose choices launch or terminate them (Weaver, 2005). In light of this, it is recommended that a PMO be installed as a program of organizational change, complete with all the necessary planning, stakeholder management, communication, and business rationale.

In general, approaching implementation in stages is a good idea, focusing on tasks that provide top management immediate visibility. For instance, a list of ongoing projects and initiatives can be a significant "eye-opener," illuminating for the 1st time the scope and importance of the organization's portfolio.

SUMMARY

A centralized department or group inside an organization called the PMO monitors and enhanced program and project management procedures throughout the company. A PMO's main duty is to establish a framework for standardizing project management processes to ensure that projects are finished on schedule, within budget, and to the requisite quality standards. The PMO often supports project managers by providing project managers with tools, templates, methods, and best practices that expedite the project management process. PMOs come in various forms, such as supporting, controlling, and directive. Ultimately, the PMO is crucial to increasing an organization's success rate for projects and programs and generating economic value.

REVIEW QUESTIONS

1. What is a PMO, and what is its role in project and program management?
2. How does a PMO support project/program managers and team members?
3. What are the key challenges of implementing a PMO, and how can they be addressed?
4. How does a PMO measure its effectiveness?
5. What are some best practices for establishing and maintaining a successful PMO?

MULTIPLE CHOICE QUESTIONS

1. What does PMO stand for?

a. Project Management Outsourcing
b. Project Management Office
c. Project Management Operations
d. None of the above

2. What is the primary function of PMO?

a. To manage projects directly
b. To provide support to project managers
c. To create project teams
d. To set project goals

3. What are the different types of PMOs?

a. Supportive, controlling, and directive
b. Tactical, strategic, and operational
c. Functional, matrix, and projectized
d. None of the above

4. **What are some best practices for establishing a successful PMO?**
   a. Establish clear goals and objectives
   b. Align the PMO with the organization's strategic goals
   c. Provide adequate resources and funding
   d. All of the above
5. **Due to the rapid expansion of your company, your boss decides to establish a project management office (PMO) within the company and asks you to take the lead. According to the PMBOK guide, to be the ideal PMO you can do which of the following? Select one:**
   a. Speed up a specific ongoing project.
   b. Find opportunities for collaborative project management.
   c. Reassign the resources that have been assigned to ongoing projects.
   d. Reduce the assigned resources to existing projects.

Answers to Multiple Choice Questions

1. (b); 2. (b); 3. (a); 4. (d) 5. (b)

REFERENCES

1. Alexandrova, M., Stankova, L., & Gelemenov, A., (2015). The role of project office for project portfolio management. *Economic Alternatives, 1*(1), 19–30.
2. Al-Zwainy, F., & Al-Marsomi, M., (2023). Structural equation modeling of critical success factors in the programe of development regional. *Journal of Project Management, 8*(2), 119–132.
3. Aubry, M., Hobbs, B., & Thuillier, D., (2008). Organizational project management: An historical approach to the study of PMOs. *International Journal of Project Management, 26*(1), 38–43.
4. Aubry, M., Hobbs, B., & Thuillier, D., (2009). The contribution of the project management office to organizational performance. *International Journal of Managing Projects in Business, 1*, 4–6.
5. Baughn, M. K., & Finzel, P. A., (2009). A clash of cultures in a merger of two acquisition project offices. *Engineering Management Journal, 21*(2), 11–17.
6. Bernstein, S., (2000). Project offices in practice. *Project Management Journal, 31*(4), 4–6.
7. Bourne, L., (2016). *Stakeholder Relationship Management: A Maturity Model for Organizational Implementation* (Vol. 1, pp. 6–9). Routledge.
8. Carvalho, V. G., Barbalho, S. C. M., Silva, G., & Toledo, J. C., (2018). Benefits management as a path for project management offices contribute to programs and influence on project performance. *Business and Management Studies, 4*(1), 20.

9. Chen, T., Fu, M., Liu, R., Xu, X., Zhou, S., & Liu, B., (2019). How do project management competencies change within the project management career model in large Chinese construction companies? *International Journal of Project Management, 37*(3), 485–500.
10. Dai, X. C., (2002). *The Role of the Project Management Office in Achieving Project Success* (Vol. 1, pp. 3–7). The George Washington University.
11. Darling, E. J., & Whitty, S. J., (2016). The project management office: It's just not what it used to be. *International Journal of Managing Projects in Business, 9*(2), 282–308.
12. Fernandes, G., Pinto, E. B., Araújo, M., & Machado, R. J., (2020). The roles of a program and project management office to support collaborative university–industry R&D. *Total Quality Management & Business Excellence, 31*(5, 6), 583–608.
13. Gareis, R., (2010). Changes of organizations by projects. *International Journal of Project Management, 28*(4), 314–327.
14. Gasik, S., (2019). A proposal of governmental project management maturity model. *PM World Journal, 8*(9), 8–25.
15. Gassmann, O., & Von, Z. M., (1998). Organization of industrial R&D on a global scale. *R&D Management, 28*(3), 147–161.
16. Haukka, M., & Lyytikäinen, M., (2020). Assessing and improving program management maturity. In: *Gower Handbook of Program Management* (Vol. 1, pp. 575–583). Routledge.
17. Hobbs, B., Aubry, M., & Thuillier, D., (2008). The project management office as an organizational innovation. *International Journal of Project Management, 26*(5), 547–555.
18. Hu, Y., Chan, A. P., & Le, Y., (2015). Understanding the determinants of program organization for construction megaproject success: Case study of the shanghai expo construction. *Journal of Management in Engineering, 31*(5), 05014019.
19. Jones, D. A., & Lucey, M. C., (2009). PMO success and value. *Governance An International Journal of Policy and Administration, 1*, 1–10.
20. Jordan, M. M., & Hackbart, M., (2005). The goals and implementation success of state performance-based budgeting. *Journal of Public Budgeting, Accounting & Financial Management, 1*, 5–10).
21. Koria, M., (2009). Managing for innovation in large and complex recovery programs: Tsunami lessons from Sri Lanka. *International Journal of Project Management, 27*(2), 123–130.
22. Laufer, A., & Tucker, R. L., (1987). Is construction project planning really doing its job? A critical examination of focus, role and process. *Construction Management and Economics, 5*(3), 243–266.
23. Martinsuo, M., & Hoverfält, P., (2018). Change program management: Toward a capability for managing value-oriented, integrated multi-project change in its context. *International Journal of Project Management, 36*(1), 134–146.

24. Monteiro De, C. M., (2013). An investigation of the role of communication in IT projects. *International Journal of Operations & Production Management, 34*(1), 36–64.
25. Owen, J., (2006). Integrating knowledge management with program management. *International Journal of Knowledge Management (IJKM), 2*(1), 41–57.
26. Pellegrinelli, S., & Bowman, C., (1994). Implementing strategy through projects. *Long Range Planning, 27*(4), 125–132.
27. Pellegrinelli, S., & Garagna, L., (2009). Towards a conceptualization of PMOs as agents and subjects of change and renewal. *International Journal of Project Management, 27*(7), 649–656.
28. Pemsel, S., & Wiewiora, A., (2013). Project management office a knowledge broker in project-based organizations. *International Journal of Project Management, 31*(1), 31–42.
29. Pilkaitė, A., & Chmieliauskas, A., (2015). Changes in public sector management: Establishment of project management offices–a comparative case study of Lithuania and Denmark. *Public Policy and Administration, 14*(2), 291–306.
30. Rondinelli, D. A., (1983). Implementing decentralization programs in Asia: A comparative analysis. *Public Administration and Development, 3*(3), 181–207.
31. Salameh, H., (2014). A framework to establish a project management office. *European Journal of Business and Management, 6*(9), 19–26.
32. Sanchez, H., Robert, B., Bourgault, M., & Pellerin, R., (2009). Risk management applied to projects, programs, and portfolios. *International Journal of Managing Projects in Business, 2*(1), 14–35.
33. Scanlin, J., (1998). The internet as an enabler of the Bell Atlantic project office. *Project Management Journal, 29*(2), 6, 7.
34. Shao, J., (2018). The moderating effect of program context on the relationship between program managers' leadership competences and program success. *International Journal of Project Management, 36*(1), 108–120.
35. Shen, L. Y., Platten, A., & Deng, X. P., (2006). Role of public private partnerships to manage risks in public sector projects in Hong Kong. *International Journal of Project Management, 24*(7), 587–594.
36. Teller, J., Unger, B. N., Kock, A., & Gemünden, H. G., (2012). Formalization of project portfolio management: The moderating role of project portfolio complexity. *International Journal of Project Management, 30*(5), 596–607.
37. Thiry, M., & Deguire, M., (2007). Recent developments in project-based organizations. *International Journal of Project Management, 25*(7), 649–658.
38. Too, E. G., & Weaver, P., (2014). The management of project management: A conceptual framework for project governance. *International Journal of Project Management, 32*(8), 1382–1394.
39. Unger, B. N., Gemünden, H. G., & Aubry, M., (2012). The three roles of a project portfolio management office: Their impact on portfolio management execution and success. *International Journal of Project Management, 30*(5), 608–620.

40. Weaver, P., (2005). Effective project governance the tools for success. In: *Project Management Institute of New Zealand, Annual Conference, Auckland,* (Vol. 1, pp. 2–7).

41. Yeong, A., & Lim, T. T., (2010). Integrating knowledge management with project management for project success. *Journal of Project, Program & Portfolio Management, 1*(2), 8–19.

CHAPTER 6

MANAGING RISKS AND OPPORTUNITIES

UNIT INTRODUCTION

Any potential uncertainty, hazard, or incident that could prohibit someone from reaching a company's objectives and advantages is a risk. Timeframe, price, quality, or advantages could all be impacted. There is a certain risk involved in every endeavor, and the degree of that risk varies greatly.

Opportunity is the potential for a project to proceed more successfully than anticipated (Akintoye et al., 2008).

Figure 6.1 illustrates where opportunity and risk fit concerning other project controls (Wideman, 2022). When an event happens, a risk will become a problem. Problems might be fixed within the project's scope or by altering the project itself. Similarly to risk, an opportunity might have positive effects instead of negative ones. An opportunity will become a problem if the occurrence happens, much like a danger. Figure 6.2 also demonstrates that once a project is well along, the danger, or "downside," is typically greater than any opportunities or "upside" available (Lacy & Pickard, 2008).

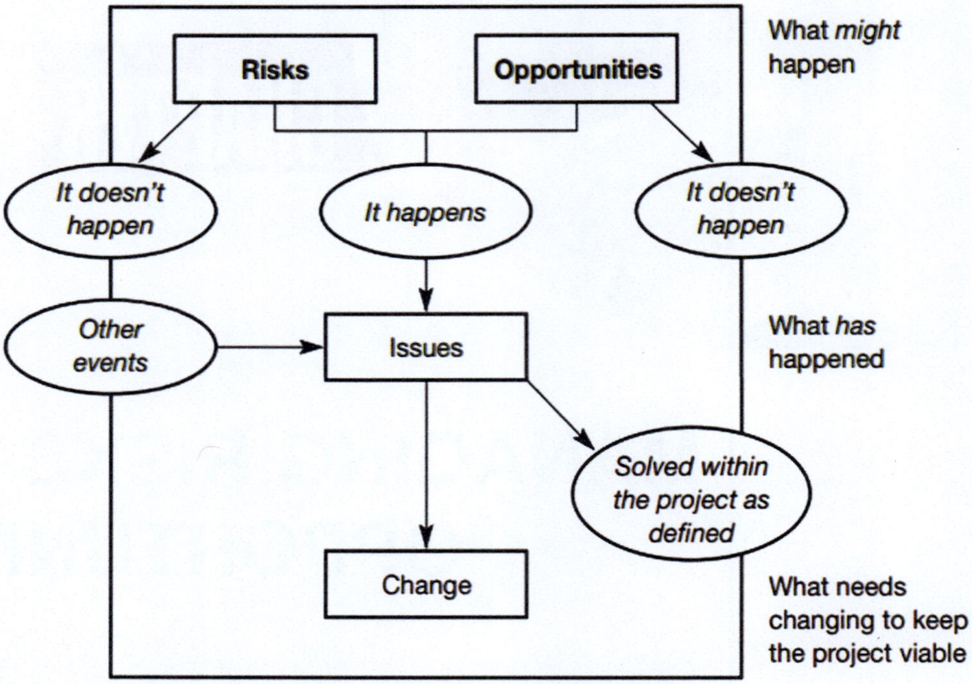

Figure 6.1. Illustration of opportunities, risks, issues, and change.

Source: Robert Buttrick, creative commons license.

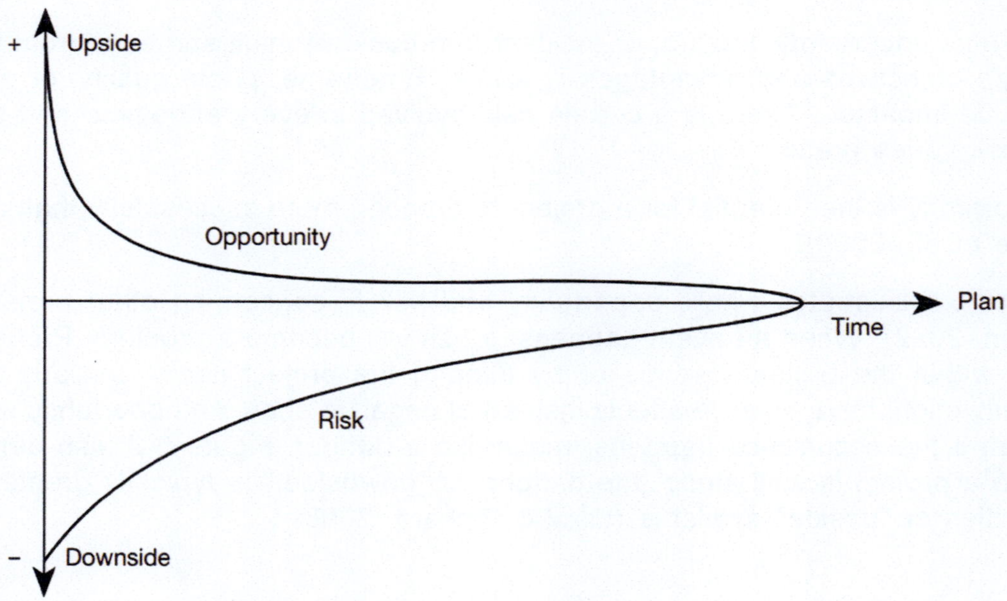

Figure 6.2. Graph of upside and downsides to a project.

Source: Jim Reynolds, creative commons license.

Opportunity and risk management work to make sure that:

i. Project risks and opportunities are recognized and assessed consistently.

ii. Risks to the project's success are acknowledged and handled, and important opportunities are utilized without delay (Greenall, 2004).

Although risk cannot be eliminated through risk management, it can sometimes be avoided or reduced by careful planning. But what if the risks that were found do not come to pass? What if a novel strategy emerges that advances a company's goals more effectively than anticipated? There are two choices:

i. The original strategy may be adopted because something completely out of control could still go wrong and ruin the efforts to save time and money (Colicchia et al., 2019).

ii. The newly discovered possibility can be included in the project (Rolstadås et al., 2019).

Even if the former strategy has historically been considered more cautious, this does not always imply that it is the best course of action.

Learning Objectives

At the end of this chapter, readers will be able to learn the following:

1. Considering possible risks and opportunities
2. Addressing risks and opportunities at the start of a project or program
3. Monitoring once the project or program is in progress
4. More sophisticated risk evaluation techniques

Key Terms

- Brainstorm
- Contingency
- Event
- Likelihood
- Opportunities
- Optimistic
- Pessimistic
- Risks

6.1. ADDRESSING RISK AT THE START OF A PROJECT

Risk management should be addressed whenever the project is originally set up at the Early Inquiry Stage (Chapman & Ward, 2003). Risk plays a significant role in the definition of a project; whenever a project sponsor authorizes a project, the researcher does so with full awareness of the risks presented, and acceptance of the repercussions should something go wrong. Since the person filling this function is the main risk taker, the project sponsor must accept the risks.

Did you Know?

The concept of risk management dates back to ancient times. The Code of Hammurabi, a set of laws from ancient Babylon, included provisions for merchants who wanted to insure their goods against loss or damage during transportation.

People are frequently excellent at detecting what could go wrong with creating deliverables but less adept at evaluating what could go wrong with the benefits gained (Taroun, 2014). Whenever projects seem to be truly business-driven, both aspects are crucial. To avoid forgetting this, consider a risk regarding project and enterprise risks. Project risks include those that affect project delivery, while business risks include those that impact the realization of project benefits. A project risk, such as a substantial project delay, can also have a negative impact on benefits. Do not be too rigid! The key is to understand that certain risks, such as fluctuations in the currency rate or rival action, are not related to project completion but rather to benefits.

The steps are:

i. List every risk that could compromise the project's success. Do not forget to mention both those the project team can influence and those that are mostly beyond the control. Once the brainstorming is over, add checklists to the list (Cooper et al., 2005).

ii. Examine every risk individually:

a. Evaluate the risk's likelihood of happening;

b. Identify the impact's potential severity on the project (Pritchard & PMP, 2014).

iii. Find the "risk category" using a risk matrix like the one below (low, medium, high).

iv. When there are high risks involved, think about how to prevent or avoid the situation, lessen its impact, or transfer the risk to another party. Planning for contingencies is a last resort, but because the danger is great, the researcher might want to consider making a "contingency plan" the main one (Levine, 2005).

v. Use reduction, preventative, or transfer measures for low to medium risks. If it does not work, make a backup plan.

vi. Keep an eye on low dangers because they might increase in importance. Depending on a specific situation, decide if additional action is necessary (Zhong et al., 2018).

Taking proactive measures to lessen the potential effects of risks is a sign of excellent project management rather than pessimism (Table 6.1).

There are numerous approaches to managing risk, including:

- **Prevention:** Protective measures are implemented to stop the threat or problem from materializing or having any impact (Gotterbam, 2002).
- **Reduction:** When the activities either lessen the risk's likelihood of happening or keep its effect on the project within reasonable bounds (Meredith et al., 2017).

Table 6.1. Risk Matrix

Risk Matrix	**Likelihood of Event Occurring**			
Severity of impact	Very unlikely < 5%	Unlikely	Likely >50%	Very likely >75%
Minor impact on project schedule or cost. No impact on benefits	Low	Low	Medium	Medium
Major impact on project schedule or cost. Minor impact on benefits.	Medium	Medium	Medium	High
Major impact on project schedule or cost. Major impact on benefits.	Medium	Medium	High	High

Source: Alan Crean, Creative Commons License.

- **Transference:** Expert risk mitigation is when the effects of risk are passed to another entity, typically a contractor or insurance company (Schwartz et al., 2014). The risk can also be transferred to a more senior member of the company, who then acts as an "insurer" for several initiatives. This course of action is helpful because it will likely lessen the sum set aside for emergencies.
- **Contingency:** When precautions are taken, they will take effect as soon as the risk materializes.
- **Acceptance:** The organization moves on, acknowledges the risk's potential occurrence, and is prepared to take the results (Atkinson et al., 2006).

Furthermore, keep in mind the following:

i. Risky operations are brought to the front of the schedule to lessen the impact of any delays on the project's conclusion.
ii. It is changing the project's requirements to eliminate elements that carry a high risk, such as brand-new, cutting-edge technology.
iii. Considering necessary cost and time contingencies
iv. Pilots and prototypes are used to determine the viability of new strategies (Kutsch & Hall, 2010).

Remember

Project and program managers must constantly balance risks and opportunities in order to ensure the success of their initiatives.

Once a project has passed the development gate, it typically should not have any significant risks. If so, the project plan must be reevaluated to reduce the total risk by adopting a different strategy or introducing measures to lessen the expected impact. The "log" depicted in Figure 6.3 is an easy approach to keeping track of risk.

6.2. BEWARE THE DIFFICULTIES OF RISK CONVERSATIONS

i. **To Bring up the Subject of Risk Means not to Admit Failure:** Cultures that view risk conversation as a sign of failure need to be altered as soon as possible. Attempting to manage risk by pushing it 'underground' is not effective. Sharing risks and learning about the steps to manage them is beneficial if the researcher is in charge. Risks should be tackled with "eyes wide open" since this is crucial in guaranteeing a good project outcome (Meyer-Stamer, 2002).
ii. **Things Still go Wrong:** Risk management is not perfect. A project could yet be destroyed by something (Wolburg, 2001). For example, it is impossible to forecast the illogical behavior of members of an organization, rival companies, or the government. The most challenging behaviors and acts to manage are frequently emotional ones (Table 6.2).

Table 6.2. A Typical Risk Log

Ref No	Description of Risk	Date Raised	Probability of occurrence	Severity	Risk Category	Risk Management: Action	Risk Management: by/date
1	Seigathon might introduce a brand-new item to the same target market.	2/3/10	Unlikely	3	Medium	Monitoring market activities in Seigathon	G. Smith 1/5/10
2	The accomplishment of Project X is necessary for the product launch. It could potentially be postponed.	13/4/10	Unlikely	2	Medium	Monitor the progress of Project X.	F. Kent 1/7/10
3	Due to a shortage of resources and other business obligations, the project's contractor has been unable to deliver on time.	20/6/10	Very Likely	2	Medium	Establish a connection with the contractor. Locate a different supplier and factor in extra time for emergencies.	G. Smith 1/8/10
4	The warehouse management system will be released once the testing has already begun.	29/6/10	Certain	2	High	During the early testing, provide paper-based systems and procedures.	J. Arnold 1/7/10
5	Beyond the scheduled commencement of testing, the introduction of the credit control system will be postponed.	29/6/10	Very likely	2	High	Create a three-month contingency in the schedule.	F. Kent 1/8/10

Source: Robert Buttrick, Creative Commons License.

6.3. IDENTIFYING RISKS

The project team must participate in this exercise.

- To come up with as many potential dangers as possible, utilize brainstorming or other innovative approaches. Anything that somebody desires to bring up should be included. By incorporating them in the process, the team's issues can be better understood, and the confidence level in other team members or departments can be improved. Group members would also hear one another's worries, which aids in team formation. Do not allow anyone to critique or comment on every danger mentioned; note ideas. Hint: Consider any presumptions and constraints that were applied.

- Once each risk is mentioned, write it down on a Post-It Note; if anyone has questions or needs clarification, that's fine, but no additional discussion should be allowed (Effah Ameyaw & Chan, 2013).
- Each Post-It Note should be posted on a board so everyone can see it. Create risks till the team has nothing else to contribute.
- Examine the dangers and categorize them into comparable groups (Maguire, 2002). Technology, people, the law, employee relations, money, etc., could all be involved. Choose whatever clusters "fit" the circumstance.
- Put the dangers into perspective by combining some, explaining or restating others, and numbering each risk.
- After evaluating every risk using the matrix, plot all the medium and high hazards onto a flip chart (Chapman, 2001).
- Give the team some time to evaluate the results so far. Are there any recurring patterns in the hazards or how they are grouped? Are there any specific project elements that stand out as being problematic?
- Start with the highest risks and come up with potential solutions. Allow for the raising of all alternatives. Just record the potential risk management steps for subsequent consideration without evaluating them.
- After evaluating the options, decide which risk-management strategy must be used and who manages each specific risk (Tang & Musa, 2011).

6.4. ADDRESSING OPPORTUNITIES AT THE START OF THE PROJECT

Opportunities must be addressed during the Early Inquiry Stage when the project is being set up. Opportunities like risk may impact the entire project plan and strategy. The project manager ought to:

i. List all the possibilities that could make the project more successful.
ii. Examine each possibility in turn:
a. Evaluate every likelihood of happening;
b. Evaluate how it will affect the project if it happens (Almarabeh & AbuAli, 2010).

iii. To identify the opportunity category, utilize an opportunity matrix like the one below (Table 6.3).

Table 6.3. Opportunity Matrix

Opportunity matrix	**Likelihood of Event Occurring**			
Impact	Very unlikely < 5%	Unlikely	Likely >50%	Very likely >75%
Minor impact on project schedule or cost. No impact on benefits	Minor	Minor	Medium	Medium
Major impact on project schedule or cost. Minor impact on benefits.	Medium	Medium	Medium	Major
Major impact on project schedule or cost. Major impact on benefits.	Medium	Medium	Major	Major

Source: Dr. Eddie, Creative Commons License.

i. Consider revising the baseline strategy to incorporate significant opportunities from the beginning.
ii. Provide a rough description of a contingency plan for medium-sized possibilities.
iii. Do not act immediately for insignificant opportunities; stick to the current action (Zhang et al., 2020).

Numerous opportunities may take advantage of, such as:

i. Adjusting the project's timeline such that, must a risky component of the project goes off without a hitch, the benefits and release date can be pushed ahead;
ii. They were utilizing time and money saved to combine previously discarded outputs.

Opportunities can be presented as a "log," much like the risk log in table 6.2, which is a practical approach (Davenport et al., 1996). The researcher may use the same record for both, identifying them as risks or opportunities. It is quite comparable to the risk log.

6.5. IDENTIFYING OPPORTUNITY

The project team must participate in this exercise. Maybe perform this after the risk workout (Section 6.3) to make the project look better.

i. Design the project strategy and method appropriately without sacrificing a risk-management plan to position to take advantage of possibilities!

ii. Investigative efforts should be incorporated into a plan to transform minor chances into large ones.

iii. Keep a log of opportunities (similar to Table 6.2).

6.6. MONITORING ONCE THE PROJECT IS IN PROGRESS

As soon as the project begins, the project manager ought to:

i. Keep a risk and opportunity log that resembles the illustration in Table 6.2 (Kerzner, 2022).

ii. Reevaluate the impact's seriousness and likelihood of occurrence regularly while monitoring them with the team.

iii. New opportunities and risks should be noted, categorized, and reported, together with the steps to address them.

iv. The regular project status report includes new, high risks, and potential big opportunities.

One of the following things could occur throughout a project:

i. An "event" involving a risk or opportunity must be recorded in the "action" column, and a similar entry must be made in the problems log.

ii. A risk or opportunity event passes, meaning the project moves forward, and the occurrence doesn't happen. "None" must be entered as the category (Al-Jibouri, 2003).

The log entry must be darkened both times to indicate that the event has been "closed" and no longer needs management attention.

6.7. TIPS ON USING THE RISK AND OPPORTUNITY LOG

- Ensure that risks are actually hazards and not just fears.
- Has only one opportunity or risk per "line;" combining them may make management challenging.
- Do not contribute to already-written entries unless to clarify something.
- Cross-reference the problems log whenever an event occurs.
- Maintain visibility of all possibilities and dangers, even those that have already passed or taken place. It serves as a safeguard in case other people's perceptions disagree. It is evident which hazards and opportunities are active and which are not by shading past ones (Diebold et al., 2000).

6.8. MORE SOPHISTICATED RISK EVALUATION TECHNIQUES

People can use the basic approach to risk described in this chapter on any project. It requires no special tools or technical or statistical knowledge (Klammer & Walker, 1984). In many cases, it is the most powerful and effective approach, relying on the creativity and common sense of the team. Nevertheless, there are occasions where other tools and techniques are very valuable for supplementing intuitive analyzes.

6.8.1. Sensitivity and Scenario Analysis

Everyone on any project may utilize this chapter's fundamental risk management strategy (Covello & Mumpower, 1985). It doesn't call for any specialized equipment or technical or statistical expertise. Depending on the team's inventiveness and common sense, it is frequently the most powerful and successful strategy. Nonetheless, there are times when using additional tools and methodologies is a great way to support intuitive analysis (Table 6.4).

Using a sensitivity analysis, one can examine how various inputs could affect a project. It will help to determine which assumptions are crucial to the argument and require additional investigation. Here's how it's done:

i. Identify the assumptions.
ii. Decide on a range of values for each assumption.
iii. Review the calculation (business model) using such numbers to examine the impact of changing that specific assumption on project viability.
iv. Determine the assumptions that will have the biggest impact and record them as risks.
v. Choose how someone will react to such risks (Aven, 2016).
vi. The project viability, for instance, is more susceptible to percentage changes in tariff than expenses, as seen in the accompanying table.
vii. By considering potential futures, scenario analysis goes beyond sensitivity analysis. A scenario is a collection of assumptions that represent the future and are selected based on risk and sensitivity analysis (Renn, 1998). To apply the various assumptions consistently, it is frequently necessary to build a model. For instance, fewer customers may result in a lower cost of sales, while fixed expenses may stay the same. Three scenarios need to be looked into:

- optimistic.
- most likely.
- pessimistic (Klinke & Renn, 2002).

Table 6.4. Tabular Data of Project Viability to Changes in Cost and Tariff

Assumption		–20%	–10%	+10%	+20%
Change in cost	NPV ($)	215k	416k	764k	978k
	IRR	14%	32%	52%	67%
Change in tariff	NPV ($)	10k	234k	865k	1234k
	IRR	9%	17%	16%	102%

Source: Chris Worseley, Creative Commons License.

So, in a gloomy scenario, the researcher might foresee a later-than-expected project completion date, a cost overrun, slower client adoption and usage, and more-than-expected downward price pressures. Tabulating this, for instance (Table 6.5):

Table 6.5. Comparison of Different Scenarios for Project Completion

Parameter	**Pessimistic**	**Most likely**	**Optimistic**
Timing of RFS	2 months late	On time	2 weeks early
IT cost	$450k	$340k	$320k
Customer take-up	+5%	+12%	+15%
Usage	35 mins/day	50 mins/day	65 mins/day
Tariff erosion	–15% annual	5% annual	–5% annual
IRR%	–6%	40%	87%
NPV ($k)	–1767	2990	3875
Payback	No payback	3 years	2 years

Source: Dr. Eddie, Creative Commons License.

Sensitivity analysis aims to give decision-makers a clear picture of potential outcomes of moving forward with the project, allowing them to weigh potential benefits against associated risks (Tummala & Schoenherr, 2011).

6.8.2. Risk Simulation

The most delicate characteristics and possible outcomes of a project can be examined using risk simulation. It depends on applying various times, expenses, and advantages of a certain project component. Entering this as:

i. The lowest likely value.

ii. The most likely value.

iii. The highest probable value (Berg, 2010).

Following a network analysis, the simulation software would determine expected costs and durations using a set of probabilities. Critical chain scheduling software includes probability, risk, and distributions to allow for a rigorous plan's development, testing, and implementation.

ACTIVITY 6.1.

Assume any project or program and make a list of potential risks that could impact the success of that project or program.

SUMMARY

An important component of project and program management is managing risks and opportunities. It entails identifying potential threats and opportunities to the project's success, evaluating their likelihood and impact, and implementing methods to reduce risks and take advantage of chances. Risk and opportunity management, risk assessment, risk mitigation, opportunity evaluation, and opportunity exploitation are important ideas in managing risks and opportunities. A proactive and systematic approach is needed for effective risk and opportunity management to recognize possible threats and opportunities during a project or program.

REVIEW QUESTIONS

1. What is risk management, and why is it important in project and program management?
2. How can project and program managers identify and assess potential risks and opportunities?
3. What is opportunity exploitation, and what are some common strategies for exploiting potential opportunities?
4. What are some best practices for managing risks and opportunities throughout the life cycle of a project or program?

MULTIPLE CHOICE QUESTIONS

1. What is risk management?

a. Identifying and taking advantage of potential opportunities
b. Identifying, assessing, and mitigating potential risks
c. Identifying and mitigating potential risks and taking advantage of potential opportunities
d. None of the above

2. Which of the following is a key component of risk management?

a. Evaluating potential opportunities
b. Identifying potential stakeholders
c. Assessing the likelihood and impact of potential risks
d. None of the above

3. What is opportunity exploitation?

a. Developing strategies to take benefit of opportunities
b. Identifying potential risks

c. Assessing the likelihood and impact of potential risks
d. None of the above

4. Which of the following is a key component of opportunity management?

a. Developing strategies to reduce the likelihood of risks
b. Assessing the potential value and impact of opportunities
c. Identifying potential stakeholders
d. Developing contingency plans

5. "Risk" usually _______ as the project progresses.

a. A increases
b. B reduces
c. C remains same
d. D becomes negligible

Answers to Multiple Choice Questions

1. (b); 2. (c); 3. (a); 4. (b) 5. (b)

REFERENCES

1. Akintoye, A., Beck, M., & Hardcastle, C., (2008). *Public-Private Partnerships: Managing Risks and Opportunities* (Vol. 1, pp. 4–8). John Wiley & Sons.
2. Al-Jibouri, S. H., (2003). Monitoring systems and their effectiveness for project cost control in construction. *International Journal of Project Management, 21*(2), 145–154.
3. Almarabeh, T., & AbuAli, A., (2010). A general framework for e-government: Definition maturity challenges, opportunities, and success. *European Journal of Scientific Research, 39*(1), 29–42.
4. Atkinson, R., Crawford, L., & Ward, S., (2006). Fundamental uncertainties in projects and the scope of project management. *International Journal of Project Management, 24*(8), 687–698.
5. Aven, T., (2016). Risk assessment and risk management: Review of recent advances on their foundation. *European Journal of Operational Research, 253*(1), 1–13.
6. Berg, H. P., (2010). Risk management: Procedures, methods and experiences. *Reliability: Theory & Applications, 5*(2(17)), 79–95.
7. Chapman, C., & Ward, S., (2003). *Project Risk Management Processes, Techniques and Insights* (Vol. 1, pp. 2–6). John Wiley & Sons Ltd.
8. Chapman, R. J., (2001). The controlling influences on effective risk identification and assessment for construction design management. *International Journal of Project Management, 19*(3), 147–160.

9. Colicchia, C., Creazza, A., Noè, C., & Strozzi, F., (2019). Information sharing in supply chains: A review of risks and opportunities using the systematic literature network analysis (SLNA). *Supply Chain Management: An International Journal, 24*(1), 5–21.
10. Cooper, D. F., Grey, S., Raymond, G., & Walker, P., (2005). *Project Risk Management Guidelines* (Vol. 1, pp. 5–9). Wiley.
11. Covello, V. T., & Mumpower, J., (1985). Risk analysis and risk management: An historical perspective. *Risk Analysis, 5*(2), 103–120.
12. Davenport, T., Jarvenpaa, S., & Beers, M., (1996). Improving knowledge work processes. *MIT Sloan Management Review, 1*, 6–9.
13. Diebold, F. X., Schuermann, T., & Stroughair, J. D., (2000). Pitfalls and opportunities in the use of extreme value theory in risk management. *The Journal of Risk Finance, 1*(2), 30–35.
14. Effah, A. E., & Chan, A. P., (2013). Identifying public-private partnership (PPP) risks in managing water supply projects in Ghana. *Journal of Facilities Management, 11*(2), 152–182.
15. Gotterbam, D., (2002). Reducing software failures: Addressing the ethical risks of the software development lifecycle. *Australasian Journal of Information Systems, 9*(2), 1–5.
16. Greenall, D., (2004). *The National Corporate Social Responsibility Report: Managing Risks, Leveraging Opportunities* (Vol. 1, pp. 7, 8).
17. Kerzner, H., (2022). *Project Management Metrics, KPIs, and Dashboards: A Guide to Measuring and Monitoring Project Performance* (Vol. 1, pp. 6–10). John Wiley & Sons.
18. Klammer, T. P., & Walker, M. C., (1984). The continuing increase in the use of sophisticated capital budgeting techniques. *California Management Review, 27*(1), 137–148.
19. Klinke, A., & Renn, O., (2002). A new approach to risk evaluation and management: Risk-based, precaution-based, and discourse-based strategies 1. *Risk Analysis: An International Journal, 22*(6), 1071–1094.
20. Kutsch, E., & Hall, M., (2010). Deliberate ignorance in project risk management. *International Journal of Project Management, 28*(3), 245–255.
21. Lacy, P., & Pickard, S., (2008). Managing risk and opportunity: The people imperative. *Journal of Corporate Citizenship*, (30), 139–146.
22. Levine, H. A., (2005). *Project Portfolio Management: A Practical Guide to Selecting Projects, Managing Portfolios, and Maximizing Benefits* (Vol. 1, pp. 3–9). John Wiley & Sons.
23. Maguire, S., (2002). Identifying risks during information system development: Managing the process. *Information Management & Computer Security, 10*(3), 126–134.
24. Meredith, J. R., Shafer, S. M., & Mantel, Jr. S. J., (2017). *Project Management: A Strategic Managerial Approach* (Vol. 1, pp. 4–7). John Wiley & Sons.

25. Meyer-Stamer, J., (2002). Clustering and the creation of an innovation-oriented environment for industrial competitiveness: Beware of overly optimistic expectations. *International Small Business Journal, 20*(3), 1–23.
26. Pritchard, C. L., & PMP, P. R., (2014). *Risk Management: Concepts and Guidance* (Vol. 1, pp. 3–5). Auerbach Publications.
27. Renn, O., (1998). Three decades of risk research: Accomplishments and new challenges. *Journal of Risk Research, 1*(1), 49–71.
28. Rolstadås, A., Johansen, A., Bjerke, Y. C., & Malvik, T. O., (2019). Managing risk and opportunities in complex projects. In: *Advances in Production Management Systems. Towards Smart Production Management Systems: IFIP WG 5.7 International Conference, APMS 2019, Austin, TX, USA, September 1–5, 2019, Proceedings, Part II* (Vol. 1, pp. 631–639). Springer International Publishing.
29. Schwartz, J. Z., Ruiz-Nuñez, F., & Chelsky, J., (2014). Closing the infrastructure finance gap: Addressing risk. *Financial Flows Infrastructure Financing, 14*(1), 6–11.
30. Tang, O., & Musa, S. N., (2011). Identifying risk issues and research advancements in supply chain risk management. *International Journal of Production Economics, 133*(1), 25–34.
31. Taroun, A., (2014). Towards a better modelling and assessment of construction risk: Insights from a literature review. *International Journal of Project Management, 32*(1), 101–115.
32. Tummala, R., & Schoenherr, T., (2011). Assessing and managing risks using the supply chain risk management process (SCRMP). *Supply Chain Management: An International Journal, 16*(6), 474–483.
33. Wideman, R. M., (2022). *Project and Program Risk Management a Guide to Managing Project Risks and Opportunities* (Vol. 1, pp. 2–6). Project Management Institute, Inc.
34. Wolburg, J. M., (2001). The "risky business" of binge drinking among college students: Using risk models for PSAs and anti-drinking campaigns. *Journal of Advertising, 30*(4), 23–39.
35. Zhang, Z., Hummel, J. T., Nandhakumar, J., & Waardenburg, L., (2020). Addressing the key challenges of developing machine learning AI systems for knowledge-intensive work. *MIS Quarterly Executive, 19*(4), pp. 1–5.
36. Zhong, W., Qin, S., & Li, X., (2018). Addressing challenges in construction project management process. *International Journal of Innovation, Management and Technology, 1*, 33–36.

CHAPTER 7

FUTURE TRENDS OF PROJECT AND PROGRAM MANAGEMENT

UNIT INTRODUCTION

Innovations now take place anywhere, without regard to location. They grow and bring about significant adjustments. Such changes are occurring at an extremely rapid rate, posing a different challenge to society's advancement. It is possible to see project management as a method for accelerating the development of innovations (Missig et al., 2010). Expanding knowledge about project manager instruction and significant financial expenditure in project management and behavior courses are other indicators of the discipline's growing importance.

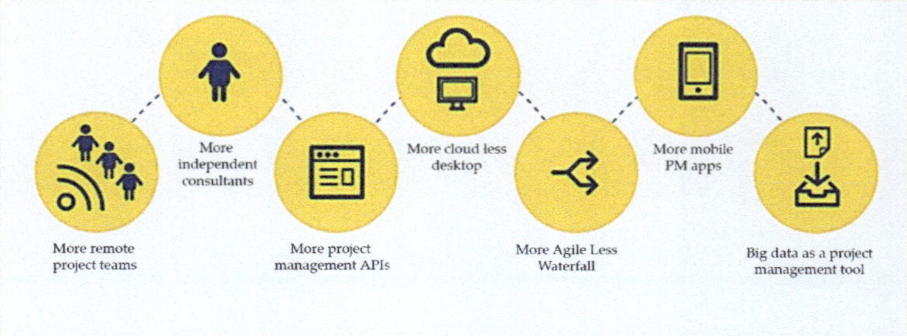

Figure 7.1. Image of future trends in project and program management.

Source: Filip Kitundu, creative commons license.

The organization must improve at discovering, choosing, and assessing successful project criteria due to various projects. Project success metrics are one of the characteristics that set average firms apart from great ones. A complex project process needs a flexible approach. Achieving value in project management is more crucial than meeting the three limitations.

Learning Objectives

At the end of this chapter, readers will be able to learn:

- Future trends in project management.
- Future of research and project management.
- The human component of project management in the future.
- Project management and commercial operations.
- Organizational aspects of project management.
- Concept of Green project management.

Key Terms

- Commercial operations
- Future trends
- Green Project Management
- Organization
- Research

7.1. FUTURE TRENDS IN PROJECT AND PROGRAM MANAGEMENT

A prominent aspect of management employing projects is equitable and sustainable development, which serves as the foundation for the growth of contemporary society. The issues society is currently facing have an impact on how it develops. Loss of moral principles and the business manners accompanying them cause market drops, company bankruptcies, and, more lately, intense economic decline and immigration to regions with a plentiful supply of cheap labor. Due to industrial closures in wealthy nations, more people now lack jobs and the chance to use knowledge with a minimum shelf life (Royer et al., 2004). These phenomena need to be handled, and reasonable societies should act accordingly. To identify the causes of the current problem, it is first essential to investigate the background and development of how society as people understand it now developed. By doing so, people may learn about past patterns and occurrences (Figure 7.1).

According to D. Zelenovic's (2011) chart, civilization has developed from the beginning of the industrial revolution until now, with a prediction out to the year 2200. The new era is defined by diversity in the fullest meaning of the word (from the population via societal expectations to a resolution for goods, individuals, and activities), creativity, adaptability, reliability, price, efficiency, and finally, the range of market needs.

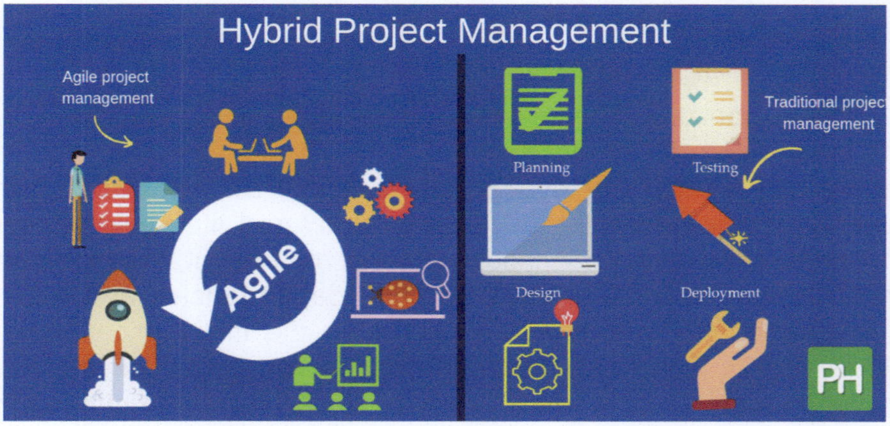

Figure 7.2. Image of hybrid project management.

Source: Vartika Kashyap, creative commons license.

Finding a successful strategy to reach goals that the business turns into a new stage of expansion and growth requires all of the elements above. It is widely acknowledged that computer technology is a tool that improves connectedness and productivity and gives everyone access to the media and trends. It is obvious how strong and massive the tsunami of problems brought about by computer technology has been and how similar in severity it is to the changes that occurred during the Industrial Revolution and in the past (Jiang et al., 2001) (Figure 7.2).

From utterly unorganized management via Total Quality Management (TQM) and integrated design to aligning key performance measures with organizational effectiveness, management has been through various phases (Kerzner, 2013). Considering the phases, it is clear that the model management process follows the same patterns in corporate control and oversight of assistance programs, which is a difficulty that arises naturally from a long history of the project and corporate leadership approaches. The extraction of reengineering stages, the life cycle costs, cross-cultural collaboration, long-term planning, six sigma, Agile philosophy, and the effects of the process management sustainable approach are all fascinating.

Remember

From the steam engine to Ford's assembly line, changes were inspired by technological solutions of individuals and groups of people.

It was essential to spend on project managers' education, and today the majority of investments are made in project management and behavior courses. Instead of being near the conclusion of this stage, project leaders are currently involved in the early stages of initiation. Today's project managers also make commercial decisions. In research about project management patterns, Crawford et al. (2006) identified three key patterns:

a. Leadership in agile projects;
b. Personal inventiveness; and
c. Size of the project.

The organization must improve at recognizing, deciding on, and assessing the indications of project success due to the variety of projects. For over three decades, traditional programs generally characterized and had well-structured life cycle phases, and criteria for every step saw the use of project management. Previous research has shown the inter-dependencies and effects of international development initiatives on the Information Society (Wirth, 1992). Future studies could go in two paths, as the data show connections between these two effects. It was crucial to look into how international development programs affected different spheres of society. Evaluating how development projects will affect the country's information society is vital to have a thorough picture. Numerous national initiatives are underway that are concerned with establishing new companies, applying creativity, and the growth of the Information and Communications Technology (ICT) sector through marketing, institutional capacity, and finances to develop collaborations with international nations. It is essential to look at the interconnections and dependencies that result from such projects and the numerous others that have a national impact on the digital age. The Ministry of Foreign and Domestic Trade and Telecommunications, the Authority for Investments and Export Promotion Agency, the Serbian Chamber of Commerce, the Ministry of Finance and Economy, the Ministry of Education, Science, and Technology Development, etc., are just a few of the organizations whose projects must be included.

Only after the creation of the agile manifesto paper in 2001 the application of the agile method in project management has grown in recent years (Dingsoyrn et al., 2012). Agile project and program management is used by lesser clubs that work together to achieve the following goals:

a. Producing results progressively enhancing new features
b. Prioritizing projects in line with requirements and budget
c. Carrying out the project number of iterations in accordance only with the client's input creates the best significance.

SCRUM, Extreme Programming (XP), the Crystal Family, EVO, and Dynamic Systems Development Method (DSDM) are a few of the most influential agile approaches (Kloppenborg & Opfer, 2002).

i. Decrease in innovative capability (29%)
ii. Decline in quality (31%)
iii. Withdrawal or delay of significant efforts (27%); (Project Management Institute, 2013).

Prior studies established a connection between corporate intelligence, organization, and program preparedness, indicating the need for further regional research among the two axes. The horizontal axis points toward the direction of in-depth studies, the neighborhood of application of the project strategy as a whole management of the company (Turner, 1999), thru the thorough layout of all special events in projects utilizing the research methods and the stages accomplished by such operations. The vertical axis denotes extensive investigation into additional components of intelligence that may be fostered in many ways inside the company (Zelenovic, 2011). The result is that the region nearer to the x-axis relates to the organizational plan. In contrast, the area more nearly to the y-axis refers to establishing a philosophic and tactical foundation for advancing knowledge. The plane depicted in Figure 7.3 is restricted to the field of intelligent procedure and the needs of an organization and does not incorporate studies in the area of cognitive computing (business analysis) or the ground of machine learning, robotics, or other systems; however, it cannot be relied upon seriously without these systems within an organization.

Figure 7.3. Graph of future research directions.

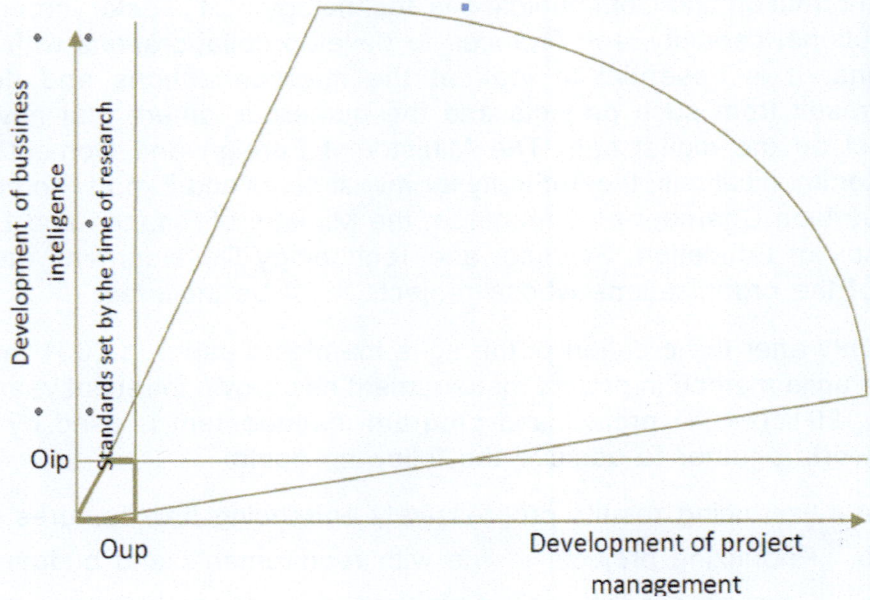

Source: Milos Jovanovic, creative commons license.

The relationship between business analytics and project preparation is significant, and the project's successful execution benefits business intelligence (BI).

According to the established relationship between organizational intelligence and project preparation, the natural continuation of study in this field involves the development of organization and project preparedness, assessing, and constructing a value system (Rumeser & Emsley, 2018).

7.2. FUTURE RESEARCH AND PROJECT AND PROGRAM MANAGEMENT

The intelligence of business and manufacturing systems is a subject comprised of several sub disciplines that may be seen as complementary in describing intelligence transmitted from the humanoid creature to the concept of designing the production system (Kwak & Anbari, 2009).

To locate a clever person and the pattern of intelligence that ought to be copied, it is required to investigate a variety of highly smart natural systems, like ant species, honey bees, and dolphins. The species above are famed for their intellect, but another trait inspired the designers of the intelligent firm idea.

Companies that effectively establish criteria have several profitable business options (Thannhuber, 2005). There are several research problems whose solutions should help the construction of circumstances for creating smart groups, especially intelligent economic sectors based on the theory of living entities (Zelenovic, 2011). In the future study of intelligence systems, based on previously investigated areas; it is feasible to split activities into two primary directions:

i. Study in the field of BI using data technologies in the domain of decision-making support networks.
ii. Study of the intelligence platform as a generic element comprised of individuals technology and synergies among diverse environmental factors that involve producing value for businesses.

An earlier study on organizational and project preparedness and their influence on the manifestation of intelligence in organizations has given the framework and built the foundation for future research. In addition, a foundation for future study on the influence of project tasks on smart output in the organization is developed as a bridge between the two written based on primary themes. Based on the present patterns and the notion that "The future is already here—it's just not evenly distributed" (Gibson, 2003), it is possible to recognize the research problem that starts the region of fast expansion at the innovation level and the involvement of intellectual ability in a given fad, the region starting to emerge from the vanishing of borders among industrial and research subjects, and (Dingsøyr et al., 2012) the neighborhood of nanotechnology as a new place to discover in legal terms and ethics.

Did you Know?

Dolphins, have the ability to connect small parts of their vision as the information in the brain with the broader concept of display regions that are around them. That concept is directed towards the development of intelligence in management/business navigation system by integrating a lot of information into a single picture of a good review and the potential for management and maintenance.

7.3. PROJECT AND PROGRAM MANAGEMENT APPROACH ORGANIZATIONS

Integrating project methods into the management of a firm or institution is a research-worthy topic. Several of the concerns stated and the available literature provide a solid foundation for researching to establish the viability of employing project management tools and methods in organization management.

There is a spot in this discipline when project management, training, and business model converge (Krahn et al., 2009). Study problems such as how operating a program, that is, a collection of projects, is comparable to managing a project-oriented organization, the role of assets in programs, and the process of picking initiatives for portfolios are all relevant and inevitable research topics. There ought to be a separate field of future study devoted to the organizational status of projects in non-project-oriented firms.

7.4. HUMAN COMPONENT OF PROJECT AND PROGRAM MANAGEMENT

The relevance of the role of the project leader in determining project success has been established in several pieces of research (Jiang et al., 2001). Personal traits of leaders, groups, agility, collaboration, and the overall human aspect of project management are all fundamental issues that give a foundation for study on the aforementioned subject. Project meetings on and on the ground also represent a continuously growing possibility motivated by the endless opportunities for communication, virtualization, and information dissemination through international reach. The endless opportunities for interaction, configuration management, and information dissemination through global reach inspired this potential. The project method is used to study leadership and collaboration in decision-making, negotiating, creating power, resolving conflict, skills acquisition, and control of particular areas of interest. In the future, human influence will have a more noticeable effect on project management, but this will take place within the context of honoring the based on culture, cultural, technical, and other specific details of various regions (Wong et al., 2007). These regions are home to interested parties, funders, workgroups, clients, and consumers of the project outcomes.

The derived research questions might be categorized under their sources—missing et al. (2010) motivation of the structure. This structure of the project personnel; Royer et al. (2004) rationality thru the team decision-making; Dingsøyr et al. (2012) resolution of interpersonal conflict; Kerzner (2013) institutional capacity from the existing resource workgroups (Wong, 2007). When one considers the centuries that have come before and those that are still to come in the 21st century, which are regarded to be the era of the dominance of information and intelligence, it is logical to conclude that the most massive change in the conceptual analysis of project management is connected to the intelligent and effective project management as the economic crisis challenge that is rooted in human possibility. This conclusion can be reached after considering the past and the centuries that are still to come in the 21st century.

7.5. "GREEN" PROJECT MANAGEMENT

The study questions that need to be posed also took into consideration certain additional restrictions resulting from the "triple constraints." These new constraints are mirrored in the kinds of resources used, the process by-products, and the end product supplied. Both biotechnology and nanotechnology provide a wide variety of possibilities; however, these possibilities can only be realized if they are included in the manufacturing process and the protection of natural resources (Maltzman & Shirley, 2011). As a consequence of concerns about ethics in research, the field of ecological sustainability in project management may be embraced, at least to some degree (Figure 7.4).

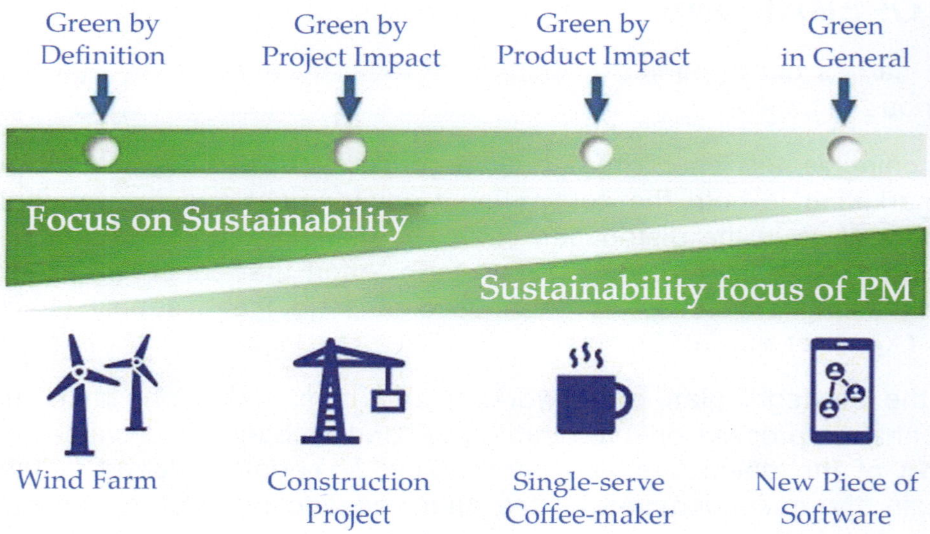

Figure 7.4. Illustration of green project management.

Source: Rich Maltzman, creative commons license.

7.6. TECHNICAL ASPECTS OF PROJECT AND PROGRAM MANAGEMENT

Technically, survey questionnaires in the future advancement of project and program management that are focused on the creation of theoretical bases will include the following:

a. Problems associated with designing and development projects;
b. The relation between manufacturing and projects with a focus on new product innovation;
c. The managerial staff of specific specifications during the new environments;
d. The managerial staff of technical specifications during periods of intense technological advancement;
e. Evaluation in uncertain circumstances (Söderlund, 2004).

A separate region for in-depth studies, which would assist in better understanding the needs in product design in such a complex responsibilities distribution, is the questionnaire method of the connection between the lifetime of a product and the task. This line of inquiry concerns the product's lifetime and research work (Kwak & Anbari, 2009).

7.7. PROJECT AND PROGRAM MANAGEMENT IN COMMERCIAL OPERATIONS

A corporation carries out a significant portion of today's engagement with the market in various initiatives.

This reasoning is the basis for the emergence of new study issues in selling and marketing in both the conventional environment and the Internet ecosystem, as well as in the distribution chain, bargaining, market, contracts, and legal structure of project execution. The term "effort that concentrates on building or enhancing processes" is often used in project and supply chain management (Ayers et al., 2010).

To help the strategic plan of networking and communication, such as partners, to enhance process-oriented strategies, and recognize the causative factors instead of the diagnoses and implications of negative deeds in the system or chain, the questionnaires for the future advancement of the project strategy in the distribution network are centered.

The relationship between the supply chain and the cost structure, which reflects a two-dimensional position of the commercial entity when seen through a design approach, may be determined via research in a specific domain. Because the relationship between a project and a corporation is universal, it is feasible to use methods and tools applicable to project management when running a company, even as methods and tools tried to apply to project management could be utilized in the management of a company (Hansen & Ahmed, 2012). Future studies of approaches and strategies must be oriented toward the advanced concepts of management.

The Lean methodology is among the effective methods, the application of which should be shown in the context of the project environment. This is necessary since the concept offers guidance for reducing costs and the effective execution of projects. Specifying the study topics in the region where the essential areas overlap is feasible.

The Theory of Constraints, Critical Chain Project Management (also known as CCPM), Total Quality Management (often known as TQM), and Six Sigma are the three domains that fall under this category (Leach et al., 2005) (Figure 7.5).

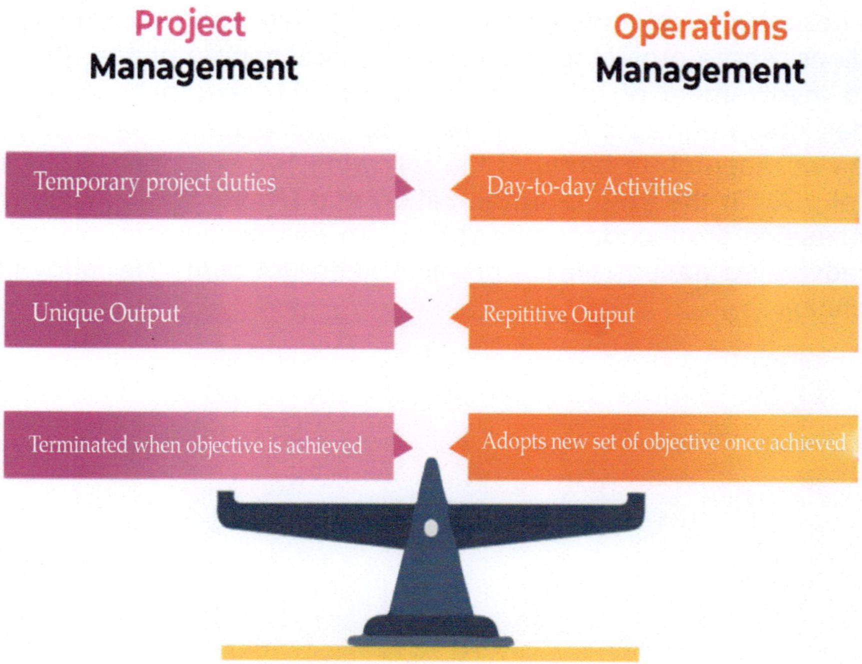

Figure 7.5. Schematic of comparison between project management and operation management.

Source: Lucy Brown, creative commons license.

7.8. ORGANIZATIONAL ASPECTS OF PROJECT AND PROGRAM MANAGEMENT

Organizational components of project and program management open research issues that must address the challenges of trying to shape the life cycle of business and social construction projects and the functional growth of a society described by the technique of product lifecycle project (Project Cycle Management) as a replacement for the balance of nature that appears to exist between both the funder and the implementer of the project where numerous donor organizations have the position of sponsors (Marcom et al., 2007).

The logical Framework Matrix is a field that has been almost entirely undiscovered in the context of the scientific method. As a result, there are many research questions, the answers that will result in the corresponding matrix in connection with the circumstances of achievement, the kinds of projects, and the relevant expected outcomes. To make the project implementation process more efficient and successful, the organizational components include further assessment, the creation of an organization, and assigning responsibilities. Particularly in advanced economies in which projects do not symbolize innovative techniques, unlike in underdeveloped nations where project ideology is in its preliminary phase, the role and involvement of the Office of Project Management in various types of organizations must be taken into account as a modern area of research in terms of the following two segments: (Missing et al., 2010) the project organization and (Royer et al., 2004) the processing/production organization. This is particularly important in advanced nations where projects need not comprise innovative techniques.

ACTIVITY 7.1.

Conventional construction projects are energy oriented and consume huge amount of energy in their development. As a project manager of a construction company you are given a task to develop a project charter and project management plan by applying the concept of "Green Project Management."

SUMMARY

An association between an organization's intelligence and organizational preparedness has been supported by prior research. It has been amply demonstrated that if the extent of adaptation to the situations of the environment is among the elements of the system project, the organization's level of willingness directly impacts the acknowledgment of organizational innovation and flexibility. This is because it is necessary to respond quickly to changing environmental conditions. By demonstrating the relationship between each element of organizational readiness and each component of project preparation using canonical correlation analysis, the possibility of a connection between organizational and project availability was investigated. As anticipated, the relevant corporate and project preparedness components showed the most significant degree of association (leadership in the organization – leadership in the project management system, the project management system, etc.).

REVIEW QUESTIONS

1. Describe some future trends in project management.
2. What is the future of research and its relationship with project management?
3. Explain the human component of project management in the future.
4. Describe project management and commercial operations in the future.
5. What are the organizational aspects of project management in the future?
6. Define and explain the concept of Green Project Management.

MULTIPLE CHOICE QUESTIONS

1. Milestones established by the customer must be adhered to by:

a. Project manager
b. Functional managers
c. The customer
d. Both a and b

2. Successful project managers spend most of their time

a. Planning with their personnel
b. Planning with the top management
c. Communication with the project team
d. Studying project results.

3. Which of the following is the most efficient means of product quality inspection

a. Acceptance sampling
b. 100% inspection

c. Variable sampling

d. a and c

4. From an HR perspective, the project manager's responsibility in the planning role includes the:

a. Hiring the team

b. Developing work schedules

c. Forecasting

d. Feedback sessions

e. Both b and c

5. Which of the following is a main reason why project managers need to understand their organization's mission and strategy?

a. They can better focus on the immediate customer

b. They can make appropriate decisions and adjustments

c. So they can be effective project advocates

d. Both b and c are correct

Answers to Multiple Choice Questions

1. (d); 2. (c); 3. (c); 4. (d) 5. (d)

REFERENCES

1. Aliu, E., Aune, T., Beilicke, M., Benbow, W., Boettcher, M., Bouvier, A., & VERITAS Collaboration, (2011). Multiwavelength observations of the previously unidentified blazar RX 0648.7+ 1516. *The Astrophysical Journal, 742*(2), 127.
2. Alvarez-Dionisi, L. E., Turner, R., & Mittra, M., (2016). Global project management trends. *International Journal of Information Technology Project Management (IJITPM), 7*(3), 54–73.
3. Boesch, D. F., Boynton, W. R., Crowder, L. B., Diaz, R. J., Howarth, R. W., Mee, L. D., & Turner, R. E., (2009). Nutrient enrichment drives Gulf of Mexico hypoxia. *Eos, Transactions American Geophysical Union, 90*(14), 117-118.
4. Crawford, L., Pollack, J., & England, D., (2006). Uncovering the trends in project management: Journal emphases over the last ten years. *International Journal of Project Management, 24*(2), 175–184.
5. Dingsøyr, T., Nerur, S., Balijepally, V., & Moe, N. B., (2012). A decade of agile methodologies: Towards explaining agile software development. *Journal of Systems and Software, 85*(6), 1213–1221.
6. Gibson, C., (2003). Cultures at work: Why 'culture' matters in research on the cultural industries. *Social & Cultural Geography, 4*(2), 201–215.

7. Hansen, Z. N. L., & Ahmed-Kristensen, S., (2012). Connecting engineering operations to strategic management: A framework for decision making in engineering offshoring. *International Journal of Product Development, 17*(3, 4), 204–227.

8. Jiang, J. J., Klein, G., & Chen, H. G., (2001). The relative influence of IS project implementation policies and project leadership on eventual outcomes. *Project Management Journal, 32*(3), 49–55.

9. Jochims, H. W., Schwell, M., Baumgärtel, H., & Leach, S., (2005). Photoion mass spectrometry of adenine, thymine, and uracil in the 6–22 eV photon energy range. *Chemical Physics, 314*(1–3), 263–282.

10. Kerzner, H., (2013). Strategic planning for a project office. *Project Management Journal, 34*(2), 13–25.

11. Kloppenborg, T. J., & Opfer, W. A., (2002). The current state of project management research: Trends, interpretations, and predictions. *Project Management Journal, 33*(2), 5–18.

12. Krahn, A. D., Healey, J. S., Chauhan, V., Birnie, D. H., Simpson, C. S., Champagne, J., & Gollob, M. H., (2009). Systematic assessment of patients with unexplained cardiac arrest: Cardiac arrest survivors with preserved ejection fraction registry (CASPER). *Circulation, 120*(4), 278–285.

13. Kwak, Y. H., & Anbari, F. T., (2009). Availability-impact analysis of project management trends: Perspectives from allied disciplines. *Project Management Journal, 40*(2), 94–103.

14. Lee, S. H., Beamish, P. W., Lee, H. U., & Park, J. H., (2009). Strategic choice during economic crisis: Domestic market position, organizational capabilities, and export flexibility. *Journal of World Business, 44*(1), 1–15.

15. Maltzman, R., & Shirley, D., (2011). Project manager as a pivot point for implementing sustainability in an enterprise. In: *Sustainability Integration for Effective Project Management* (pp. 261–278). IGI Global.

16. Marcom, P. K., Isaacs, C., Harris, L., Wong, Z. W., Kommarreddy, A., Novielli, N., & Ellis, M. J., (2007). Combining letrozole and trastuzumab as first or second-line biological therapy produces durable responses in a subset of HER2-positive and ER-positive advanced breast cancers. *Breast Cancer Research and Treatment, 102*(1), 43–49.

17. Missig, G., Ayers, L. W., Schulkin, J., & Rosen, J. B., (2010). Oxytocin reduces background anxiety in a fear-potentiated startle paradigm. *Neuropsychopharmacology, 35*(13), 2607–2616.

18. Mustaro, P., & Rossi, R., (2013). Project management principles applied in academic research projects. In: *Proceedings of the Informing Science and Information Technology Education Conference* (Vol. 1, pp. 4–30). Informing Science Institute.

19. Padalkar, M., & Gopinath, S., (2016). Six decades of project management research: Thematic trends and future opportunities. *International Journal of Project Management, 34*(7), 1305–1321.

20. Royer, D. L., Berner, R. A., Montañez, I. P., Tabor, N. J., & Beerling, D. J., (2004). Co_2 as a primary driver of phanerozoic climate. *GSA Today, 14*(3), 4–10.
21. Rumeser, D., & Emsley, M., (2018). A systematic review of project management serious games: Identifying gaps, trends, and directions for future research. *The Journal of Modern Project Management, 6*(1), 2–10.
22. Shenhar, A. J., Dvir, D., Levy, O., & Maltz, A. C., (2001). Project success: A multidimensional strategic concept. *Long Range Planning, 34*(6), 699–725.
23. Söderlund, J., (2004). Building theories of project management: Past research, questions for the future. *International Journal of Project Management, 22*(3), 183–191.
24. Spasojević, M., Ribić-Zelenović, L., & Maričić, A., (2011). The phase structure and morphology of electrodeposited nickel-cobalt alloy powders. *Science of Sintering, 43*(3), 313–326.
25. Thannhuber, M. J., (2005). Background: Discussion of the state-of-the-art. *The Intelligent Enterprise: Theoretical Concepts and Practical Implications, 1*, 13–22.
26. Wirth, I., (1992). Project-management education: Current issues and future trends. *International Journal of Project Management, 10*(1), 49–54.

CHAPTER 8

CHALLENGES FOR PROJECT AND PROGRAM MANAGEMENT IN THE 21ST CENTURY

UNIT INTRODUCTION

One could see challenges as opportunities for achievement. Project and program leaders face problems due to uncertainty in various sectors, rapid technological progressions, talent scarcity, poor communication, and other factors. Even though effectively utilizing project management proficiency has been a hot topic of debate for the past few decades, companies continue to fight over how to implement this strategy shift in their ventures (Atkinson et al., 2006; Khan et al., 2018).

The development of program managers' capabilities in coping with resources and expanding their project management knowledge body is critical to the effective execution of projects. Acknowledging the severe influence of initiatives, and thus the impact of project management skills, on the economy and society has been increasing and developed to become essential to European nations in 2007 with the worldwide recession. In line with this, the international project market is enormous, and curiosity in project operation and management as an essential knowledge body is growing (Figure 8.1).

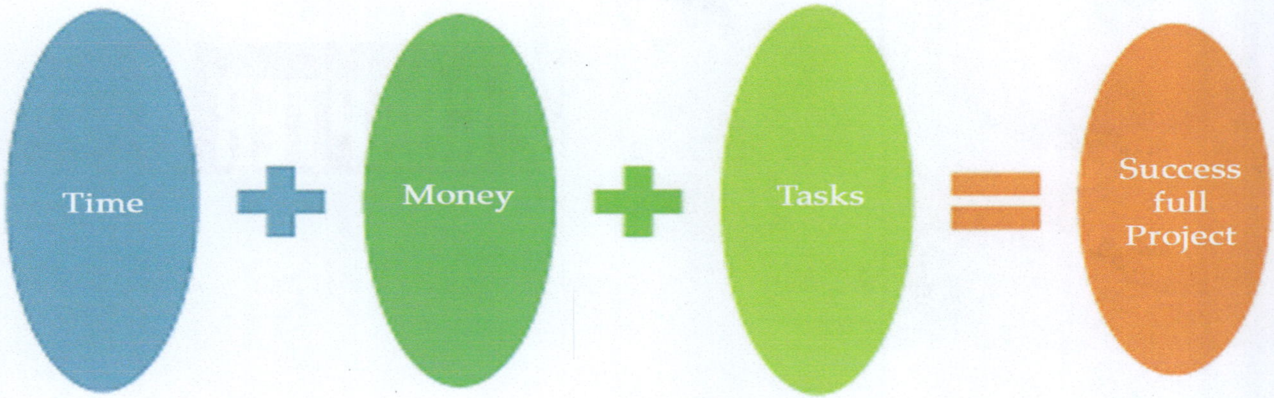

Figure 8.1. Image of a practical project.

Source: Gaurav Vasantrao Patil, creative commons license.

Being Lean and Seen is a 4-year, EU-H2020-funded, cooperative, diverse research exchange initiative between ten foreign partners (2017 to 2020). From a broader viewpoint of expanding knowledge of project management through investigative study, the curriculum deepens and broadens the field outside its existing knowledgeable foundations and links it more directly with the issues faced by current practices. The work's multidisciplinary approach transcends the traditional bounds of the PM knowledge base to establish a holistic framework that will facilitate the effective execution of projects in the present and future. It rests on three essential pillars:

i. Being Lean: Due to the demand for project productivity and effectiveness, management approaches from other industries should be adapted, improved, and advanced.

ii. Begin Seen: Emphasize the psycho-social components to include the viewpoint of those in charge of project delivery.

iii. Being Lean and Seen: Projects should be adjusted to dynamic surroundings to maintain a reasonable edge over the long term with strategic flexibility, and project management techniques should be adapted to developing nations.

To get things rolling, the purpose of this chapter is to draw attention to a few of the myriad challenges project management experts have been up against over the past few decades. These challenges may be compiled into a list of the most significant roadblocks. Despite the possibility that the obstacles that have been outlined here are not all-encompassing, resolving the most pressing problems offers the push necessary to transform difficulties into options.

Learning Objectives

At the end of this chapter, readers will be able to learn the following:

- Significant challenges of project and program management
- Unidentified goals as a challenge to project and program management
- Changes in scopes as a challenge to project and program management
- Improper risk management and impossible deadlines as a challenge

Key Terms

- Challenges
- Changes in Scopes
- Impossible Deadlines
- Risk Management
- Unidentified Goals

8.1. SIGNIFICANT PROJECT AND PROGRAM MANAGEMENT CHALLENGES

There is an increasing demand for project management to be associated with organizational strategy and to upsurge performance. Identifying the common issues that organizations encounter while handling projects might help us create a brighter prospect for this vital body of knowledge.

Following comprehensive literature research, some of the primary issues for project managers have been recognized, including, but not restricted to, scope administration, information systems, team composition, client satisfaction, lean management, communication, and reliability. Table 8.1 points out the top 15 difficulties mentioned in the existing literature. The characteristics of the problems are also identified and shown in this table. Risk Assessment, Human Resource Management, and Scope Statement and Planning are placed first in studies according to the number of recurrence of problems in the literature and diverse points of view by researchers. Innovation is thus regarded as one of the essential areas for improvement, as the invention that will arise from progress cannot be predicted until the project begins. Consequently, creativity in agile projects is commonly linked to high-tech businesses, like those involved in IT initiatives.

Table 8.1. Top 15 Issues for Project and Program Management

S. No	Issues	Factors	References
1	Risk Assessment	Financial risk Political threat Technological risk Operational risk Force majeure Construction risk	Hwang & Ng (2013); Sawhney et al. (2014); Padalkar & Gopinath (2016)
	Human Resource Management	Issues of staff enrollment Collaboration of team members Virtual teams Cultural problems Labor associated issues Cross-cultural leadership expertise Revolutionary leadership	Mir & Pinnington (2014); Hwang & Ng (2013); Padalkar & Gopinath (2016); Ainamo et al., (2010)
	Description and Planning of Project	Scope Management Project Location	Hwang & Ng (2013); Khan et al. (2018)

2	Knowledge Administration	Knowledge capabilities in project firms Information distribution contexts Implicit knowledge attainment and sharing Integration procedures in cross-functional ventures Knowledge creation in multidisciplinary project teams	Padalkar & Gopinath (2016); Dogbegah et al. (2011)
3	Performance Management	Association amongst guidelines and performance The process of aligning vague results Systematic biases and the impact of culture on the results of the project Project management maturity Main performance parameters	Sawhney et al. (2014); Padalkar & Gopinath (2016); De Reyck et al. (2005)
4	Value Management and Sustainability	Energy Effectiveness Water Effectiveness Ecology Quality of Life Health Transportable Availability Affordability	Sawhney et al. (2014); Zhang et al. (2011)
5	Investors Management	Internal & External Stakeholders Stakeholder Association Building of Trust Information Distribution	Aarseth et al. (2014); Hwang & Ng (2013); Padalkar & Gopinath (2016)
	Active Project Management	Variation of costs of materials Scarcities of materials Alterations in material requirements and type Communicating varying culture and mindset	Hwang & Ng (2013); Ameh et al. (2010)
7	Price Management	Price Approximation Price Observation and Managing Value examination Life Cycle Price of Building	Niazi et al. (2016); Padalkar & Gopinath (2016)
8	Health and Safety Management	Leadership mentality and corporate obligation Life cycle method to OH, investment in substructure and management systems	Hwang & Ng (2013); Sawhney et al. (2014)

9	Clash and Disagreement Management	Clash management approaches Recognizing the source of the clash Clash and Invention	Hwang & Ng (2013); Sawhney et al. (2014)
8	Claim Management	Unpredictable Service Delivery Increasing Client Demand Dealer Performance	Dogbegah et al. (2011)
10	Communication Management	The quick progression of information and communication technologies Virtual communications	Hwang & Ng (2013); Padalkar & Gopinath (2016)
11	Procurement Management	Contract reports Sub-contract management Supplier Pre-selection System	Padalkar & Gopinath (2016)
12	Information Technology Management	BIM adaptation Customer demand Absence of BIM skills and proficiency in technical and system specifications Substantial adoption cost to executing BIM	Aarseth et al. (2014); Haron et al. (2017)
13	Ethical Management	Personal Level Organizational Level Professional Level	Dogbegah et al. (2011)
14	Quality Management	Plan Quality Management Perform Quality Assertion	Sawhney et al. (2014)
15	Novelty and creativity	Culture of originality in the project Develop agreement on a set of goals in a steering group with different interests	Maghsoudi et al. (2015)

Source: Amin Akhavan Tabassi, Creative Commons License.

In addition to those mentioned above, a collectively organized team composing function is a growing concept in establishing high-functioning virtual teams in several industries.

Most team-building activities aim to provide the group with a pressure-free setting to carry out their duties. As a result, the project manager's role is that of a mediator.

They must understand the social differences and potential sensitivities of various individuals to achieve association and cooperation among the team members so that they can work collectively on the projects currently underway and those that are still to come (Figure 8.2).

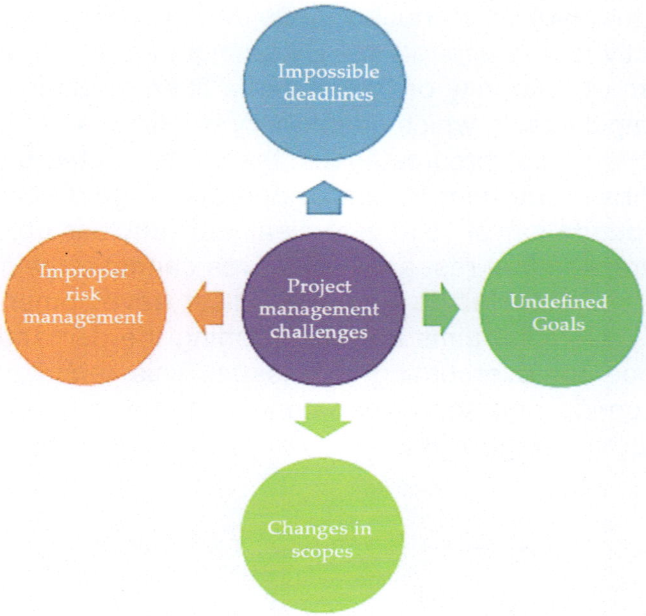

Figure 8.2. Illustration of project management issues.

Source: Amin Akhavan Tabassi, creative commons license.

The nature of relationships and the outcome of managing conflict are substantially influenced by the team members' perspective of how their intended goals might well be impacted by the behavior of others or the program managers (Tabassi et al., 2017). Previous research has shown that when there are cultural differences between the parties, the dispute is more likely to happen and worsen (Fisher et al., 2011). Thus, handling multicultural teams while dealing with diverse cultures that might also employ various dispute-resolution techniques is one of the critical issues faced by project managers working on foreign projects (Tabassi et al., 2017).

8.2. UNDEFINED GOALS

When goals are not correctly understood, the entire organization and team can be disappointed. When higher administration cannot approve or support hazy goals, the referenced initiative has little chance of succeeding. The project leader should ask genuine questions to create and assimilate stated goals. In the event of unknown aims, the desire for essentials does not require districts to cancel complete programs and substitute them with hurriedly drafted efforts to achieve as-yet undefined purposes (Voyten, 1978). Furthermore, the paper identifies three problems that restrict the dependability and state-to-state comprehensibility of state-estimated costs: (i) unclear goals, (ii) underutilized technology, and (iii) insufficient preparation (Ward, 1975). Many people may find themselves seriously considering previously specified future objectives and aspirations. By ambiguous, it is meant the unaltered nature of humanity or the lack of a fixed personality made possible by emptiness, in which adaptability is infinite and ultimate (Zhenping, 2012). In most circumstances, the 1st step of the planning procedure comprises the compilation of operational and strategic planning or the foundation of relatively clear and unclear objectives. It should be stressed that research objectives cannot remain unclear, nor can they be restricted to methodological development alone (Stolber, 1971). Defining aims and establishing the demands is the simplest method for overcoming this issue. This technique may be time-consuming and seem monotonous, but it is generally an essential procedure (Figure 8.3).

Figure 8.3. Image of blunders in defining goals.

Source: Ceyda Güzelsevdi, creative commons license Gaurav Vasantrao Patil.

8.2.1. Too Big to Accomplish

When a project leader happens to come across a scenario in which the ultimate aim is too large to be completed within timeframes, too large to be finished by the team, and too large to be finished with the available resources, it becomes unimaginable for the project leader to accomplish the goal, and it typically results in the failure of the entire planning for the future for that project (Clark, 1985).

8.2.2. Numerous Goals

There are times when a project or program manager is faced with a challenge in which he is expected to fulfill an excessive number of targets within a limited amount of time.

8.2.3. Absence of Detailing

A project or program manager may occasionally encounter a scenario where the goal's accurate description is vague. The project manager must spend extra time working out the anticipated things due to the absence of specificity. Occasionally, the project might be postponed due to follow-up with the customer over the same.

8.2.4. Goals Not Highlighted

When a project begins without setting appropriate goals, it gradually messes up the entire project flow. Therefore, keeping track of anticipated targets is crucial.

8.3. VARIATIONS IN SCOPES

This happens when expansion management permits the project's expansion to exceed its original aims. Clients and administrators might demand modifications to a venture, and it takes a capable program manager to assess every request, decide whether or not to execute it and communicate the repercussions to the budget and schedule. In the case of degree shifts, such a worldwide sequence of estimating allows for the investment required to identify an external assault, assess inspiration and intentional expectancy and then govern the necessary responses.

> **Remember**
>
> What's the fact of being competent with tasks if they're the wrong ones? Set aside some time to list and categorize your goals in this manner. In addition, whenever you examine your schedule, consider which tasks fulfill the most important purposes.

Although these goals are admirable, it may be prudent to examine the needed pace of advancement in novel program expenditures and the level of development (Clark, 1985). In the past, innovators tended to favor more intricate and rapid change; nevertheless, today's extent of growth is significantly more inconspicuous, and alterations are encountered that are not much complicated and strung out over a more extended period (Uzman, 2010). The obstruction has been caused by several powers, one of which is a supplementary and pragmatic tendency.

This tendency, which emphasizes the study of convincing compliance to progression, has restricted the scope of progression theory and investigation (Ryan, 1965). This paper suggests that exchange costs and competencies are, on a fundamental level, entangled in the confirmation of vertical degree, and it identifies the critical components of their co-development. In addition, the report suggested that exchange costs and competencies are fundamentally entwined in the confirmation of horizontal degree. Researchers have investigated the breadth and depth of these shifts in the labor market and the myriad ways they impact different categories of workers in the United States (Smith, 1997) (Figure 8.4).

Figure 8.4. Schematic of alterations in scope.

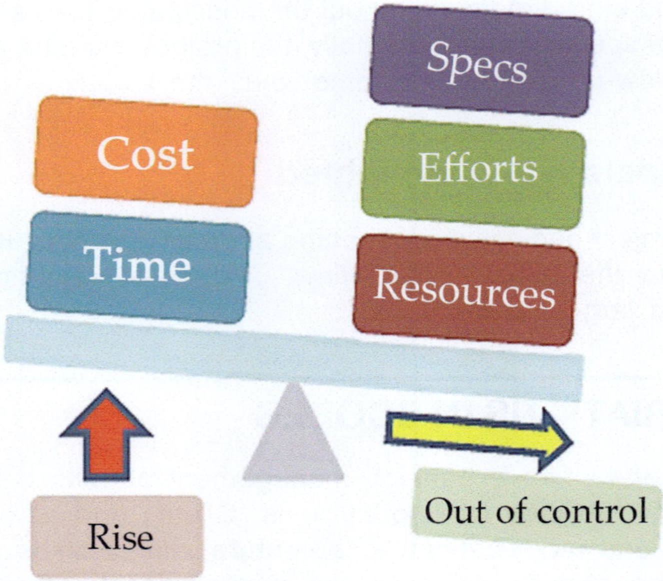

Source: Kissflow, creative commons license.

8.4. INAPPROPRIATE RISK MANAGEMENT

Another critical aspect of venture administration preparation is learning to control and prepare for risk. Chance tolerance is an appealing venture administrator feature because projects do not always go as planned. Gathering information, building trust, and recognizing which aspects of a business are off track are all part of the initiative director's job. Poor risk management is highly detrimental to the entire venture. According to the author, the basis of functioning hazard administration might well be traced back to the course of wellness building, which is primarily linked with the physical harm that might also happen as an outcome of inappropriate equipment or administrator implementation (Raz & Hillson, 2005). Firms will most likely be inflated if they attempt to use risk organization to lessen the profit uncertainty concerning money streams and if they function in countries where bookkeeping figures will most likely be used as a tightening component. However, the company leaders have instigated to embrace the notion of risk management aggressively (Tufano, 1998). Managers are trained to comprehend the outer limits of each strategy and to syndicate them to design specific risk management techniques in a particular situation. Recognizing the hazard is the first step in managing threats so appropriate solutions can be implemented (Schmidt et al., 2001). Banks do not fail due to changes in interest rates; instead, they flop because of poor risk management, inadequate capital, or other types of misconduct, all of which fall under the purview of the bank regulatory (Figure 8.5).

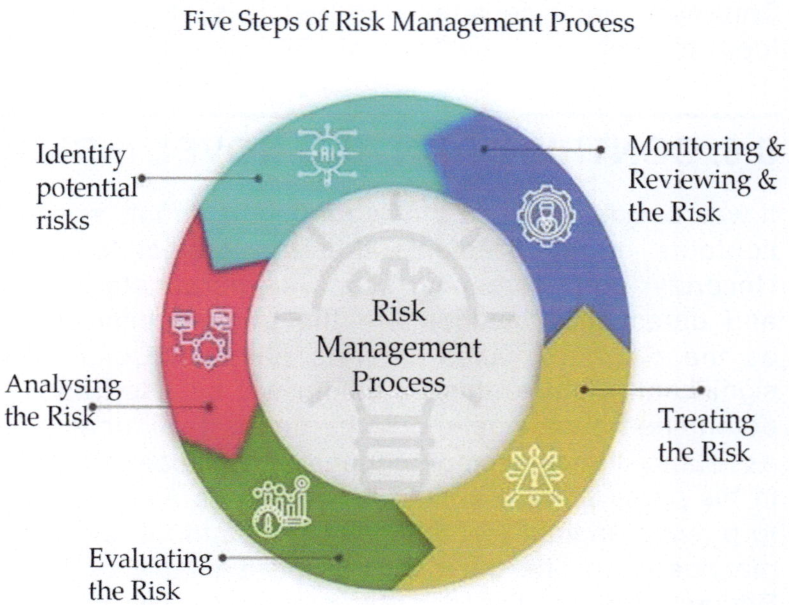

Figure 8.5. Diagram of components of risk management.

Source: HSE Watch, creative commons license.

The four steps of risk management are identification, analysis, control, and reduction.

8.5. UNMANAGEABLE DEADLINES

A good project manager understands that contacting a team for the unthinkable numerous times can rapidly lead to a loss of trust and effectiveness. The prospects of magnificently concluding a project under unrealistic timelines are, for the most part, unattainable goals. Challenging deadlines established by additional statutory requirements might do more than slow guidance to complete and lack to determine agency objectives; they may also inflict direct expenses on the private sector. So, whenever some poor slob has a valid need for an extension, do not impose onerous timelines or retort, "Not my issue, counselor" (Nolan, 2009). They put up with unreasonable timelines and never-ending "rush" work, and they have continued fighting and, it is believed, effectively to improve The Labor Lawyer's technical precision and quality. The interruption after ten minutes developed a noticeable time situation without leaving the impression that completing the activity by the tighter timeline was unattainable. The writer frequently pondered why it was he who took on the most responsibility, who was constantly willing to go the additional mile, and who, time and again, completed challenging deadlines peacefully and effectively. This was many decades ago, yet it is still valid when timelines loom frightening (Tabassi et al., 2019).

ACTIVITY 3.1.

Suppose a project manager of a bags manufacturing company is fired form the company due to various problems that he has caused in project management implementation including, unidentified, variations in scopes, inappropriate risk management, unmanageable deadlines.,

Company has hired you as a new project manager to rectify the existing issues, without causing delays in the timeline, and to achieve the desired goals. How would you plan project man agent charter to achieves company's desired goals?

8.6. CONTRIBUTION AND NOVEL INSIGHT

It was decided to build a new model that would specify the specific contours of the problems that the project leader would face. Uncertain goals, creeping scope, inappropriate risk management, and unrealistic timelines are the primary difficulties highlighted, as the diagram makes clear to observe. Before beginning any significant venture, this paradigm will be used as a reference to determine how things should be done. It will unquestionably be of assistance to the project manager in overcoming obstacles that lie in his path. Current studies and theories were critically examined to provide original theoretical insights into the difficulties of project management. The databases made available by the University of Bridgeport were utilized in this procedure. The diverse selection of journals was obtained through university databases, the Journal of Marketing, JSTOR, and Google scholar (Figure 8.6).

Figure 8.6. Illustration of challenges for project and program management.

Source: Kissflow, creative commons license.

SUMMARY

The research identifies the following as the main demotivating factors that affect project managers' ultimate performance and effectiveness in several projects: Attempting to set up the primary evaluation criteria, project management intellect at the project and organizational levels, the absence of financial reward techniques, the process to harmonize intangible results, the lengthy decision-making procedure by customers, systematic prejudices and the impact of culture on program results, the delay in replying to information requests, and the unclear association among standards and effectiveness.

In conclusion, the preliminary review of the literature was undertaken over a wide variety of journals, but very few articles showed unique drifts and issues within initiatives. A second, more targeted literature review was conducted across the expert Project Management journals, including the International Journal of Project Management, the Journal of Management in Engineering, Construction and Architectural Management, and the International Journal of Managing Projects in Business. This resulted in the retrieval of 264 papers focusing primarily on topics and trends within projects; nevertheless, none of these articles addressed the perspective or opinions of specialists in project management. Therefore, they were of inadequate help when creating pre-coding structures for research.

REVIEW QUESTIONS

1. Define and explain some significant challenges of project management.
2. How are unidentified goals challenging to project management?
3. How are changes in scope a challenge to project management?
4. Describe improper risk management and impossible deadlines as a challenge to project management.

MULTIPLE CHOICE QUESTIONS

1. What are the three interpersonal roles of managers?

a. Figurehead, leader, and liaison
b. Spokesperson, leader, coordinator
c. Director, coordinator, disseminator
d. Communicator, organizer, spokesperson

2. At what level of an organization does a corporate manager operate?

a. Functional
b. Operational
c. Middle level
d. Top-level

3. Which one is not a recognized critical skill of management?

a. Conceptual skills
b. Human skills
c. Technical skills
d. Writing skills

4. Which of these is not part of the recognized challenges for modern managers?

a. Micro-managing the workforce
b. Managing communications
c. Managing change
d. Managing the learning organization

5. During project estimation, project manager estimates following

a. Project duration
b. Project effort
c. Project cost
d. All of the above

Answers to Multiple Choice Questions

1. (a); 2. (d); 3. (d); 4. (a) 5. (d)

REFERENCES

1. Akhavan, T. A., Bryde, D. J., Mustafa, K. E., Dowson, J., & Michaelides, R., (2019). Challenges for project management in the 21st century. *The European Proceedings of Multidisciplinary Sciences, 1*, 2–6.
2. Atkinson, R., Crawford, L., & Ward, S., (2006). Fundamental uncertainties in projects and the scope of project management. *International Journal of Project Management, 24*(8), 687–698.
3. Bourne, L., & Walker, D. H., (2008). Project relationship management and the stakeholder circle™. *International Journal of Managing Projects in Business, 1*, 125–130.
4. Clark, J., (1985). Policy diffusion and program scope: Research directions. *Publius: The Journal of Federalism, 15*(4), 61–70.
5. De Reyck, B., Grushka-Cockayne, Y., Lockett, M., Calderini, S. R., Moura, M., & Sloper, A., (2005). The impact of project portfolio management on information technology projects. *International Journal of Project Management, 23*(7), 524–537.
6. Dogbegah, R., Owusu-Manu, D., & Omoteso, K., (2011). A principal component analysis of project management competencies for the Ghanaian construction industry.

Australasian Journal of Construction Economics and Building, 11(1), 26–40.

7. Dziadosz, A., Tomczyk, A., & Kapliński, O., (2015). Financial risk estimation in construction contracts. *Procedia Engineering, 122*, 120–128.
8. Fisher, R., Ury, W. L., & Patton, B., (2011). *Getting to Yes: Negotiating Agreement Without Giving in* (Vol. 1, pp. 5–10). Penguin.
9. Huang, J. C., & Newell, S., (2003). Knowledge integration processes and dynamics within the context of cross-functional projects. *International Journal of Project Management, 21*(3), 167–176.
10. Hwang, B. G., & Ng, W. J., (2013). Project management knowledge and skills for green construction: Overcoming challenges. *International Journal of Project Management, 31*(2), 272–284.
11. Khan, M. A., Peters, S., Sahinel, D., Pozo-Pardo, F. D., & Dang, X. T., (2018). Understanding autonomic network management: A look into the past, a solution for the future. *Computer Communications, 122,* 93–117.
12. Niazi, M., Mahmood, S., Alshayeb, M., Qureshi, A. M., Faisal, K., & Cerpa, N., (2016). Toward successful project management in global software development. *International Journal of Project Management, 34*(8), 1553–1567.
13. Nolan, K. P., (2009). *May It Please the Court* (Vol. 36, p. 57). Litig.
14. Odusami, K. T., (2002). Perceptions of construction professionals concerning essential skills of influential project leaders. *Journal of Management in Engineering, 18*(2), 61–67.
15. Olander, S., & Landin, A., (2005). Evaluation of stakeholder influence in the implementation of construction projects. *International Journal of Project Management, 23*(4), 321–328.
16. Padalkar, M., & Gopinath, S., (2016). Six decades of project management research: Thematic trends and future opportunities. *International Journal of Project Management, 34*(7), 1305–1321.
17. Raz, T., & Hillson, D., (2005). A comparative review of risk management standards. *Risk Management, 7*(4), 53–66.
18. Ryan, B., (1965). The resuscitation of social change. *Social Forces, 44*(1), 1–7.
19. Sawhney, A., Agnihotri, R., & Paul, V. K., (2014). Grand challenges for the Indian construction industry. *Built Environment Project and Asset Management, 4*(4), 317–334.
20. Schmidt, R., Lyytinen, K., Keil, M., & Cule, P., (2001). Identifying software project risks: An international Delphi study. *Journal of Management Information Systems, 17*(4), 5–36.
21. Smith, V., (1997). New forms of work organization. *Annual Review of Sociology, 23*, 315–339.
22. Stolber, W. B., (1971). The objective function in program budgeting some basic outlines. *Zeitschrift für die Gesamte Staatswissenschaft/Journal of Institutional and*

Theoretical Economics, 127(2), 213–229.

23. Tabassi, A. A., Ramli, M., & Bakar, A. H. A., (2012). Effects of training and motivation practices on teamwork improvement and task efficiency: The case of construction firms. *International Journal of Project Management, 30*(2), 213–224.
24. Tabassi, A. A., Ramli, M., Roufechaei, K. M., & Tabasi, A. A., (2014). Team development and performance in construction design teams: An assessment of a hierarchical model with mediating effect of compensation. *Construction Management and Economics, 32*(9), 932–949.
25. Tabassi, A. A., Roufechaei, K. M., Bakar, A. H. A., & Yusof, N. A., (2017). Linking team condition and team performance: A transformational leadership approach. *Project Management Journal, 48*(2), 22–38.
26. Tufano, P., (1998). Agency costs of corporate risk management. *Financial Management, 27*(1), 67–77.
27. Uzman, M., (2010). Romanization in Uzbekistan past and present. *Journal of the Royal Asiatic Society, 20*(1), 49–60.
28. Voyten, R. T., (1978). Back to basics and the social studies: Making program decisions. *American Secondary Education, 8*(1), 4–6.
29. Ward, P. S., (1975). Needs survey: More questions than answers. *Journal (Water Pollution Control Federation), 47*(3), 422, 423.
30. Zhenping, W. A. N. G., (2012). Undefined man: Sartrean reading of American novelist walker Percy's the moviegoer. *Intercultural Communication Studies, 21*(3), 138–156.
31. Zimmermann, M., Althaus, H. J., & Haas, A., (2005). Benchmarks for sustainable construction: A contribution to developing a standard. *Energy and Buildings, 37*(11), 1147–1157.

INDEX

C

D

E

F

G

H

I

J

K

L

M